Switch to a Mac

—No Problem!

Publisher's Acknowledgments

Some of the people who helped bring this book to market include the following:

Editorial and Production

VP Consumer and Technology Publishing Director: Michelle Leete

Associate Director—Book Content Management: Martin Tribe

Associate Publisher: Chris Webb

Assistant Editor: Colleen Goldring

Publishing Assistant: Ellie Scott

Project Editor: Juliet Booker

Series Editor: Louise Barr

Development Editor: Louise Barr

Technical Editor: Jonathan Hill

Copy Editor: Sarah Price

Marketing

Senior Marketing Manager: Louise Breinholt

Marketing Executive: Chloe Tunnicliffe

Composition Services

Compositor: Frog Box Design

Proof Reader: Sarah Lewis

Indexer: Robert Swanson

Switching to a Mac
—No Problem!

Dwight Silverman

A John Wiley & Sons, Ltd, Publication

This edition first published 2010
© 2010 John Wiley & Sons, Ltd

Registered office
John Wiley & Sons Ltd, The Atrium, Southern Gate, Chichester,
West Sussex, PO19 8SQ, United Kingdom

Editorial office
John Wiley & Sons Ltd, The Atrium, Southern Gate, Chichester,
West Sussex, PO19 8SQ, United Kingdom

For details of our global editorial offices, for customer services and for information about how to apply
for permission to reuse the copyright material in this book please see our website at www.wiley.com.

ISBN 978-0-470-71015-9

A catalogue record for this book is available from the British Library.

Set in 11pt ITC Berkeley Oldstyle Std and ITC Highlander Std, by Frog Box Design
Printed in Great Britain by Bell and Bain, Glasgow

For Jack and Jessie, who may have wondered why their father
vanished for seven months. Here you go.

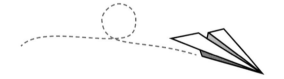

About the author

Dwight Silverman is a veteran computer columnist, technology blogger, and online editor for the Houston Chronicle and its website, `chron.com`. He also co-hosts *Technology Bytes*, a weekly computer help call-in show on KPFT-FM in Houston. He's also a frequent guest on the popular *This Week in Tech* podcast with Leo Laporte.

Dwight has been a tech junkie since the age of 5, when he became notorious for compulsively pushing any button he could reach. He's been writing about personal technology since the mid-1980s, and considers himself fluent in both Mac and Windows. Follow him on Twitter at `twitter.com/dsilverman`, and read his blog at `blogs.chron.com/techblog`. This is his third book.

Acknowledgments

Conventional wisdom says writing is a solitary pursuit, but in the case of penning a computer book, conventional wisdom is wrong. It's a collaborative effort.

Big thanks go out to my agent, Claudette Moore, who's got my back at every turn. I'm also incredibly grateful to Louise Barr, this book's editor and the creator of the **No Problem!** series—she's as brilliant as she is nice.

Also in need of a good thanking are Barrett and Amanda Canon, whose wedding made for some great screenshots in the iMovie chapter; and my Technology Bytes co-host Jay Lee, whose Mac conversion happened while I was writing this book.

Then, there's the support group. I owe so much to my lovely wife, Elise Gunst, who agreed to do the dishes after each night's dinner so I could grind away at the keyboard. Ditto for my managers at the Houston Chronicle, and particularly my boss, Scott Clark, for patience and encouragement. Thanks for the slack.

Finally, big thanks to the Mac-savvy users of Twitter, who were able to answer questions and solve mysteries with impressive speed and accuracy. You guys are the best.

Contents

Contents

Contents

Contents

How to use this book

You want to learn new skills. You want to learn them fast. And you want to remember more, too. You don't have time to wade through any more books over and over because the information didn't stick.

⇨ Can you learn things fast and still remember them?

⇨ Can a book help you learn better and remember more?

No Problem!

No Problem! books are aimed at anyone who needs to get up and running fast. **No Problem!** takes advantage of your natural learning rhythms to help you:

⇨ Learn faster and solve your problems sooner.

⇨ Remember new information better and for longer.

⇨ Follow a variety of paths through that suit your style of learning.

Your brain's already wired for this type of learning, so there's no complicated system to learn, nor any one-size-fits-all method. Choose the features within the book that feel most natural for you, making your learning experience as unique as you are.

Learn *your* way

No Problem! books have multiple learning paths so you can choose how you learn. Select the path that works for you, or use all of them, No Problem!

→ In a rush? No Problem! For a *quick path*, look out for the highlighted text to learn just what you need to know to get moving.

→ Prefer to *take notes* while you learn? No Problem! We've already sprinkled loads of notes and quick tips throughout the book, and left you plenty of room to take your own.

→ Like to learn by doing? No Problem! The Play with it and Experiment features give you the hands-on guidance you need.

→ Need a detailed step-by-step guide? No Problem! Combine *all* the learning paths for a comprehensive workshop.

How do each of these features work and how will they help you learn your way and remember more?

Active learning helps you remember

Did you ever see a swimming class shivering pool-side while the instructor drew diagrams on a whiteboard? No! You learn to swim by *swimming*.

Remembering is experiential. This is a very powerful learning tool because you remember:

| 10% of what you *read* | 15% of what you *hear* | 80% of what you *experience* |

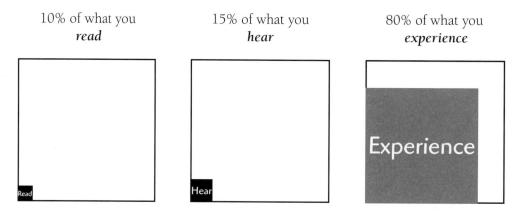

So the trick is to **experience** Switching to the Mac by *doing* it. How can we help you with that?

Skip right to the good parts

The chapters in **No Problem!** skip all the historical detail and the stuff you don't need so you **learn just the stuff you _do_ need**. You already know about working with Windows. So although some of the Mac terminology or functionality is different, you've got a great base to work from. In fact, the differences between how a PC and a Mac do the same thing can be quite memorable in themselves.

As you work your way through a chapter try out the topics for yourself. As you do, you'll be using multiple senses:

→ **Sight and spatial awareness**—understanding where on screen your cursor should be or where the cable from your Mac to your Time Machine drive needs to be plugged in.

→ **Touch**—the feel of the keyboard and the action of plugging in the cable or using the Apple mouse.

→ **Hearing**—did you get an alert? Have you got some rockin' tunes on in the background?

→ **Taste**—have you got a pot of strong coffee on the go? Maybe you're snacking or chewing gum.

> **Note:** Make a list, keep a diary, or write in a notebook to record your progress and discoveries as you work through this book.
>
> Writing (rather than typing) notes helps your brain store information. Plus, being able to revisit the "Aha!" moments when you review the chapter triggers all kinds of related feelings and memories to help you store and recall the information better.

Combining any of these makes the learning experience richer and that helps your brain connect the new knowledge to different areas and increases your chances of recalling it later.

But what about completely new information?

Play and Experiment

Playing with a topic or related topic, and experimenting more deeply shortly after you've read about it, is called "elaborative rehearsal." It gives your brain the chance to build on what it's just learned. This enhances your memory of the topic and helps you recall it later.

Play with it

The more you can test your new knowledge, the better it will stick, so once you're done experimenting you should apply what you learned in a chapter to your own projects.

Link new knowledge to what you already know

Throughout the chapters, we suggest places for you to "Make a link." This is the key information you need to learn about a topic, and the best way to do that is to link it to something you already know.

Sometimes a link is suggested, but if you can think of a better, more vivid or personal link, no problem. Your own links are *way* more memorable than anything we could ask you to remember. But how do you make links from new information to older stuff you already know?

Make stronger links

You've probably heard the phrase "Spring forward, fall back" to remember which way the clocks shift when daylight saving starts or ends. This is a mnemonic, a short phrase or term that's easier to remember than the thing it stands for.

Another kind of memory aid uses vivid imagery to add new information to a familiar sequence. Try linking the new information with something you already know well, like a daily journey. Break the journey into ten steps: you wake up, grab some breakfast, take a shower, get dressed, leave the house, walk to the coffee shop, grab a coffee to-go, arrive at the station, buy a ticket, and get on the train. It should be easy to recall each step.

Got that? Great. Now, say you have to remember some letters that you have to post, your sports bag for a workout, and a birthday gift for a friend you'll see later in the day. Imagine each item mixed into a step of the journey. The more vividly you can imagine each step and the new, linked information, the better.

You wake up under a huge pile of mail. The letters are surprisingly comfortable to sleep under. You consider going back to sleep in your gently rustling paper nest, but you're really hungry. So you make your way to the kitchen. When you reach into the cupboard for the cereal, you're surprised to find a box wrapped in bright paper that says "Happy Birthday" all over it. You tear it open to find… your cereal box, but it's filled with the most delicious gift-shaped pieces you've ever eaten. Everything's going great until, on your way to the bathroom to shower, you fall over your sports bag and stub your toe. Man, that smarts! …

There are two things at work here.

1. You're telling a sequential story and your brain loves those *because* the story is easier to remember than the list of items. Why? The main story is broken down into sequential and easy to remember steps.

2. Even better, each step is vivid. It has the new information coded into the original step with impressions from your senses as well as a good dose of emotional content. The rustle of the warm letters, the taste of the cereal, and the painful toe are all easy to recall. While the emotional content of being warm and cozy in bed, surprised at breakfast, and hurt on your way to the bathroom give your brain another pathway to not only learn, but also recall the new information.

Make a link

Ask yourself, what mnemonics can I use to help me recall the information later?

▶ Is there a common acronym or rhyme to get it to stick, or can I make up my own and make it really vivid?

▶ Can I picture myself using this new knowledge to achieve something?

▶ Is this new knowledge *like* something that I already know about? Can I tell a sequential story with new information vividly mixed with stuff I already know well?

Why "take a break" before the end of the chapter?

Taking a break before the end of the chapter sounds completely counterintuitive, huh? But, just like dreaming is your brain's way of sorting through the day's experiences while you sleep, taking a break during your learning time helps your brain make better links. Your brain likes to sift through all the new material and store it away. It stores stuff away best until around 10 minutes *after* you stopped learning.

Learn. Review. Repeat.

Your brain needs to repeat new information to save it to long-term memory for good. All the playing and experimenting with your new understanding and the time you spend making links to it helps make it more memorable, so you're already a good way towards helping your brain remember this information for the long-term. Another way to save even more of what you learn is to review it often.

Take some time at the end of each day to review your notes from that day's learning. That helps your brain realize this is stuff it needs to keep around. We added a Review to every chapter to help you along.

Do another Review in a week's time, then another after a month, and another after six months and so on and your knowledge and recall will quickly become rock solid.

> **Tip:** Reviewing isn't a big deal. Take a few minutes at the end of every chapter and make notes on what you remember, then compare them with the notes you made at the time. Write any information you missed in the Review and any new notes (your brain will have thought of new things in the meantime—it's constantly learning!) in the margin of your original notes.

Review

In this document, you learned how to help your brain remember better.

↺ **No Problem!** books have .... through the content, allowing you to learn in a way that suits you.

↺ .... learning helps you learn up to .... % more than reading alone.

↺ Make .... from what you already .... to new knowledge you want to ....

↺ Taking a break helps your brain ....

And you did it all by understanding how the brain works to help your brain learn faster, naturally.

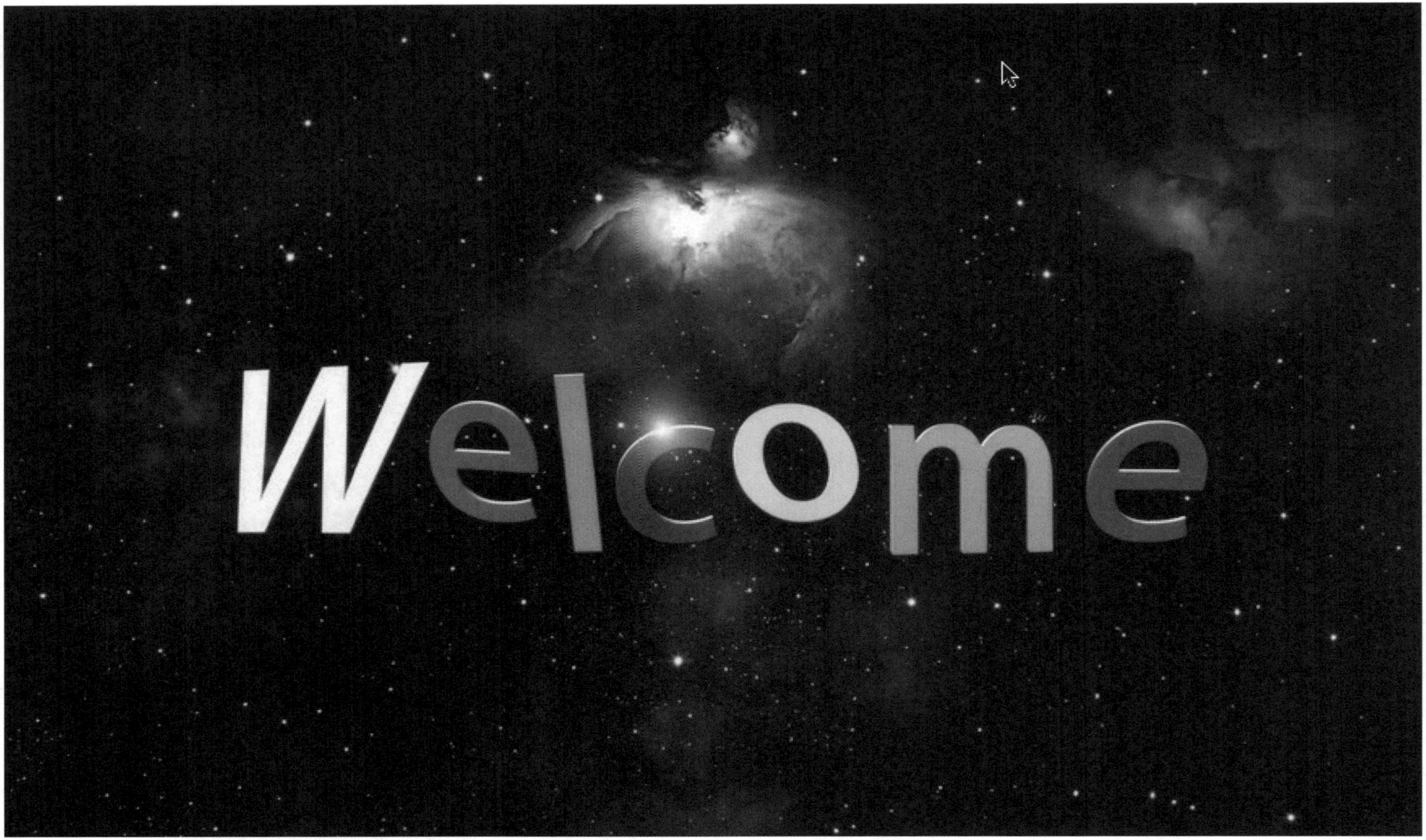
Welcome

1 Apples and ~~oranges~~ Windows PCs

Switching to a Mac is a journey for Windows users, and now that you've picked one out and it's in your hot little hands, turning it on and setting it up is the first step. It's also the first point at which you'll enter foreign territory filled with new features that you need to learn like:

⇨ The Dock

⇨ The Menu Bar

⇨ The Finder

⇨ The Apple Menu

Will it be hard to work with your new Mac if it's all so *different*?

No Problem!

There are differences, sure, but you're not a newbie. You found your way around Windows, and you can use what you know about that operating system and computers in general to get started with your new Mac. The similarities can help you make your way past the differences.

Warning
Throughout this book, we've figured you're using a new Mac running Snow Leopard, or Mac OS X 10.6, or later. If you've switched to an older machine or version of Mac OS X, some features may not be available or work quite the same way as we describe.

1

Step through the setup process

When you turn on your Mac for the first time, you're greeted with a video welcoming you to your new machine.

When it's completed, you'll move through a series of setup screens that will help configure your computer. Most of them are self-explanatory, such as the language your Mac will use, the keyboard layout, registering your Mac with Apple and how you connect to the Internet.

That peppy little tune that plays during the intro movie, by the way, is *Exodus Honey* by the California band Honeycut.

The latter process is smart: if your Mac senses wireless networks, it will present a list of them. If you've got an existing home wireless network, select it and enter its security password or alphanumeric key.

If you're connected via an Ethernet cable, you won't get any prompts to connect. When your Mac comes up, you'll be on the Internet. What could be simpler?

You'll need to pay attention to two of the screens in the setup process:

1. Set up an account

If you've set up a Windows XP, Vista or Windows 7 PC, you've been asked to pick a login name, and the Mac operating system (Mac OS) does the same thing. But the Mac asks you for two things:

→ A **long name**, which is your formal name.

→ A **short name**, which is used to label your Home folder, where all your applications and data are stored.

Easy to change.   Hard to change, so choose wisely.

Choose carefully. The long name can be changed, but the short name can't easily be changed.

You'll also be asked to choose a password and a hint that will be shown in case you forget the password. Choose a strong password, particularly if you're setting up a laptop that you'll carry around.

Tip: Your password should be memorable, but someone who knows you shouldn't be able to guess it. Strong passwords should be at least 8 characters long, mixed case, with at least one number and one symbol.

You'll be asked to set up an Apple account, too. *If you've been using iTunes on Windows, use the same e-mail address and password you use to access that account.* Otherwise, you can set up a fresh Apple account here, or hold down the Command key and press Q to quit the registration process and continue with the setup.

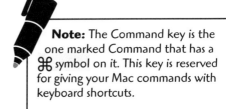

Note: The Command key is the one marked Command that has a ⌘ symbol on it. This key is reserved for giving your Mac commands with keyboard shortcuts.

2. Join MobileMe

Watch out for the screen that invites you to join MobileMe.

The second screen to watch for invites you to join **MobileMe**, a service from Apple that synchronizes files and e-mail between multiple computers, iPads and iPhones. It works with both Mac and Windows computers.

What you need to know now

The service currently costs **$99 a year** (and may be discounted the first year to $69, depending on how you bought your Mac). If you're not sure about whether you want to sign up for this service, don't worry, **you can say "No" now and come back to it later**.

Once the setup process is over, you're taken to the Mac desktop, which looks different from the Windows version... but not *too* different.

What are the first things you notice about the desktop? How does the layout of items differ from your Windows machine? Are there any similarities in the layout?

Load and unload at the Dock

What was the first thing you noticed about your Mac's desktop? Chances are, it's the row of brightly colored icons at the bottom of the screen. This is the **Dock**. Think back to Windows, what does the Dock remind you of?

If you said, "The Windows Taskbar," you're right. And if you said, "The Start menu," you're also right. But how can the Dock be like both the Start menu and the Taskbar *at the same time*?

Take another look at the Dock. Right now it's acting like the Start menu and holding icons for applications Apple thinks you'll use frequently (don't worry, it's easy to change these). So how can the Dock be like the Taskbar and show you the applications that are

running at the same time? Take a closer look. See the smiley face icon on the far left of the Dock? That's the Finder, and it's always running. You can tell that because there's a little blue light under the icon.

Note: On your Mac, *programs* are called **Applications**. It's a small change, but one well worth remembering when you're trying to find your Programs list!

On the Mac, the Dock is where the action is. The Windows 7 Taskbar works a lot like the Dock, but if you're coming from Windows XP and Vista, the Dock is like a hybrid Windows Start menu and Taskbar, as it contains both running applications, shown by a blue light underneath the icon, and icons for applications you use frequently.

Play with it

The little blue light under an icon indicates the application's running. Those that don't have the light aren't active, but can be launched with a single click. Try it now. Click the icon that looks like a compass.

You just launched Apple's web browser, Safari. Check the Dock. The Safari compass icon now has a blue light underneath it.

Click the compass icon in the Dock to launch Apple's web browser, Safari.

Something much more subtle happened to your screen when you launched Safari. Did you notice any other parts of the screen change when you started the application?

Click the Finder icon in the Dock and look at the top left of your screen. What do you see? Now click the Safari icon and check the top left of your screen again.

This is the start of the menu when the Finder's your active application.

This is the start of the menu when your active application is Safari.

What's on the Menu?

You just discovered the **Menu Bar**. It's always at the top of the screen and the items it contains change depending on the active window (the one topmost on your screen).

This is a big difference from Windows, where application menus are available in each window, but it soon becomes second nature to work with files from the top left of the screen. You'll always work from the same place, regardless of where the application's windows are placed on your screen.

On the right side of the Menu Bar are various **status indicators**. This area is similar to the System Tray, a.k.a. the Notification Area, in Windows.

Make a link

Think about it like this. Most classy restaurants have a menu in the window. The menu is always in the same place, but depending on what ingredients are in season, what's on the menu will change. Relax; it soon becomes second nature to look up for the Menu Bar because you'll do it for every application.

Where did the window controls go?

So the Dock is like a Taskbar/Start menu hybrid and there's no menu bar in the windows. These differences are weird, but did you notice the really strange thing about the Mac windows? There's no big X at the top right of every window... So if there's no close button, how will you close the windows on your Mac?

Apple's design for opening, closing and resizing windows is quite different from Microsoft's. Did you notice those three buttons at the top left of every window? Click the Safari icon in the Dock and then click the Finder icon. See those three buttons on the windows in both applications? Roll your cursor over them. What happens?

The **red** button on the left, with a little X in it when you move the cursor over it, **closes** the window; the **yellow** button in the middle, with a – when you move the cursor over it, **minimizes** the window; while the **green** button on the right, that gets a little + when you move the cursor over it, lets you **zoom** in.

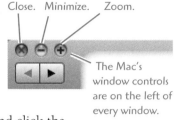

Close. Minimize. Zoom.

The Mac's window controls are on the left of every window.

Give it a shot, make sure you're in the Finder window and click the Zoom button. What happens? Click it again. What happens?

Zoom to see more of a window's contents

The **zoom button** is similar to the Windows Maximize button except that in most applications on your Mac, zoom means, "make the window big enough to show as much of the contents as possible," while the Windows Maximize button means "fill the entire screen with this window."

Tip: The green button doesn't always expand a window. In iTunes on the Mac, for example, it switches between the full view of the program to the "mini-player," which just has the playback controls showing. As you open various Mac programs, click on the green button to see just what it does in that application.

Minimize a window

Now try the **minimize button**. What happens? Let's take a look at the process.

→ When you clicked the minimize button, the window was minimized the way you'd expect it to be, but it was animated like a genie being forced back into a bottle, or in this case, the Dock.

→ Check the Dock. The minimized window now appears on the right-hand side of the Dock with a tiny icon showing you what application it's associated with.

The Dock acts like the Windows Taskbar when it holds an icon for the window you just minimized. Click the icon to restore the window.

→ To **restore** the window, just click the icon in the Dock.

Tip: You can also minimize any window by double-clicking the title bar of the window, or pressing Command+M to command your Mac to minimize. Whatever way you minimize, you'll still have to click the icon in the Dock to restore the window.

Close a window and open it again

Have you restored your Finder window? If you haven't, do it now by clicking on its icon on the right side of the Dock, then try the **close button**. What happens? Is the Finder still running? How do you know?

There are four ways to open a new Finder window.

1. Click the **Finder icon** in the Dock. Try it now.

This method works when you don't have any Finder windows open. If you've got a minimized Finder window, clicking the Finder icon restores that window.

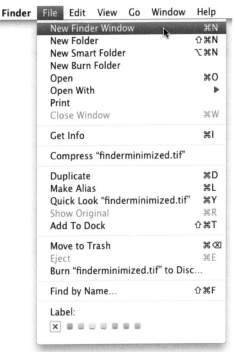

2. Click the desktop, then in the **Finder menu** (remember, it's at the top left of the screen), choose **File > New Finder Window**.

3. Use the keyboard shortcut **Command+N** to **command** your Mac to open a **new** Window.

> Methods 2 and 3 will open a new window or file in almost all the applications you'll run on your Mac, though, of course, for 2 the route will be File > New [whatever the application lets you do].

4. Double-click the **Macintosh HD icon** at the top right of your desktop.

Although you can set preferences so that a specific folder is in focus whenever you open a new Finder window, if you click the Macintosh HD icon on your desktop, you'll always get a Finder window with the HD at the top level.

Note: Did you see the **keyboard shortcuts** listed in the File menu? Shortcuts are listed there just the same as in Windows, but don't worry about trying to learn all the new Mac keyboard shortcuts. For now, just "translate" the ones you're used to (Open, Close, Save, Minimize, Cut, Copy, and Paste are the most common), which all use the same letter on the Mac as they do on Windows. Remember, you're *commanding* your Mac, so press Command, instead of Ctrl.

Wait a second, what exactly does the Finder do?

Does Finder sound like a complicated search tool? Or maybe it does exactly what the name suggests and helps you, uh, *find* things? The Finder is the equivalent of Windows Explorer. It's how you navigate network shares, drives, folders and the files they contain.

Whichever way you choose to open up a Finder window, it shows the contents of folders and drives on the right, and other places you can access on the left—other drives, other computers on your network and often-used folders, such as Documents and Pictures. Click on any item on the left, and the pane on the right changes to reflect its contents *just like Windows Explorer*. We'll come back to the Finder in a little while.

Quitting's easy when you know how

When you want to quit Safari, closing all the windows (if you didn't already, close the window you opened before) does **not** close the application. Check the Dock. The running light underneath its icon means Safari's still running, it just happens not to have any windows open right now. So how do you close down an application?

There are three ways to quit an application.

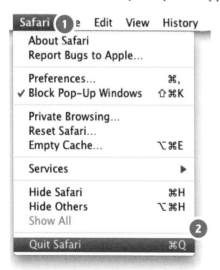

Hold down the Control button and click the Dock icon to get a contextual menu that lets you Quit.

1. Use the menu. To quit Safari, **click Safari > Quit Safari**. Try it now; you can always relaunch the application with the click of its icon in the Dock.

2. Use the keyboard shortcut **Command+Q**.

3. Hold down the **Control** button when you **click** the **Dock icon** and choose **Quit Safari**.

Don't worry, if you're in an application and you've made changes to a file (maybe you edited a text file or entered some text in a field on a web page in Safari), the application will ask you if you want to save before it quits.

Take a break

Okay, that's a good place to pause. Choose your exit, then go have some fun. Have a short break. Feel like taking a short walk? Thirsty? Go take your walk or grab a drink. When you come back, you'll learn how to customize your Mac and make it your own.

Right now you're probably thinking, "Wait. To carry on learning I need to stop and take regular breaks? That seems totally counterintuitive, how could that possibly help me learn?"

If you want to help your brain learn faster, regular breaks are a must. They keep your brain fresh; a quick walk, even as far as the kitchen to grab a drink, gets your blood pumping and sends oxygen to your brain. That helps your brain stay focused and interested in the topic.

Review

To help the new information about the Dock, Menu Bar, Finder and window controls stick in your brain, do a review of what you've learned in this chapter.

Dock

↺ The Dock is like the Windows .... and ....

↺ If an application's running you see a .... underneath the icon.

↺ To launch an application from the dock, you ....

Menu

↺ Where is the menu? ....

↺ What happens to the menu bar when you switch between open applications?

Window controls

↺ Where are the window controls on your Mac's windows? ....

↺ The middle button .... a window?

↺ The button on the right is colored .... It ....

Continues, flip the page

○ Name the three ways to open a new window:

1. ....

2. ....

3. ....

The Finder

○ The Finder behaves like the Windows ....

○ What shape is the window control to hide or show the Finder's toolbar and sidebar? ....

Quit applications

○ Name two ways you can quit an application.

1. ....

2. ....

How did you do?

If you'd like to improve your recall on any of these you should spend a little more time on that part of the chapter. You'll get more familiar with the new information faster if you take a little time to make some strong links to the new information you're learning.

Practice often to improve your recall

It's also a good idea to go over the review questions again in a day's time, then try the questions again in:

→ a week's time

→ a month's time

→ six months' time

→ a year's time and so on.

> If you find anything's missing or harder to remember, take some time to work on just those bits and make stronger links.

Experiment

The best way to really cement these features and techniques into your long-term memory and to expand on the techniques you learned in the chapter is to use them and take them a step further.

The Apple Menu

So if the Dock is a Taskbar/Start menu hybrid, where are the options to log in or shut down? This is another difference between Windows and your Mac. Did you notice the little Apple icon to the left of the menu? Did you notice how it doesn't change, regardless of the active application? Try switching between the Finder and Safari again, what happens to the in the menu? What do you think that means? Is this just Apple's way of reminding you you're on a Mac every time you look up at the menu?

About This Mac
Software Update...
Mac OS X Software...

System Preferences...
Dock   ▶

Recent Items   ▶

Force Quit...   ⌥⌘⌃

Sleep   ⌥⌘⏏
Restart...
Shut Down...

Log Out LeVeau...   ⇧⌘Q

Well, maybe that's a part of it, but the Apple is actually a pretty useful button. Try clicking it. The **Apple menu** gives you access to core features of the Mac OS, such as Software Updates, the configuration of your Mac, recent documents/applications/folders you've accessed and power options.

Make a link

The **Apple menu** is at the *top* of the screen, not the bottom like the Windows Start menu. It's higher because apples grow on trees.

Since we're at the end of the chapter, let's take a look at the four choices related to exiting the system:

→ Sleep

→ Restart

→ Shut down

→ Log Out [your long name]

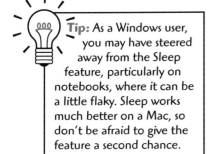

Tip: As a Windows user, you may have steered away from the Sleep feature, particularly on notebooks, where it can be a little flaky. Sleep works much better on a Mac, so don't be afraid to give the feature a second chance.

These options are similar to the ones used to shut down or log out from the Windows Start menu. (Note that there's no Hibernate option on the Mac, though.) Experiment with them to see what they do and how they do it.

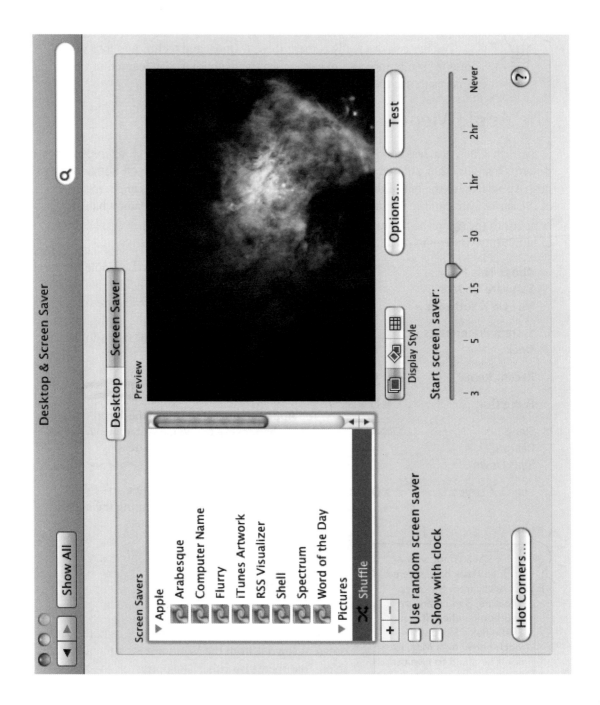

2 Make your new Mac... YOUR Mac

So you've got this shiny new Mac, fresh out of the box. It's connected to the Internet, registered with Apple and the unsullied virgin desktop is staring at you. Yes, it's a thing of beauty, but you know what? It's not *yours*. Yet.

You need to personalize it and make it your own. But where to start?

No Problem!

You know how to get Windows looking just the way you like it, right? Although the names and the design may be a little different, the process for customizing your Mac is very similar. Just as on the PC, you can change the look and behavior of many of the Mac's features. On the Mac you can:

⇨ Change the background.

⇨ Choose a screen saver.

⇨ Change some sound effects.

Many tweaks are done from one central "toolbox," a place in the Mac where you can tweak dozens of features. Sound familiar?

System Preferences is the new Control Panel

When you work with Microsoft Windows, where do you usually go when you want to change something about the operating system? Yes, when it's time to tweak, the Control Panel is your best friend.

Now that you're on the Mac, meet your new best friend: **System Preferences**. To launch System Preferences look for this icon that Apple conveniently places on the Dock.

Just like the Windows Control Panel, System Preferences is a one-stop-shop when you want to make changes.

If you've got an iPhone or iPod Touch, that icon should look familiar. Apple uses it for the same purpose on those handheld devices, but there it's labeled simply Settings.

Click the icon and System Preferences launches. Does it remind you of the Windows Control Panel?

There are a lot of icons here. It would be easy to get lost in System Preferences, but for now we're going to concentrate on just the parts that let you customize your Mac.

Look at the layout of the icons on the System Preferences window. See how they are organized by the kinds of features they control? This makes it easy to find just the setting you're looking for. Clicking any of the icons launches a settings window called a **preference pane**.

Personalize your desktop

To personalize your desktop we're going to focus on some of the preference panes in the top two rows of icons.

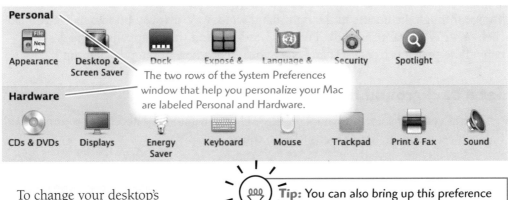

The two rows of the System Preferences window that help you personalize your Mac are labeled Personal and Hardware.

To change your desktop's background, which is called wallpaper in the Windows world, which option do you think you'd click? Yep, click **Desktop and Screen Saver**.

Tip: You can also bring up this preference pane by holding down the Control key and clicking an open area on the desktop. Choose "Change Desktop Background..." from the pop-up menu to launch the pane.

What do you see when you get into the Desktop and Screen Saver preference pane? At the top of the pane are buttons marked Desktop and Screen Saver and one of them will be highlighted in blue. Is Desktop highlighted? If not, click on it. We'll come back to Screen Saver later. Your preference pane should now look like this:

Click the Desktop button to change your desktop background.

On the left side, there's a list of folders with background art organized by type of image. Click on the folders and the thumbnails in the right side of the pane change to show you the folder's contents. The Preview window in the upper left corner shows you the current selection, which is Aurora, the default background that comes on the Mac.

Do you want to change the background? Click on the various category folders and browse through the images in the right-hand window. When you find an image you like, click on it. What happens to the Preview window? And what happens to the desktop behind the preference pane? There. Now you've got a new desktop background.

Set a background from the Web

What if you find something cool on the Web you want to use as a background image? Can you get an image from a website onto your desktop?

Actually, saving an image from the Web as your desktop background works just the same way on the Mac as it does in Windows. If you know how to do it on your Windows PC, how do you think it works on the Mac?

Try it out and see if you were right:

1. Open Safari by clicking on its icon in the Dock.

2. Find a cool picture. Try typing this into the address bar at the top of the Safari window: `http://www.flickr.com/groups/skylines`

    Explore the images until you find one you like.

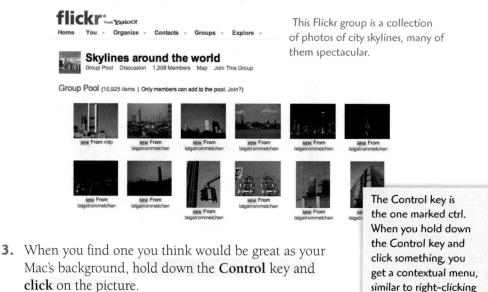

This Flickr group is a collection of photos of city skylines, many of them spectacular.

FLICKR and the FLICKR logo are registered trademarks of Yahoo! Inc.

3. When you find one you think would be great as your Mac's background, hold down the **Control** key and **click** on the picture.

> The Control key is the one marked ctrl. When you hold down the Control key and click something, you get a contextual menu, similar to right-clicking on a PC.

4. Choose **Use Image as Desktop Picture** from the menu that pops up. What happens to the desktop background this time?

Open Image in New Window
Open Image in New Tab
Save Image to the Desktop
Save Image As...
Add Image to iPhoto Library
Use Image as Desktop Picture
Copy Image Address
Copy Image
Inspect Element

Play with it

Modern browsers can display almost any kind of image; they're a bit like a photo preview application. You can drag images onto them, and they'll display the picture. With that in mind, how could you use a Web browser to get any kind of photo onto your background, even if it's on your computer and not on the Web?

Change your desktop background automatically

Before we move on, one more thing: what if you want different backgrounds to show up over time? Can you do that on the Mac?

You bet. Let's go back to the **Desktop preference pane**. Do you recall seeing some other controls on that pane? Look at the bottom of the window.

1. Check the box next to Change picture.

Checking the Change picture box makes the drop-down next to it active

2. Click the Change picture drop-down box and choose a time interval you like.

3. If you would like the background to change in a random sequence, check the Random order box.

4. Choose the folder in the left-hand pane you'd like the process to pull from.

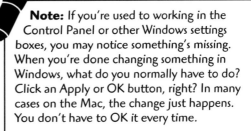

Note: If you're used to working in the Control Panel or other Windows settings boxes, you may notice something's missing. When you're done changing something in Windows, what do you normally have to do? Click an Apply or OK button, right? In many cases on the Mac, the change just happens. You don't have to OK it every time.

Set up a screen saver

The same preference pane used to change your desktop background also is used to select a screen saver. To get there from here, what do you think you'd do?

Click the **Screen Saver button** at the top of the window, and the preference pane morphs to handle screen savers.

Check the boxes to **add a clock to your screen saver**, or have different screen savers rotate randomly.

Use the **Start screen saver** slider to determine how much idle time passes before the screen saver launches.

Click the little triangle next to the **Pictures** item in the left-hand side of this window. What happens? Now try clicking the **Shuffle** item.

The drop-down menu lets you select pictures that Apple provides for the backgrounds, and they'll become part of a screen saver.

Check and uncheck some of the boxes below your selections to change how the pictures you've picked behave when you use them as a screen saver. Click OK when you're done.

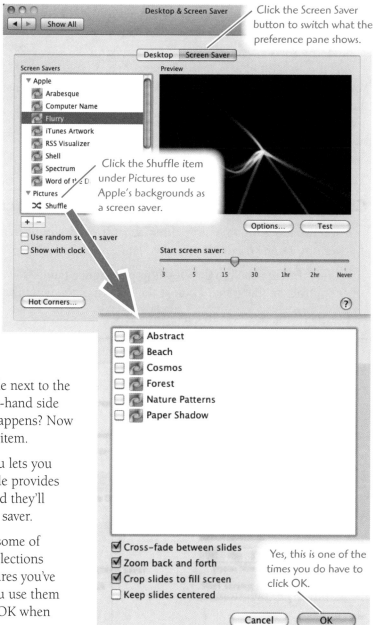

Click the Screen Saver button to switch what the preference pane shows.

Click the Shuffle item under Pictures to use Apple's backgrounds as a screen saver.

Yes, this is one of the times you do have to click OK.

The Screen Saver pane has changed again. Now you've got some controls that weren't there before under the preview on the right-hand side. Based on the icons, what do you think these controls do?

Click on each control to see what happens in the preview window. Click the Test button to see the screen saver full screen.

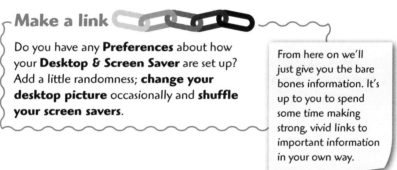

Make a link

Do you have any **Preferences** about how your **Desktop & Screen Saver** are set up? Add a little randomness; **change your desktop picture** occasionally and **shuffle your screen savers**.

From here on we'll just give you the bare bones information. It's up to you to spend some time making strong, vivid links to important information in your own way.

Change the sound effects

So far, you've focused on changing the visuals in Mac OS X. Can you customize the way your Mac *sounds*, too?

Open the System Preferences again to access your Mac's Sound preferences via the speaker icon.

The Sound preference pane controls sound effects and some other stuff we'll come back to shortly.

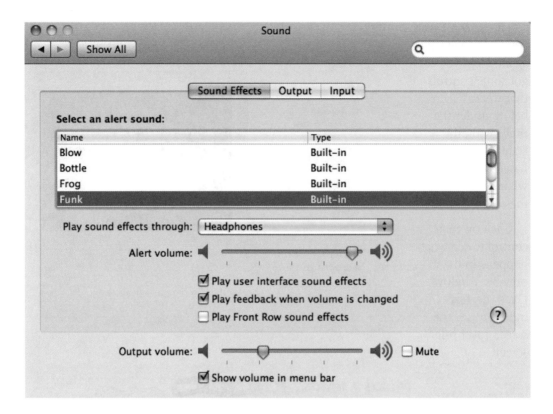

Actually, it should be called sound *effect*, singular. Mac OS X strives for simplicity, and **there's only one alert sound** that's played when something goes awry, or when an action is completed.

The highlighted sound is called "Funk," and it's the default system sound. Click on the word to see what it sounds like. Sounds kind of funky, right? Like a bass note played once. Now you know how to find out what the others sound like, click on the name once to hear each sound and when you find one you like, leave that one highlighted and it will be your new alert sound.

Wait a second... Windows has different sounds for different things. They're audible cues for what's going on with your PC. If everything sounds the same on the Mac, how will you know what's happened in different applications? For example, say you want to change the sound you hear when new e-mail arrives in the Mail application. If you can't change the sound here, how do you think you'd change it?

There's just one sound for system alerts, and that's what you can change in System Preferences. Different applications have their own sounds, which you change in the preferences for those specific programs.

Turn it up

Look at the Sound preference pane again. The **sliders** control the volume. Windows uses those, too, but they're usually vertically oriented. Why do you think there are two volume sliders here?

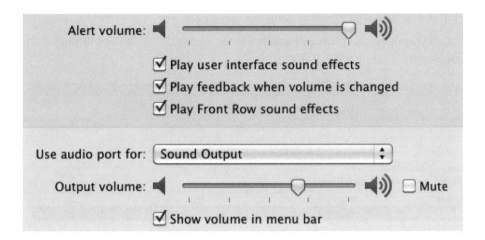

Just like Windows Vista and Windows 7, the Mac OS lets you control the volume of the system alert sounds separate from other sounds, say music or audio with movies.

What happens when you move the sliders? Those sounds let you know exactly how loud the volume will be. The demonstration sounds are different, too. The alert volume has one sound, and the output volume another. You know which one is the default alert sound. Try clicking on the alert sounds until you find the sound effect being used for the output volume.

Play with it

Of course, you don't want to open the System Preferences and then the Sound pane every time you want to turn the audio up or down. There are two, much faster ways to control the sound level.

One of them is on your desktop, the other on your keyboard. Look at both. Do you see icons that might indicate they control volume? Once you find them, play with them to see how they work. Hint: there's a clue in the Sound pane that will help you find one.

Sound sources

What if you've got speakers plugged into your
Mac. How do you control the volume of those?
And will you be deafened if you unplug your
headphones? Let's take a look at the other buttons
at the top of the Sound preferences pane.

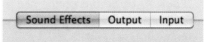

What do you think the **Output button** lets you control? Click the Output button, and
the Sounds pane changes. What do you see?

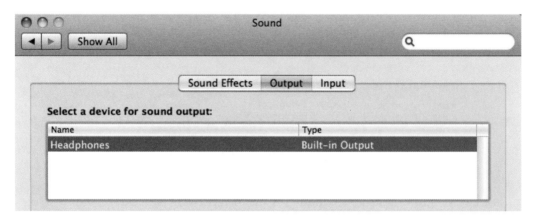

The Sound preference's **Output** option shows you the various devices connected to
your Mac that let you hear sound. The Mac in this screenshot had only headphones
connected. But if you had a Mac Pro and had speakers connected to its audio ports on
the back and headphones in the front, you'd see both in the list.

Click the **Input button**.

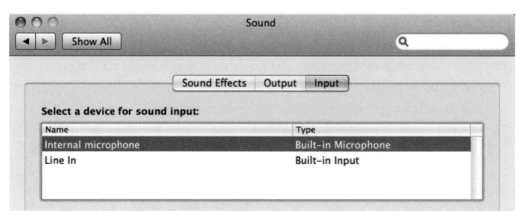

There are two devices in this Mac's Sound preference's **Input** window. Some Macs don't have internal microphones at all, so if you don't have any external mics plugged in and you're on a Mac Pro or a Mini, you won't see anything at all in this pane. What do you think is the difference between **Internal Microphone** and **Line In**?

Here's one way to tell. Make sure **Internal Microphone** is highlighted, the Input volume slider (which affects how much the mic picks up) is around mid-way on the scale, and then *say something out loud* to your Mac. Watch the Sound pane while you're talking. What happens?

Now click the **Line In** input device. What happens when you *talk to your Mac* this time?

You should see the volume level meter flash as it "hears" your words on the Internal Microphone setting. Unless you have an external, plug-in microphone connected, nothing happens in the Sound pane on the Line In setting.

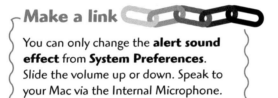

Make a link

You can only change the **alert sound effect** from **System Preferences**.
Slide the volume up or down. Speak to your Mac via the Internal Microphone.

- -

Take a break

You're near the end of the chapter and the best thing you can do right now is to take a break. Research shows that taking frequent breaks when you're learning new material gives your brain some much-needed processing time. So, do yourself and your brain a favor and find something else to do for a little while. When you're ready, come on back for the review to see how much you retained.

Review

Write down what you remember about personalizing your Mac.

System Preferences

↺ The System Preferences icon in the Dock shows ....

↺ What are preference panes? How are they organized?

Desktop backgrounds

↺ To change the desktop background, click on the ....
.... System Preferences icon.

Screen savers

↺ To show the Screen Saver preference pane, go to the System Prefs >
.... > .... button.

↺ To have different screen savers kick in randomly, go to the
.... preference pane and check the box next to
....

↺ How do you control the amount of idle time before a screen saver
launches?

....

Sounds

↺ What kind of sounds can you change with the Sound preference pane?

....

↺ What happens in the Output and Input preview windows when you
plug in new audio devices?

↺ When you talk to your Mac when Internal Microphone is selected in
the Input window, what happens?

How did you do?

If you'd like to improve your recall on any of these, you
should go spend a little more time on that part of the chapter.

Experiment

Here are some suggestions for your experiment using techniques covered in this chapter.

Change how the Finder looks

Open System Preferences again. Click the Appearance icon in the row of Personal icons. Then launch a Finder window, as described in chapter 1, and place the two windows side by side.

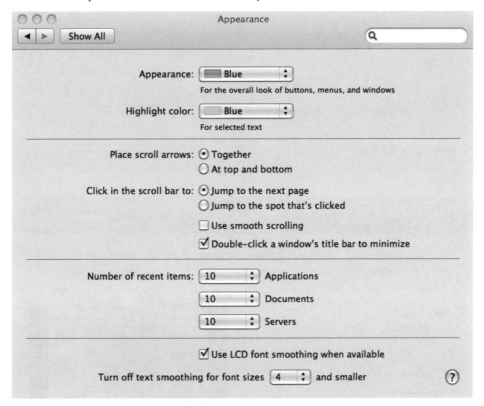

Change the settings in the Appearance preference pane and watch what happens to the Finder window. Which parts of the Finder's display can you change using the top two areas of the pane? How might some of these features help you organize your files?

Remember the Apple menu? The third area in the Appearance preference pane can change some parts of that menu. Make some changes to the number of recent items in the preference pane then check the Apple menu. What's different?

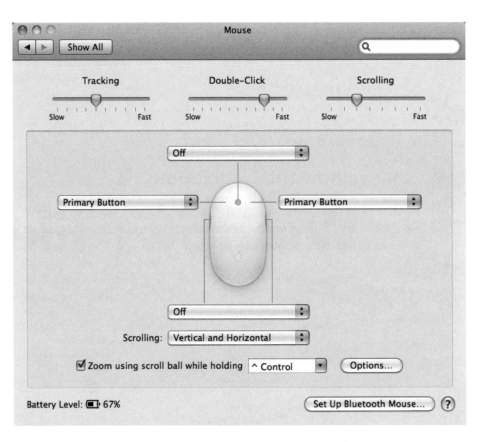

3 Make your Mac more Windows-like

You've been using Windows since forever, and you know how you like your computer to be. Sure, owning a Mac means you don't have to worry as much about viruses and spyware, and your system's going to be more reliable and stable. But still, there are certain things you miss, and doing things the Mac way seems to take forever. Is there some way to make your Mac more Windows-like?

No Problem!

Surprise! You *can* actually make your Mac behave more like a Windows PC. You won't get your Start menu or Taskbar back, but there are some things you can do that will make you feel more comfortable using your Mac:

⇨ Turn on your mouse's right-clicks.

⇨ Tweak the Finder.

⇨ Watch Windows video on your Mac.

⇨ Get applications you had on your PC.

All these things will not only make your Mac more Windows-like, but since your workflow will be closer to how it used to be, there's a good chance they'll make you more productive as well.

Enable right-click-ability

The **Magic Mouse**, which comes with iMac desktops, only appears to have one button and so does its predecessor, the **Apple Mouse**. Does that mean you'll always have to Control+click instead of being able to right-click?

Although **Apple's mice** may look like they have just one button, in fact, they've got **right-click buttons** and more. The Apple Mouse actually has *five* buttons that you can configure, while the Magic Mouse gives you left and right mouse-button functions as well as multitouch movements that replace some button functions completely.

So, how do you configure the buttons on your mouse? You just have to know where to look. Given what you learned in chapter 2, where would you look?

Mouse

Yes, in **System Preferences**. In your System Preferences window, click the Mouse icon. The Mouse preferences pane will show you the mouse you have, along with the settings available for it.

We'll start with the Magic Mouse. If you have an Apple Mouse, skip to the next page and if you have a trackpad, skip even further to page 31.

Right-click with a Magic Mouse

The wireless **Magic Mouse** has a **multitouch surface** that lets you use **gestures** instead of buttons for common actions. It connects via Bluetooth, and at this writing comes with Apple's iMacs.

What happens to the video playing in the window on the right when you move your cursor over the various options on the left of the pane,

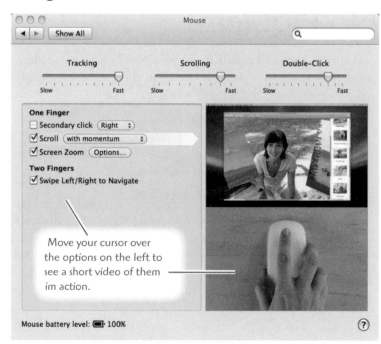

without clicking on them? Which option do you think would set up a right-mouse click on your Magic Mouse?

That's right. **Check** the box next to **Secondary click**. You're done.

> **Tip:** If you're left-handed and want the left mouse button of your Magic Mouse to invoke context menus, click the drop-down menu next to "Secondary click" and choose Left.

Right-click with an Apple Mouse

The **Apple Mouse** is a more traditional mouse with **multiple buttons**, though it has a **scroll** ball instead of a wheel. It's available both in USB/wired and Bluetooth/wireless versions. It comes with Apple's Mac Pro desktops.

> **Note:** Apple still sells what it used to call the Mighty Mouse. If you'd rather not have a touch-sensitive mouse, you can order or buy it by its new name: the Apple Mouse.

If you've got an Apple Mouse, you have more options. You can configure its buttons in different ways.

The Apple Mouse has *five* total buttons, but you can only make **four** choices. Why?

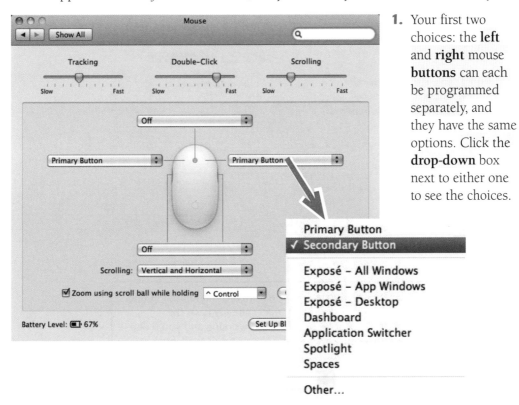

1. Your first two choices: the **left** and **right** mouse **buttons** can each be programmed separately, and they have the same options. Click the **drop-down** box next to either one to see the choices.

2. You can set up the **scroll ball** with multiple options just like you can with scroll wheels on mice used with Windows machines.

3. You need to **press the two buttons** on either side of the Apple Mouse **together** to invoke an action. That's why there are five buttons, but only four actions you can set up. Click the drop-down for the side buttons to see what they can do.

Let's turn on right mouse-clicking:

1. Click the **drop-down** for the **right** mouse button.

2. Select **Secondary Button**. You're done.

Tip: If you're left-handed and want the left mouse button of your Apple Mouse to invoke context menus, click the drop-down menu next to "Secondary click" and choose Left.

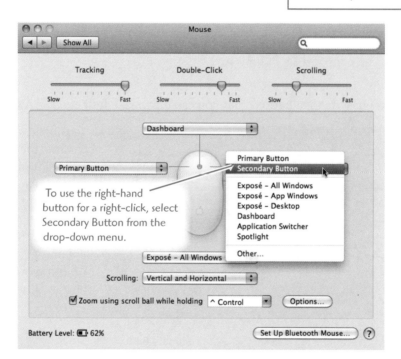

Note: You can also plug in a mouse from any manufacturer and it will most likely just work. In fact, many already have the right-click function available, but if it's not working and you'd like it to, you know where to look to see if the option's available.

Right-click with a trackpad

Even the **trackpad** on a MacBook or MacBook Pro has right-click capabilities, though it appears to have no buttons at all. Let's set up the trackpad as if you've got a notebook. Click the **Trackpad** icon in **System Preferences** and look at the options in the Trackpad preference pane.

Move your cursor over the various options on the left of the pane but don't click on them. What does the short video playing in the window on the right show you?

There are two ways to enable right-clicking to bring up a context menu:

1. Use a two-finger click on the trackpad; this is already set up for you.

2. Turn on a "corner click" using the trackpad as a button.

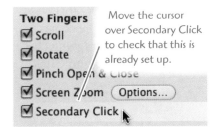

Move the cursor over Secondary Click to check that this is already set up.

Move the cursor over to check that the **Secondary Click** item under the **Two Fingers** category is set up.

Use **two fingers** to **click on** an area on your Mac's open desktop. What happens? Now try two-finger clicking on other areas of the desktop; the Macintosh HD icon and the icons on the Dock. What happens each time?

A *second* way to right-click with the trackpad

On most Windows notebooks, the right button next to the trackpad is the right-click button. If there are no buttons next to the Mac's trackpad, how can you use the trackpad to right-click?

On your Mac the entire trackpad is one big button, but *it's sensitive to the location where you press it*. Knowing that, you can set up the trackpad so that clicking the **bottom-right** or **bottom-left corner** of the **trackpad** serves as the **right-click**.

1. To use the bottom-right corner as the right-click button, click the checkbox next to **Secondary Click** under the **One Finger** category.

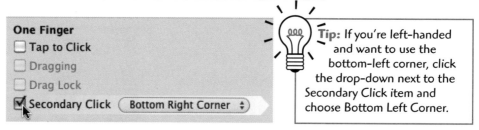

Tip: If you're left-handed and want to use the bottom-left corner, click the drop-down next to the Secondary Click item and choose Bottom Left Corner.

What do you think will happen when you **tap** the **bottom-right** or **bottom-left** of the **trackpad**? Try it. What happens? Try tapping the bottom-right or bottom-left of your trackpad on other areas of the desktop: the Macintosh HD icon, the icons on the Dock, an icon on the right side of the Menu Bar. What happens each time? Do you get the context menu every time?

Which right-click method do you prefer?

Tap and drag with a trackpad

Most Windows notebooks let you simply tap on the trackpad to do a left-click. On your Mac this feature is called **Tap to Click** and you have to turn it on.

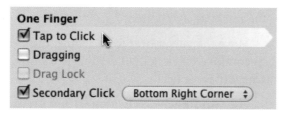

Check **Tap to Click** on the **trackpad options** and another option—Dragging—that was grayed out suddenly comes to life. **Check** the **Dragging** check box to **turn on Tap to Click**.

Play with it

Why do you think Tap to Click is required to make Dragging and Drag Lock available as options? Enable both Dragging and Drag Lock, then open a Finder window on your desktop and explore the differences by reproducing the examples you see in the video window of the preference pane.

Dragging and Drag Lock can make it easier to move objects around on the desktop, but the features may take some getting used to.

Make a link

{ Set up right-clicking for your mouse or trackpad via System Preferences. }

Note: From here on in the book when we say "right-click" anything, you can use any method you like, including Control+click to do that, but since we don't know what method you're using we'll stick with "right-click."

Tweak the Finder

You already know that the Finder is the equivalent of Windows Explorer and helps you navigate your drives, folders, files, and network shares. If you put the Finder and the Windows 7 Explorer side by side, they look a lot alike. But there's something missing from the Finder that's very useful in Windows Explorer.

Both the Finder and Windows Explorer have left sidebars for navigation and exploring, and a large right pane that shows the contents of folders and drives. And both have toolbars and a search field.

In Windows Explorer, as you navigate through levels of folders, you can see breadcrumbs at the top of the window. The name should be a hint as to the purpose: when do you leave a trail of breadcrumbs on the ground? Uh, besides when you want pigeons to follow you . . .

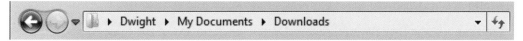

In computer navigation breadcrumbs show you the path you've taken to get to the current folder. You don't get a **breadcrumbs** view by default in the Mac OS X Finder, but you can turn it on.

1. Click the **Finder** icon on the Dock.

2. Click **View** on the Menu Bar.

3. Click **Show Path Bar** in the menu that appears.

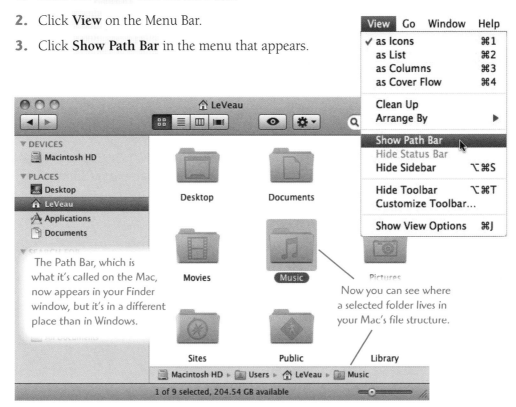

The Path Bar, which is what it's called on the Mac, now appears in your Finder window, but it's in a different place than in Windows.

Now you can see where a selected folder lives in your Mac's file structure.

Play with it

The Path Bar behaves a little differently than the Windows breadcrumbs. Click once on any folder in your main Finder window to highlight the folder. The *highlighted folder appears in the Path Bar*, even though you're not actually in it yet. How could that be useful?

You can use the Path Bar to navigate. Double-click on any of the folders shown in the path. Now that your mouse or trackpad is set up to let you, right-click on any of the folders in the Path Bar. What happens?

Get back your favorite apps

When they consider switching to the Mac, some people worry they'll miss familiar applications, that fitted in with their existing workflow. Luckily many of these apps are available for the Mac also.

Install Firefox

Say you'd like to download **Firefox®**, the popular Web browser. It's available for both Mac and Windows.

1. Open Safari and type `www.firefox.com` into the address bar then hit Return.

2. The Firefox site already knows what kind of Mac you've got and what software you're running on it, so you don't have to choose a version. Click the link to Download.

3. When the download's done, it will automatically open as a folder on your desktop, but *we'll come back to that in a moment*.

Double-click

Firefox 3.6.2.dmg

Instead, click the Downloads icon in the Dock. Do you see the Firefox Installer icon? It has a `.dmg` extension. What do you think DMG stands for?

When you double-click on a **D**isk i**M**a**G**e file, it sets up or **mounts a simulated drive** on your desktop.

But because you used Safari to download the file, you don't have to do that—Safari opens DMG files for you. Look on the right side of your desktop. See the new Firefox drive icon?

Double-click a .dmg file and it mounts a simulated drive on your desktop.

Firefox

4. Okay, it's time to take a look at the Finder window that opened when your Firefox download completed. There's the Firefox icon, but what do the arrow and the folder indicate you should do?

Firefox is a registered trademark of the Mozilla Foundation

5. Right, the arrow indicates that you should drag the Firefox icon into the Applications folder, but before you do that… Do you see the little arrow in the corner of the Applications folder icon in the Firefox window? Where have you seen arrows like that in Windows?

That little curved arrow indicates a **Shortcut**—a pointer to the "real" folder or program elsewhere in the system—just like it did in Windows. On the Mac, this feature is called an **Alias**.

The Firefox logo is a registered trademark of the Mozilla Foundation

Watch carefully: the Firefox folder tells you what to do to install Firefox on your Mac.

Since you have an alias for the Applications folder, you can drag the Firefox icon onto the alias and it will install Firefox in your Applications folder.

Note: Not every opened Disk Image folder is set up with an alias. In most cases, you'll have to drag the program's icon into the Applications folder.

6. Now what? You dragged the icon onto the Applications alias and … has Firefox installed? Check it's installed by finding its icon in the Applications folder and double-clicking it.

Eject the Disk Image

Looks like that's all working fine, but the Disk Image is still on your desktop. When you're done with a Disk Image, you need to eject it. You can do this in one of two ways:

1. **Right-click** on its **removable drive icon** and choose **Eject**.

2. **Drag the icon to the Trash** in the Dock. The Trash icon will turn into an up arrow as you drop the icon onto it.

Watch Windows Media video

Your Mac is great for watching video, but there's one area where it needs a little help. If you have any video recorded in the Windows WMV format, you'll soon discover that it won't play on your Mac. That's because WMV is a Microsoft-backed format, and while it's not as prevalent as it used to be, you'll still run into it from time to time.

Install Flip4Mac

Fortunately, there's an easy way to enable **QuickTime**—the Mac's media player—to play WMV files. **Flip4Mac®** is a free program that lets QuickTime play WMV files. Once Flip4Mac is in place QuickTime will play WMV files just as it would any other. Let's install it.

1. Open **Safari** and type
   `dynamic.telestream.net/downloads/download-flip4macwmv.htm`
   into the address bar, then hit the Return key.

2. Click the **Download Now** button.

3. Once the download has completed, click the **Downloads** icon on the Dock. Do you see a file in the folder that includes the words WM Components in its name (the version number may be different)? Does it look like the same type of file you downloaded for Firefox?

4. Double-click the file, and it will open a drive icon on your desktop.

5. Double-click the drive icon, and you'll find the Flip4Mac installer waiting for you inside.

6. Double-click the installer to launch it. Although cosmetically it's different, you'll see right away that it works in a similar way to a Windows installation. Because of that, you already know how to work your way through the installer, but there are one or two things to notice as you do.

WM Components 2.3.2.6.dmg

Make a link

Mac installers work just like Windows installers.

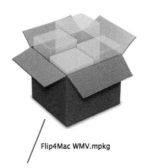

Flip4Mac WMV.mpkg

That's called a "package installer" and it's similar to installers for Windows.

7. A window appears that says "This package will run a program to determine if the software can be installed."

8. Click Continue and the Introduction page appears.

9. Click Continue, then when you're done reading the Read Me page, click Continue again to clear it.

10. Choose your language for the program. Click Continue. A window slides down inviting you to read and agree to the license agreement.

11. Click Agree to continue. The "Standard Install" page appears.

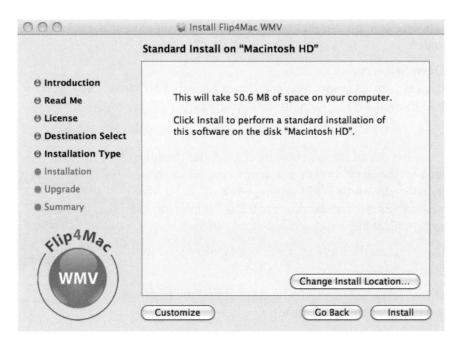

12. Click Install. You'll be prompted to enter your account password.

13. Type in your password, then click OK.

14. When you see the message "Flip4Mac successfully updated," click Continue then click Close.

From now on, whenever you come across a WMV file, QuickTime will play it automatically. There's nothing else to tweak or change. That's it!

There are three ways to receive software: zipped, as a disk image, or on a physical disk. To install the application, either follow the instructions, or drag and drop the app's icon to the Applications folder (or an alias in the installer if one's available).

.zip .sit	.dmg	DVD
Double-click the file to decompress it.	Double-click the .dmg icon to mount the disk image.	Insert the disk into your Mac's optical drive.
The files decompress into a folder in a Finder window.	A new icon is added to your desktop and it also appears as a drive in the left-hand pane of a Finder window.	A new icon is added to your desktop and it also appears as a drive in the left-hand pane of a Finder window.
Select the folder to see how the files will install.	Double-click the drive icon to see how the files will install.	Double-click the drive icon to see how the files will install.

Double-click the installer to run it.	Drag and drop the app's icon onto the alias (if one is provided) or into your Applications folder.

Choose your program

When you had a lot of programs running on your Windows PC did you use the Alt+Tab key combination to bring up icons for running programs to quickly switch to another program?

Now that you're on a Mac, you'll be happy to know there's a similar feature to cycle between open applications. Launch a few applications, then press **Command+Tab**, and *hold the Command key down*. Look familiar?

Keep holding down the Command key, and press Tab again. Each time you press Tab, you advance to the next icon in the row. Want to go backwards in the row? Hit the ` key, just above Tab, instead of Tab.

When you find the application you want to work with, release the keys and the currently selected application comes forward.

Choose your window

But what if you want to move quickly from a specific window in one application to a specific window in another? The application switcher Command+Tab won't cut it here as you'll still have to hunt through a bunch of windows in whatever application you switch to, unless the Mac handily gives you a shortcut…

To show all windows from just *one application*, click and hold on its icon in the Dock.

An even quicker way to jump from a window in one application to a window in another is to use **Exposé** to see *all* the windows that are active in all open applications.

On the current Mac keyboard, it's the F3 key, or Fn+F9. When you have several applications open, invoke Exposé to see all your windows arranged nicely on the screen. Just click the window you want to work on to bring it forward.

> 💡 **Tip:** Would you like to organize your applications into separate desktops? This can come in handy if you've got a lot of applications running at once, particularly on a small notebook screen. The Mac has a cool feature called **Spaces**, and you'll learn more about it in chapter 18.

Take a break

Phew! That was a vault of information. But now you're done. Your Mac has a more familiar feel to it, so give your brain a break. Go do something else for a while. Got a magazine to read? Need to check your e-mail? Do that now and we'll see you back here in 10, rested and ready to review, then you can dive in and experiment with some of the new skills you just learned to cement them in your brain.

Review

Turn on right-click

○ Where do you change the settings for your mouse?

....

○ Where do you change the settings for your trackpad?

....

○ You can set up a right-click on your trackpad in .... ways.

○ Use .... finger(s) to tap on the trackpad to get a context menu.

○ To set up single-tapping on a trackpad, go to the .... category and check the .... option.

○ What do Dragging and Drag Lock do on the trackpad?

....

Tweak the Finder

○ To turn on the Path Bar, go .... > .... > ....

○ What happens when you double-click a folder icon in the Path Bar?

....

Install Mac software

○ There are .... ways to install Mac software, and they depend on the program.

○ Drag a program icon to the .... folder in the "simple install" method.

○ What is a Disk Image? When launched, what does its icon look like?

○ Programs downloaded via Safari are saved to the .... by default.

How did you do?

If you'd like to improve your recall on any of these you should go spend a little more time on that part of the chapter.

Experiment

Tweak the Finder more

You can change the Finder's appearance and behavior quite a bit. You can make changes that affect every Finder window, or you can make tweaks that only affect a specific folder. There are too many customizations to include here, but you can explore them easily if you know where to look. Let's make a few changes to get you started.

To make global changes to the Finder, you'll need to go into its preferences menu.

1. Click on the desktop, or open a Finder window.

2. Click Finder in the Menu Bar then select Preferences from the menu. The Finder Preferences window appears.

The General tab is up by default, and it lets you choose:

→ what appears on your desktop when those devices are present or connected to your Mac

→ the default folder that appears when you open a new Finder window

→ whether double-clicking on a folder always opens a new Finder window.

Would changing any of these settings be useful to you? Could some of them cause problems? For example, what would happen if you unchecked the Hard disks option? What would happen to your desktop? Would that cause you any problems?

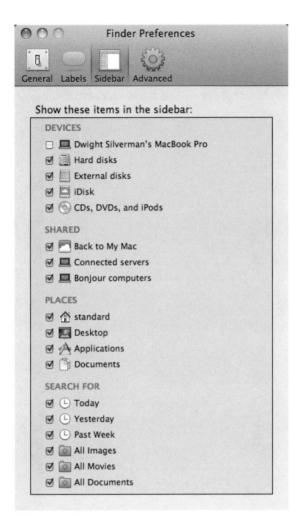

For more global changes, click the Sidebar tab. This gives you a long list of items you can add or remove from the Finder's sidebar.

Do you see any there that you think you might not need? Go ahead and uncheck them. If you decide you need them later, you can always come back and check the box again.

Take some time to play around with some of the ways in the preferences that you can tweak the Finder. You really can make the Mac OS your own.

4 Transfer files from a PC to your Mac

Right now, you've got music, word processing documents, photos, maybe a spreadsheet or two, and a few videos tucked away in folders on your Windows PC, but how will you move them onto your new Mac?

No Problem!

There are a number of ways to move your stuff from your Windows PC to your Mac. Some require that you spend some cash, one has you setting up a PC/Mac network, and one requires that you carry your precious Mac to the nearest Apple Store. Your options to move the data are:

⇨ Get someone to move your data for you.

⇨ Use an external drive.

⇨ Transfer it over a home network.

> We'll look at what to do with everything once it's on your Mac in chapter 5.
>
> Don't worry about your e-mail and contacts, we'll move those in chapter 7.

Get your files ready to move

You probably know where most things are on your PC. Most people use the pre-set folders that Microsoft provides in the Windows setup.

Have you stored any documents, music, photos and other files in non-standard folders on your PC? For example, do you have work-related Word documents in a folder on your desktop, rather than in the Documents folder?

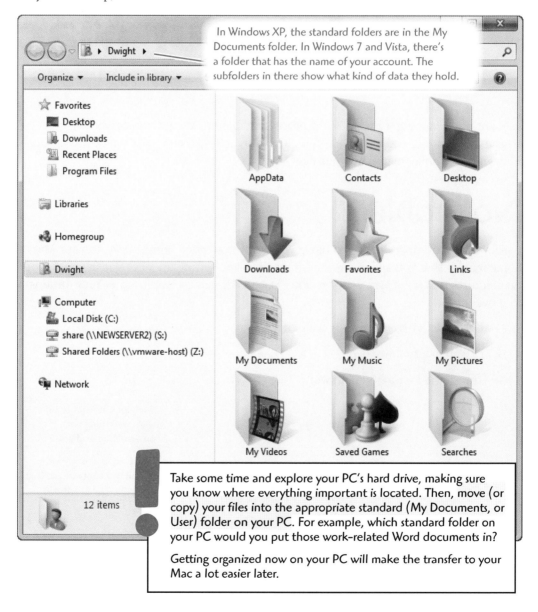

In Windows XP, the standard folders are in the My Documents folder. In Windows 7 and Vista, there's a folder that has the name of your account. The subfolders in there show what kind of data they hold.

Take some time and explore your PC's hard drive, making sure you know where everything important is located. Then, move (or copy) your files into the appropriate standard (My Documents, or User) folder on your PC. For example, which standard folder on your PC would you put those work-related Word documents in?

Getting organized now on your PC will make the transfer to your Mac a lot easier later.

Have a Genius transfer your files

Ready for the big move? Let's start with the easiest way to move your stuff from your old PC to your new Mac. Bring your Mac and PC to an **Apple retail store** and the tech support crew—known as **Geniuses**—can do the transfer for you. You may qualify for having this done free.

For $99, you can sign up for a year of **Apple's One-on-One** service, which provides training and help with projects, as well *as an expanded version of the transfer service* where the store's staff will move over everything from your PC, then *organize it for you* on your Mac.

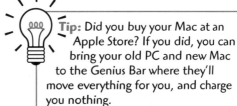

Tip: Did you buy your Mac at an Apple Store? If you did, you can bring your old PC and new Mac to the Genius Bar where they'll move everything for you, and charge you nothing.

The basic process **transfers *everything* from your PC's main data folder**—My Documents in Windows XP, or your User folder in Vista and Windows 7—and moves it **to a *single* folder on your Mac's desktop**. Go to chapter 5 to learn how to organize everything now it's on your Mac.

You don't need to have bought your Mac at an Apple Store to sign up for One-on-One.

A caveat: dragging your hardware down to an Apple Store may not be so easy if you don't live near the store. And, of course, if someone does the transfer for you, you won't learn how to do it yourself. Still, part of the Mac experience is that these services are available to you, and they can make your life much easier.

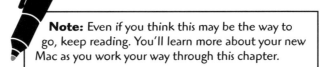

Note: Even if you think this may be the way to go, keep reading. You'll learn more about your new Mac as you work your way through this chapter.

Transfer your files with an external drive

If you buy a new external hard drive (or reformat an old one) specifically to transfer your files, when you're done moving the files over you can use the same drive to **back up your stuff** using the Mac's very cool **Time Machine** feature, which you'll learn more about in chapter 6.

You'll need a drive that:

Is big enough to copy over the contents of your Windows PC.	How much data's stored on your PC? When you've consolidated all of your PC's data into the User folder in Windows 7 or Vista, or My Documents in XP, right-click on the folder and choose **Properties** to see the folder's capacity.
Has the same capacity at least as your Mac's hard drive.	This requirement is so that you can use the drive for Time Machine when you're done. For example, if your Mac's drive is 500 GB, get at least a 500 GB external drive. (More is always better!)
Connects using USB 2.0.	Though some drives can connect in multiple ways.

How much will this cost? At this writing, a 500 GB external hard drive costs around $65; a 1 terabyte drive sells for about $100. So for the same price as, or less than, having a Genius transfer your data you get to keep the drive to use for Time Machine afterwards.

Once you've plugged your drive into a power supply, plug it into your Windows PC first. Once the drive's recognized and drivers are installed, follow the steps below to copy the data to the drive.

Windows XP

1. Click **Start > My Computer**

2. Follow this path:
   `C:\ > Documents and Settings > Your User folder`

   The name of your Windows account.

3. Again, click **Start > My Computer**

Windows 7 and Vista

1. Click **Start > Computer**

2. Follow this path:
   `C:\ > Users > Your User folder`

   The name of your Windows account.

3. Again, click **Start > My Computer**

From here, Windows XP, Windows 7 and Vista all follow the same process

4. **Find the external drive** you plugged in earlier, and double-click its icon. Move the resulting window to one side of the screen.

5. Move your User folder to the other side of the screen.

6. **Drag the User folder into the empty folder of the external drive** and release.

7. You may see several warnings pop up that indicate some files can't be moved. In each case, click Skip. These are system files that are in use by Windows, but aren't needed for what you want to do.

   The copying process may take a while, particularly if you have a lot of data or if your PC is older. Once it's complete, disconnect the hard drive from the PC.

Moving the files over to your Mac is a reversal of the process you just completed.

1. Plug the drive into one of your Mac's USB ports. A USB drive icon appears on your desktop.

2. A message asks whether you'd like to set the drive up for Time Machine.

You don't want to do this, at least not yet (we'll set up Time Machine in chapter 6). So click the **Decide Later** button.

3. **Double-click** on the **USB drive** icon to open its Finder window. What's inside?

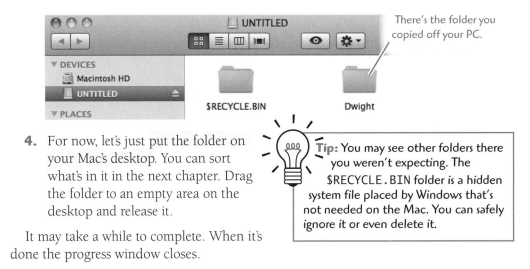

There's the folder you copied off your PC.

4. For now, let's just put the folder on your Mac's desktop. You can sort what's in it in the next chapter. Drag the folder to an empty area on the desktop and release it.

It may take a while to complete. When it's done the progress window closes.

Tip: You may see other folders there you weren't expecting. The `$RECYCLE.BIN` folder is a hidden system file placed by Windows that's not needed on the Mac. You can safely ignore it or even delete it.

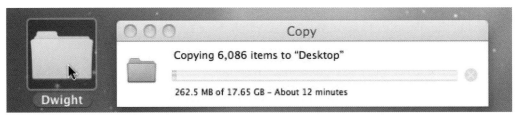

Play with it

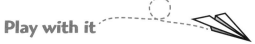

Double-click on the folder on your desktop. You want to make sure that everything copied over as expected, so spend some time exploring the folder.

Once you're certain you've copied everything over, you can delete the folder from the external drive. Drag it to the trash on your Mac, or right-click and choose Move to Trash from the window that appears.

Make a link

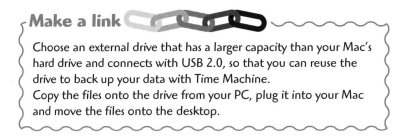

Choose an external drive that has a larger capacity than your Mac's hard drive and connects with USB 2.0, so that you can reuse the drive to back up your data with Time Machine.
Copy the files onto the drive from your PC, plug it into your Mac and move the files onto the desktop.

Use a flash drive

If you don't have a lot of stuff to transfer, and you're not interested in Time Machine (read chapter 6 to find out why you should be interested), you can make do with a USB flash drive. These are sometimes known as thumb drives.

They come in small sizes; 2, 4, 6, 8, and 16 GB. And they're cheap, starting at under $10. You can use any size, but if the amount of your data is greater than the capacity of the drive, you may have to move it in chunks.

Have you consolidated all of your PC's data into the **User folder** in Windows 7 or Vista, or the **My Documents** folder in XP? If so, **right-click** on either of those folders and choose **Properties**. You'll see the capacity of the folder, and can plan how you'll move your info—in one "trip," or piecemeal—based on the size of the drive and the amount of the data.

Follow the steps for using an external hard drive (above). They're the same for a flash drive except you won't be able to use the flash drive for Time Machine.

When you're done moving your files, if you're ready to start organizing, skip to chapter 5. To learn how to share files over a network, read on.

Use your home network to transfer your files

Maybe you're not a switcher at all. Maybe you're an "adder." Are you adding a Mac to an existing stable of computers on a home network? If so, that's a very simple way to transfer your stuff from your Windows PC.

First, follow the steps above for moving your data into the appropriate folder on your PC. Then, when you're ready, you'll need to add your Mac to your home network then connect to the PC that holds the data and transfer it across over the network.

Turn on file sharing and share a folder on your PC

If you've got an existing home network, do you have file sharing turned on so you can move files between computers? If not, you'll need to **enable file sharing** before you **share a folder**. Here's how to do that, depending on which version of Windows you have:

	Windows XP	Windows Vista	Windows 7
Turn on file sharing	Open My Computer, then Documents and Settings, and right-click on the folder with your user name. Choose **Sharing and Security** from the menu that appears. Click the tab for **Sharing**, then click the link that reads "If you understand the security risks but want to share files without running the wizard, click here." If you already have file sharing turned on, you won't see this message. A box labeled Enable File Sharing appears. Select **Just enable file sharing** and click OK.	Click Start and type "network and sharing" into the search box and hit Enter. The Network and Sharing Center appears. Click the drop-down buttons for Network Discovery and File Sharing, then make sure **Turn on network discovery** and **Turn on sharing so anyone with network access can open files** are selected. Click Apply for both.	Click Start and type "file sharing" into the search box and hit Enter. The Advanced Sharing Settings window appears. Make sure **Turn on network discovery** and **Turn on file and printer sharing** are selected. Click the Save Changes button.
Share a folder	In the next dialog box, check **Share this folder on the network**. Check **Allow network users to change my files**. Click Apply, then OK. There should now be a hand under the folder icon, indicating the folder is now shared.	Navigate to the User folder (C:\ > Users > your user folder). **Right-click** on the **User folder** and click on **Share…** At the dialog box that appears, click the Share button, then click OK.	Navigate to the User folder (C:\ > Users > your user folder). **Right-click** on the **User folder** and hover your cursor over **Share with…** In the subfolder that appears, choose **Specific people…** In the next dialog box, click the Share button. When the sharing process is complete, click Done.

That's got the network up and running on the Windows side, now let's do the same for your Mac.

Set up the PC/Mac network

Your Mac has been on the Internet since chapter 1. And if you're connecting to the Net via a home network, that means your Mac is already on the network.

But you want your Mac to talk to a Windows PC here, so let's set that up. Open a System Preferences window. Click the **Sharing** icon and take a look at the Sharing preferences.

Notice that three items are checked by default? This is why Macs can see each other immediately across a network. To see your Windows machines, you'll need to tweak some settings.

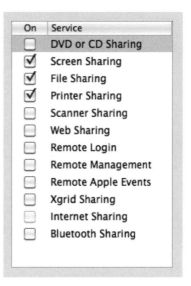

On	Service
☐	DVD or CD Sharing
☑	Screen Sharing
☑	File Sharing
☑	Printer Sharing
☐	Scanner Sharing
☐	Web Sharing
☐	Remote Login
☐	Remote Management
☐	Remote Apple Events
☐	Xgrid Sharing
☐	Internet Sharing
☐	Bluetooth Sharing

1. Select the File Sharing item in the left-hand list, then click Options.

2. Check **Share files and folders using SMB (Windows)**. This will enable Windows PCs to see your Mac's shared folders.

This Mac already has AppleTalk Filing Protocol (AFP) switched on. This means it can share files with other Macs over an Apple network.

Check the SMB box to share files with a PC running Windows.

☑ **Share files and folders using AFP**

Number of users connected: 0

☐ **Share files and folders using FTP**

Warning: FTP user names and passwords are not encrypted.

☑ **Share files and folders using SMB (Windows)**

When you enable SMB sharing for a user account, you must enter the password for that account. Sharing files with some Windows computers requires storing the Windows user's account password on this computer in a less secure manner.

On	Account
☐	Apple
☐	dwight

Warning
See the security warning in this dialog? The passwords used in Windows file sharing aren't stored in quite as secure a manner as Mac passwords. This is not a big deal if you're working on your home network. If you connect to Windows-based systems on the road, while it's unlikely that someone could access your passwords, it's something you may want to consider before checking that box.

(Done)

3. Click Done.

4. Click Show All to return to System Preferences.

    The Windows machines can now see your Mac on the network. Let's set up the
    second half of the equation, so your Mac can see the PCs.

5. Click on the **Network** icon in System Preferences.

6. In the list on the left, click the topmost item:

    →   If you connect to the network via your Mac's Wi-Fi adapter, AirPort will
        be at the top.

    →   If you have a wired connection, Ethernet will be at the top.

7. When you've selected the top item in the list, click the **Advanced...** button.

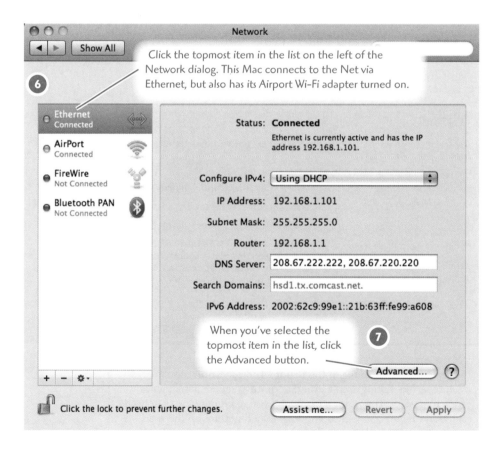

Switching to a Mac—No Problem!

8. Select the **WINS** tab.

9. Your Windows network has what's called a workgroup name. All your Windows PCs should be set up on the same workgroup. The default workgroup name for most Windows networks is WORKGROUP (some older Windows XP systems may use MSHOME). Do you know what your workgroup is called?

> **Note:** To find out the workgroup name, as well as the computer's individual name (you'll need this in a moment, so make a note of both), right-click on the Computer icon (My Computer in Windows XP) and choose Properties.

Enter the name of your Windows PCs' workgroup in the Workgroup field and click OK.

Don't be surprised if the workgroup name is already there. Mac OS X is pretty smart.

10. Click Apply, then close the Network preference pane.

Copy your data over the network

Your Mac and Windows PCs can now talk to each other. So all that's left to do is to go get your stuff. You'll need to connect to the PC on the network that holds the data you want to transfer, so open a Connect to Server window:

1. Hold down the **Command** key and then hit the **K** key. (Or click Go > Connect to Server from the Finder's Menu Bar.)

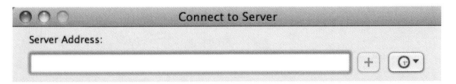

2. In the Server Address field, type `cifs://` (which is a type of network file system used by Windows) followed by the name of the Windows PC holding your stuff. Here's an example:

`cifs://Dwight-Win7-x64`

>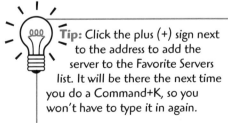
> **Tip:** Click the plus (+) sign next to the address to add the server to the Favorite Servers list. It will be there the next time you do a Command+K, so you won't have to type it in again.

3. A progress bar appears, followed by a login prompt. Enter the login and password for the Windows PC, then click **Connect**. (If your PC doesn't have a password, choose Guest.)

4. Choose the folder that contains your data in the dialog box that shows you the folders available for sharing and click OK.

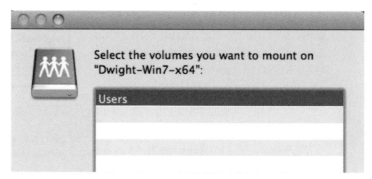

5. A Finder window opens showing the folders you can access on your Windows PC. Do you see the folder that holds your data?

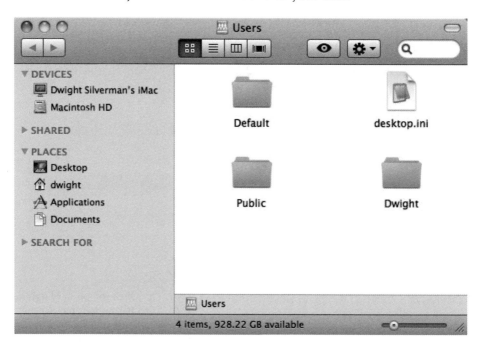

Click on the folder that holds your data and drag it to the Mac's desktop. Depending on the size, the transfer may take a while.

Play with it

There's now a connection between your Windows PC and your Mac. To see that connection hold down the Command and Shift keys, then hit K. The Network window opens and there's an icon representing your Windows machine.

Do you want to have an icon on your desktop for network drives to which you connect? Select the Finder icon in the Dock, then click Finder in the Menu Bar, then Preferences > General. Select the Connected servers box, and you'll see a blue-green drive icon with stick figures on it. That indicates you're connected to another computer on the network. What happens if you double-click it?

Dwight-Win7-x64

The network icon is Apple's little dig at Windows—a Blue Screen of Death, or BSoD, from Windows 98.

When you connect to another computer on the network, the Mac OS places an icon for that computer on your desktop. This is called mounting the drive, and it makes it easy to access it repeatedly while you're working at your computer.

Make a link

Share files between a PC and your Mac. Turn on file sharing and share the folders on your PC that hold the data. Back at your Mac, share files and folders using SMB, then connect to a server (the PC holding the files) with Command+K

Take a break

Your brain needs time to sift through what you just learned about transferring your data. Time to take a break. We're nearly at the end of the chapter. All that's left is the review and an experiment. So, walk away and find something else to do for a little while. Now is a great time to read that magazine article you've been saving.

Review

Get your files ready to move

↻ Before you can move your files over to your Mac, ensure the files are moved or copied to .... locations in Windows.

Let a Genius do it

↻ When would you *not* want a Genius to move your stuff for you?

....

Use an external drive

↻ How large does the drive you use to transfer your data need to be?

....

↻ When you're done using it for transferring files the Mac OS X .... feature can take advantage of an external drive.

↻ Your external drive should have a .... connection.

Use your home network

↻ To connect to another computer via your Mac, hit Command+ ....

↻ What appears on your desktop when you connect to another computer on your network?

....

How did you do?

Did you forget anything? It's hard to remember it all. Go ahead and re-read the sections covering anything you may have overlooked. Your brain might need a bit more time to absorb all the information and make some stronger links.

Experiment

Remember how, when you set up file sharing, you designated specific folders on your PC that you wanted to share? You can do that, too, on the Mac, and in a similar way. Right-click on a folder, choose Get Info, and from the window that appears designate that you want to share the folder.

To share a folder on your Mac, right-click it, then check the Shared folder box.

Even if you don't pick one, there's a default folder that appears when you try to connect to a Mac on a network. Try it now.

Go ahead and log into your Mac from your Windows PC, if you have them both on a network. (If you're asked for a login and password, use the same ones you use to log into the Mac when you're working on it.) What is the name of the folder you can see?

....

This folder lets you leave files for other users who don't have access to the rest of your files. Does it have anything in it?

Put some files from your PC into the folder on your Mac, then hop back on your Mac and retrieve them. Play around with moving files back and forth between the two computers.

Folder permissions

Back on the Mac, follow the path below in a Finder window:

`Macintosh HD > Users`

If you've got other users sharing your Mac, do you see their Home folders inside the Users folder? Can you double-click on one of the other users' folders to open it? Do you see the little red symbol on the folders? What do you think that symbol means?

If you double-click on a folder with a red symbol, what do you think will happen?

In the Mac OS, you can only get to *your* stuff, not to the stuff of other people who have accounts on the system. And they, most importantly, can't get to your stuff.

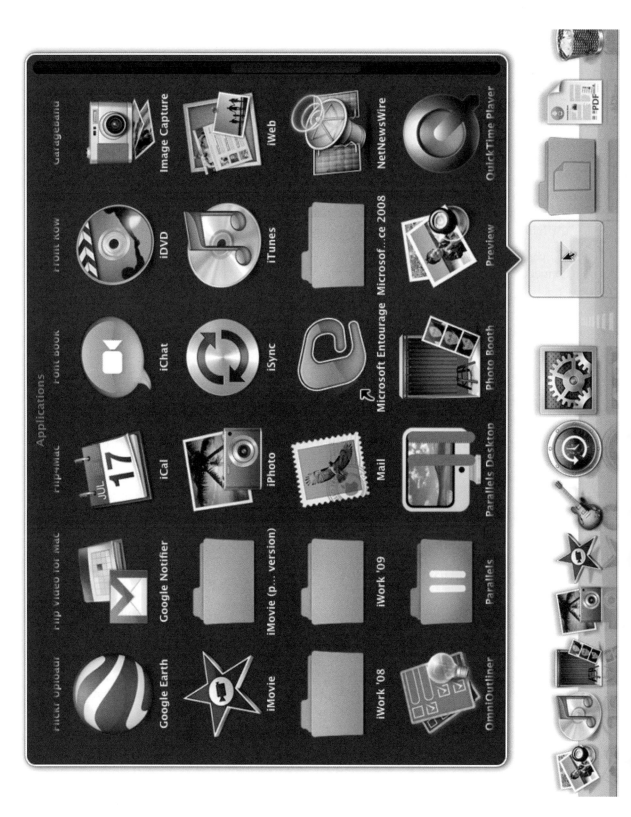

5 Settle in to your new Home

Now that you've moved the data from your Windows PC to your Mac you need to get everything off the desktop and into the right folders. You need a place for your stuff.

No Problem!

You know where things go in Windows, but putting them in the right place in Mac OS X requires knowing a little bit about where files are stored. In this chapter, you'll learn:

⇨ Where the Mac stores different types of documents.

⇨ How to add folders to the Finder.

⇨ How to set up the Dock to best access your data.

⇨ How to find your data.

Explore your new Home

If you used the pre-set folders that Microsoft provided in your Windows setup, you'll have a good idea of the Windows file structure, but how different is the Mac's file structure? Can you create a similar structure on your Mac?

Just like Windows, the Mac OS has specified places for your stuff and the setup is similar to Windows 7 and Vista. The folder with the house icon and your account's name on it is the starting point. On the Mac, this is called your **Home folder**. It's always visible in the sidebar of each Finder window, and you can get to it by following this path if you double-click the Macintosh HD icon:

`Macintosh HD > Users > your Home folder`

In your Home folder, you'll find places for specific types of data. Do you want to store your movies, music, documents and pictures in an organized way? That's what the Home folder is all about.

The standard set of subfolders in the Home folder comprises:

→ **Desktop.** Remember that the desktop is a folder itself? Here it is. Whatever's on your desktop is stored in this folder.

→ **Documents.** This is where spreadsheets, word processing documents and other "serious" files get stored. Many Macintosh applications save their data here by default, and some even create their own subfolders in here.

→ **Downloads.** The Downloads folder is where Safari saves downloaded files by default.

→ **Library.** The Library is where your individual settings are stored. Every user gets a library folder so that applications can maintain preferences for different users. You won't need to access the Library much.

→ **Movies.** All your videos are stored here, including those saved and edited in iMovie, a video-editing application that comes with your Mac.

→ **Music.** Your music files go here. iTunes, the music management application, places its files here in a subfolder called iTunes Music.

> **Note:** If you buy or rent any movies from the iTunes Store, they're not saved in the Movies, but rather in the *Music* folder.

→ **Pictures.** This folder holds the photos you save. You can either manually place photos here, or use iPhoto, a photo-editing and management application that comes with your Mac. You'll learn all about iPhoto in chapter 11.

→ **Public.** If you want to make files available to other people on your network, this is the place to put them. This is *like the Shared folder in Windows*. There's also a **Drop box** folder inside, which lets people leave files for you.

→ **Sites.** Your Mac has a web server. Files created by iWeb are stored here. You'll meet iWeb in chapter 15.

Organize your files

Now that you have your documents, music, pictures, video, and other files moved over to your Mac and you know where they'll live, let's organize them. Moving a file into a folder on Windows is a simple drag-and-drop action, right? Well, you can do that on your Mac, too. It's as easy as dragging files between folders.

1. Start fresh. Close any Finder windows that may be open now.

2. Click the **Finder** icon in the Dock to open your **Home** folder and access its subfolders.

   Move this window to the left-hand side of your screen.

3. Double-click on the icon on your desktop for the folder you copied over from your Windows PC. Does it contain category-based folders?

   Depending on the version of Windows you copied from, you may need to look in the My Documents folder to see some other topic-based folders.

   Move this window to the right-hand side of your screen.

63

4. Navigate to the **Pictures** folder in your Home folder window, then find the **Photos** folder in the folder from your Windows PC. Still in this window, hold down the **Command** key and hit the **A** key. This selects all the content *just like the Windows Control+A* command. How do you know all the files in the folder are selected?

5. Drag the highlighted items from the Photos folder to the **Pictures** folder in your Home Finder window. The files will move, rather than copy. When it's done, the older Photos folder will be empty.

Note: You can simply drag and drop the contents of the folders in the PC folder on your desktop to their new folder in your Home folder. If you have subfolders within the main folders in the PC folder on your desktop, those will be transferred, too.

6. Repeat steps 1 to 5 for each category until you've moved the rest of your files.

Play with it

You can take a peek at a folder's content before you decide to move a file into it.

1. Click on a single file you want to move, hold down your left mouse button and drag it to the destination folder, but *don't let it go!* Just hold it over the folder.

2. The folder begins to flash, then it springs open, and now you're looking inside it. This feature is called **spring-loaded folders**.

3. Is that the destination you're looking for?

   → Release the file to complete moving it to the new folder.

   → Or move the file away to close the folder.

Tip: You can control how fast folders pop open by going to Finder > Preferences > General and changing the slider for spring-loaded folders.

   Hit the spacebar to open a folder immediately with no spring-load delay.

   How useful would spring-loaded folders be if the destination folder is four or five subfolders deep? Rather than repeated double-clicking to get to the right folder, just click-and-drag and use this feature to drill down quickly to your destination.

Add your own folders

The set of folders in Documents is handy, but what if you want to add folders on your Mac to give you more control over the way your files are organized?

Creating a new folder is ridiculously easy on a Mac. Navigate to your Documents folder: `Macintosh HD > Users > Your home folder > Documents`

Did you notice there was already a file in there, called **About Stacks.pdf** when you moved your files? Find the About Stacks.pdf file. Let's create a new folder to hold that lonely little file. How would you do it in Windows? The process is similar on your Mac, but simpler.

1. **Right-click** on the **open background** in the **Documents** folder.

2. Choose **New Folder** from the menu that appears. A folder named Untitled appears.

Tip: In the Finder you can also go **File > New Folder** or **Shift+Command+N** to create a new folder.

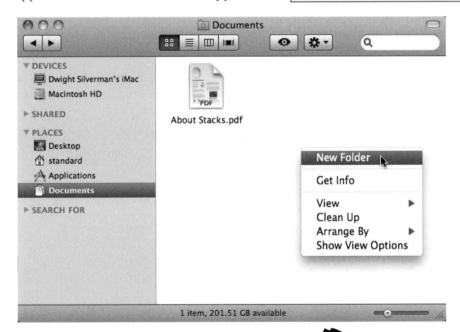

3. Without clicking on anything, just start typing a name to replace the default Untitled name. For the sake of this exercise, let's call the folder "PDFs."

4. Hit the **Return** key when you're done.

Note: If you click off a folder and want to rename it, **select its name in a Finder window, then hit Return**.

Delete the empty folder

Once you're done moving the files from the PC folder on your desktop, you can delete the empty folder. Simply drag it to the trash.

Make a link

▶ Drag and drop files or folders from one place to another to move them.

▶ Hold an item over a folder and the spring-loaded folder springs open to show you its contents.

▶ Create a new folder with a right click, from the Finder's File menu or hit Shift+Command+N in the Finder.

Actions and storage on the Dock

Now that your stuff is all safely in its new Home, you need to be able to access it, but are there faster ways to do that than open a Finder window and drill down to the right place?

You've already seen that the **Dock** functions as a kind of Windows Start menu and Taskbar hybrid. The Dock makes it very easy to get to your stuff. It provides quick access to both your data and applications.

Let's take a closer look at the Dock. The **divider** separates application icons from folder icons and it looks like a line down the middle of a highway. Hover your cursor over the icons on the right of the divider. What do you see?

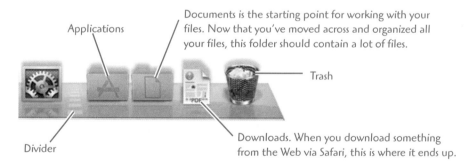

Applications

Documents is the starting point for working with your files. Now that you've moved across and organized all your files, this folder should contain a lot of files.

Trash

Divider

Downloads. When you download something from the Web via Safari, this is where it ends up.

Since the **Applications**, **Documents** and **Downloads** folders are **on the Dock** you can access any of them directly by clicking on them in the Dock just like you can with the applications. Click one of these icons. What happens? Click another one. Does it display the same way or differently?

The folders placed on the right side of the Dock are displayed in a *variety of graphical ways* called **Stacks**. There is nothing quite like this in Windows.

The different Stacks views are called:

Grid displays the contents in a grid with large icons. You can scroll through the collection.

List displays a simple list of file and folder names, and is also scrollable.

Fan displays smaller icons that curve up and right.

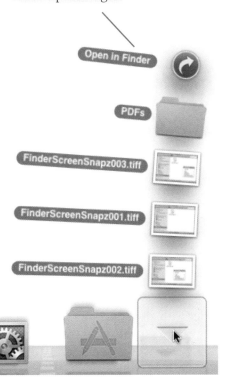

Make a link

The **Grid** Stacks view **icons** and the **List** Stacks view file and folder **names** are both **scrollable**, while the **Fan** Stacks view has **smaller** and daintier **icons** like a neat little literary heroine fanning herself.

The Stacks view changes depending on how many items are in each folder, though you can customize this for each folder. When would each one of these views be useful? When would you want to use a grid view over a fan view or a list view?

Let's **customize** the Stacks. Right-click on a folder you want to change to see your options.

To have the items in the Stack appear *in a certain order*, make a choice in the **Sort by** area.

Display as *changes the icon on the dock* to either a folder, or the icon of the first item in the folder.

To *fix the way a Stack displays* when you click on it, make a selection under **View content as**.

Right-click a folder in the Dock to customize its Stacks view.

You can remove a folder from the Dock in the Options menu.

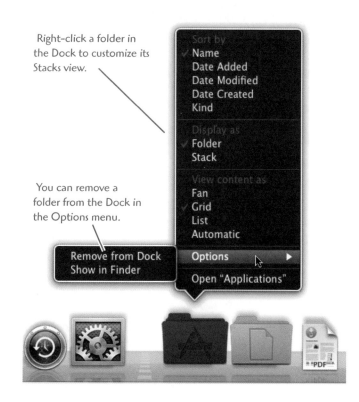

You can also use the Stacks menu to remove a folder from the Dock. In fact, let's do it. (Don't worry; you'll put it back in a second.)

1. Right-click on the **Documents** folder.

2. Hover the cursor over **Options**.

3. Click on **Remove from Dock** in the submenu. What happens to the Documents folder?

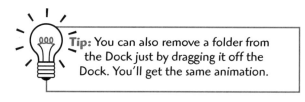

Tip: You can also remove a folder from the Dock just by dragging it off the Dock. You'll get the same animation.

Wait! Did you just delete your Documents folder with all your content in it? That content took an *age* to move from your PC then organize on your Mac...

Don't panic! The **folders on the Dock** are basically **aliases**—in Windows, they'd be called *shortcuts*. You didn't really delete the Documents folder.

It's easy to put the Documents folder back on the Dock.

1. Click on the **Finder** icon on the Dock.

2. Your Home folder opens in a Finder window.

3. Find the **Documents** folder, click on it, and **drag** it to the spot on the **Dock** where the original Documents folder sat.

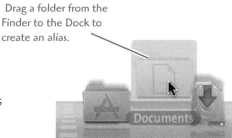
Drag a folder from the Finder to the Dock to create an alias.

4. When you bring the folder down to the Dock's base the other folders get out of its way. **Release** the folder and it will snap into position.

Now the Dock is back the way it was originally. Click on the Documents icon. What Stack view does it use?

Play with it

What if you wanted to add other folders to the Dock? What do you think would happen? How would having any folder on the Dock be useful?

Let's put all the skills you've learned together.

1. Create a new folder.

2. Drag it to the right side of the Dock and drop it into a position you prefer.

3. Change its settings so it always opens as a List.

4. When you're done, remove it from the Dock… unless you want to use it.

Find your stuff

If you have a lot of documents, music, movies, and photos, you can be as organized as possible and still not be able to find what you're looking for. Now that you've moved over your Windows data to your Mac, there are going to be times when you'll need to search for it, but uh, how do you do that?

Meet **Spotlight**. It's the equivalent to the Search box on the Windows 7 and Vista Start menu. Spotlight lives on the **far right** side of the Mac OS X's **Menu Bar**, and in the **top right-hand** corner of every **Finder window**.

To get started, click on the magnifying glass icon on the Menu Bar.

Let's try it out. Click on the Spotlight icon on the Menu Bar and type "About Stacks" into the search field.

The Spotlight search box looks a lot like the search field on a web browser, doesn't it?

There are several results, but Spotlight gives you a **Top Hit** selection, the file it thinks you're really searching for. Click on the file in the Top Hit section to open it.

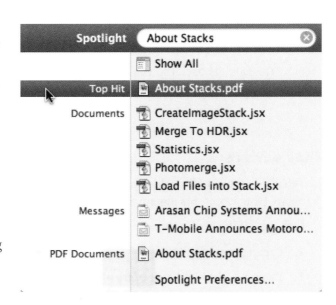

Spotlight will organize your search results by category, making it easier to find items with similar names. It's unlikely you'd have a song called "About Stacks," but if you did, it would be categorized separately than the PDF file you're really looking for. In that case, click the Show All link at the top of the search results to see them categorized so you can look deeper.

Play with it

Give the same search a try in the Spotlight field in a Finder window. As soon as you start typing, you get a bunch of buttons below the toolbar. Click one of them to tell Spotlight where to search and what to search for.

Make a link

Throw the Spotlight over your whole Mac from the Menu Bar or drill down a little more in a Finder window.

Take a break

That was a vault of information. Give your brain a break. Let your mind ponder some of the ideas discussed in this chapter. Then, when you feel rested and ready to dive in, try some of the elements out for yourself by coming back and reading on for the review and experiment.

Review

Explore your new Home

↺ Navigate to your Home folder by going .... > .... > ....

↺ Name three subfolders that are inside the Home folder by default.

1. ....

2. ....

3. ....

Add folders

↺ There are three ways to create a new Folder, name your favorite two methods.

1. ....

2. ....

↺ When you've navigated away from a new folder, how do you rename it later?

....

↺ How can spring-loaded folders help you stay organized?

....

Continues, flip the page

Do stuff and store things from the Dock

↺ The left side of the Dock lets you .... and the right side lets you ....

↺ Name the three Stacks views.

1. ....

2. ....

3. ....

↺ How can you set a specific view in a Stack folder?

....

↺ How do you remove a folder from the Dock?

....

↺ How do you add a folder to the Dock?

....

Find your stuff

↺ Spotlight is a .... and you can access it via .... and ....

↺ How do searches differ in Spotlight when they're conducted via the Menu Bar vs. the Finder?

....

How did you do?

Did you forget anything? It's hard to remember it all. Go ahead and re-read the sections covering anything you may have overlooked. Your brain might need a bit more time to absorb all the information.

If you find anything's missing or harder to remember, take some time to work on just those bits and make stronger links.

Experiment

Use some of the techniques you just read about. Here are a few ideas to get you started. You can accomplish these experiments with the knowledge you've gained in this chapter and earlier chapters.

The Dock is not only Mac OS X's most useful feature; it's also one of the most versatile. You can customize the Dock in a variety of ways to make it work the way you want it to. We've only scratched the surface here.

Want to know more? Go ahead and launch the Dock preference pane from System Preferences.

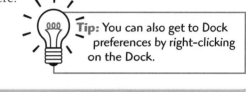

Tip: You can also get to Dock preferences by right-clicking on the Dock.

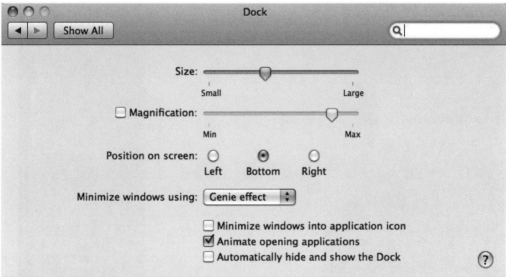

This pane lets you do all kinds of interesting things with the Dock. Looking at its controls, which one do you think:

→ Lets you change the size of the icons in the Dock?

→ Makes the icons grow when you move the cursor over them?

→ Changes where the Dock lives on your desktop?

→ Changes the animation when windows minimize and restore?

Go ahead and play with the settings here. You can always go back to the defaults. Get the Dock set up just the way you like it.

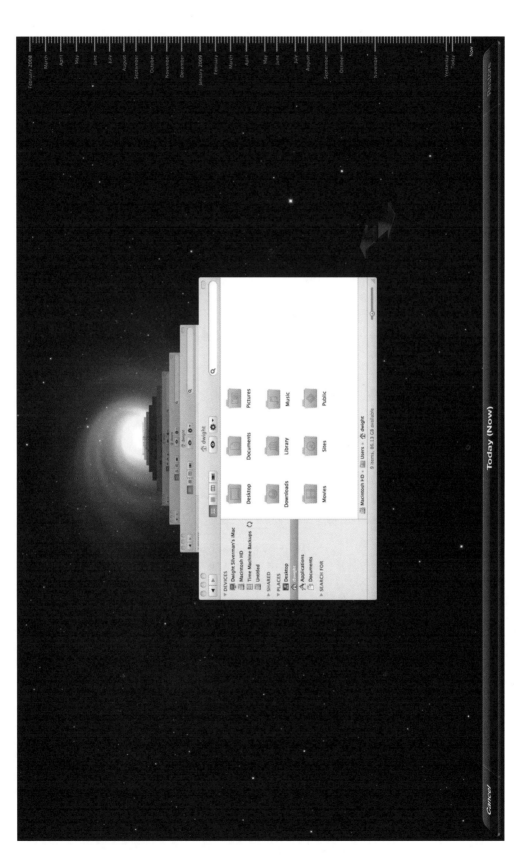

6 Hop aboard the Time Machine

Computer users are harangued again and again to back up their data, but most of them never do it. Back-burner guilt turns into full-out horror after a hard drive dies and every precious byte stored there is lost. Is there an easy way to keep your files safe without having to step through the tedious process of backing everything up?

No Problem!

Apple feels your pain, and more importantly, has a very simple solution. Time Machine. If you happen to have a spare external drive it's about to become one of the handiest tools for use with your Mac. That's because Time Machine is a set-it-and-forget-it backup. Once the drive is connected to your Mac, Time Machine:

⇨ Makes a complete backup of the current state of your Mac.

⇨ Backs up new and changed files every hour.

⇨ Consolidates hourly backups into daily and weekly backups.

⇨ Lets you retrieve individual files from earlier dates, or completely restore your Mac should the internal drive fail.

Set up Time Machine if you clicked "Decide Later" in chapter 4

Did you use this external drive to copy your files from a PC to your Mac? If you did, the process requires a few additional clicks. Time Machine has already seen the drive and asked you about it, but in chapter 4, you clicked the **Decide Later** button.

Now you've decided. You want to use the drive with Time Machine, but it's not letting you. What can you do?

1. When you plugged in your drive, an orange-colored drive icon should have appeared on your desktop.

    Even though Time Machine didn't recognize it as a drive yet, your Mac does.

2. Right-click the Time Machine icon on the Dock and select **Open Time Machine Preferences…** .

3. When the Time Machine preferences pane appears, click **Select Backup Disk**.

4. In the drop-down that appears, click on the external drive you want to use and click **Use for Backup**.

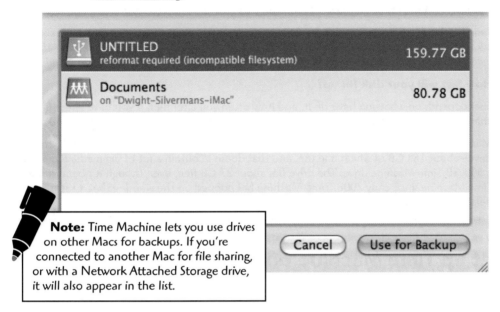

Note: Time Machine lets you use drives on other Macs for backups. If you're connected to another Mac for file sharing, or with a Network Attached Storage drive, it will also appear in the list.

5. The backup process begins. You can close the Time Machine preferences window. A progress bar will appear to let you know the initial backup's status.

Once the backup starts, look at the clock icon on the right of the Menu Bar. Yeah, the one that until now was grayed-out. What's it doing now?

Is it running counterclockwise? That lets you know a backup is in progress. Most times, because the application runs quietly in the background, this little icon may be your only indication that Time Machine is doing its job.

What do you think will happen when you click the icon? Go ahead and click it to see if you were right.

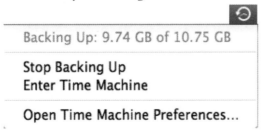

The icon launches a dialog. Do you see the amount that's being backed up, and how much has been backed up so far? This value will change with each hourly backup, based on how many files you've added or changed in the past hour.

> **Note:** If Time Machine makes backups every hour, and consolidates those hourly backups to daily and weekly backups over time, won't your external drive eventually fill up?
>
> Time Machine handles this in different ways. When your backup drive is full, a dialog box will ask how you want to handle the overflow. By default, Time Machine will start *deleting the oldest backups*, but you can also tell the application to start *using a different backup disk*.
>
> **How fast will your disk fill up?**
>
> That depends on what you have on it, and how often you alter files. If you have larger files that change often—say, video files you edit and save—the external drive can fill up pretty quickly.
>
> Many users won't need to worry much. For example: the author's iMac with a 320 GB hard drive—about 168 GB of which is in use, and that doesn't contain a lot of big media files—has a 500 GB Time Machine drive. The drive has about 27 GB free, even though it's been running Time Machine since early 2008. Time Machine has popped up the warning that it's starting to delete old files, but files dated back to early 2008 can still be retrieved.

Set up Time Machine on a new external drive

If you have a new external drive, Time Machine is so simple to use that it requires just two steps to set it up.

Make sure the drive has a storage capacity equal to or greater than your Mac's hard drive.

1. **Plug in an external hard drive.** A dialog box asks if you want to use the drive for Time Machine backups.

2. Click the **Use as Backup Disk** button.

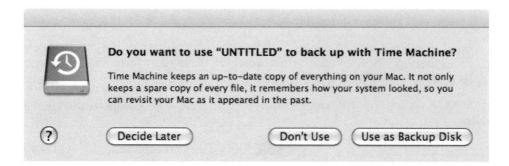

That's all there is to it. Time Machine begins to back up your entire Mac. Depending on how many files are on your drive, it could take a while (though on a brand-new machine with no additional data, it typically takes about 15 to 20 minutes). When the initial backup is complete, your settings, programs, and all your stuff are backed up.

Go back in time

Suppose you accidentally delete a document. It's easier than you think; lots of people get that "must empty the trash" reflex. You can't un-empty the trash and you didn't save the document as a copy, so what can you do?

Apple called its backup feature Time Machine because you really can go "back in time" to get older versions of files, or to a time when a now-deleted file was still present on your Mac. Here's how it works:

You need the document you deleted . . . **Time Machine, will let you go back in time** and retrieve the document—and in a very cool way.

Play with it

When you've set up Time Machine, delete the About Stacks.pdf file that we created a folder for in chapter 5. Don't worry if you hadn't read it yet, you'll be able to retrieve it with Time Machine.

When you've dragged About Stacks.pdf to the trash, right-click the trash icon and choose Empty Trash to be sure the file's really gone.

1. Click the **Time Machine** icon in the Dock. Your Mac's desktop slides down to reveal a line of Finder windows marching off into what looks like a swirling galaxy.

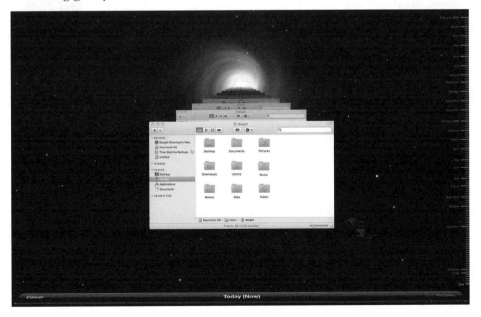

2. If you had no Finder windows open at the time, the default window will show your Home folder. If you do have a window open, Time Machine will launch with that window in focus. Double-click the folder you think contains the file you need—in this case, the PDFs folder in the Documents folder. The PDFs folder opens.

3. Do you know the approximate **date** that you created the PDFs folder that contains the About Stacks.pdf file? If you do, move your cursor to the **right** side of the screen. The Timeline bulges outward to show a backup date. Most of the lines represent a week in a month.

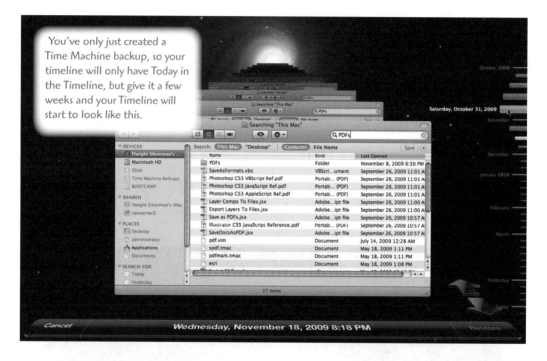

Move your cursor toward the **bottom** of the Timeline. How do the dates shown change? Because Time Machine archives by hour, then by day and then by week, the lines closest to the bottom of the screen will show the most recent set of backed-up files.

4. Find the date closest to when you think the original About Stacks.pdf file was still saved on your Mac and click it. The Finder windows march forward to show the PDFs folder from that period.

5. If you see the file you think you want, click on it. Not sure it's the right one? Hit the space bar.

Note: Hitting the space bar invokes Quick Look. As the name implies, it lets you see the contents of a file quickly, without actually launching the application that works with this type of file.

Quick Look is available anywhere you see documents listed; in Mail, the Finder, and so on. It works with almost any kind of document file type—just click on it, then hit the space bar. What do you think would happen if you tried this on a music file? On a video? On a Word document? Or a PDF? Try it and see!

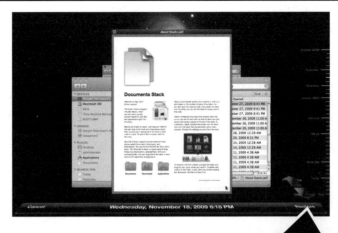

6. When you've Quick Looked and you're sure the file is the correct one, click on the **Restore** button on the lower right-hand side of the screen.

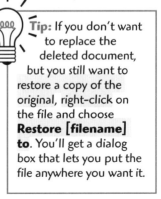

7. Your desktop slides back into place.

   If the document you restored has a *different name* than all the other files already in the target folder, it will be placed in the target folder automatically. Go look in the PDFs folder to see if the About Stacks.pdf file is really there.

   But what if you want to restore an older version of a file that still exists? If you're restoring an older file, that means a *duplicate file name* would appear in the folder, so you'll be asked if you want to replace it.

Tip: If you don't want to replace the deleted document, but you still want to restore a copy of the original, right-click on the file and choose **Restore [filename] to**. You'll get a dialog box that lets you put the file anywhere you want it.

8. Click the button that best fits your needs. Your document is restored.

Play with it

What happens if you don't see the file you want? Or you can't remember the date you saved it? Or you have so many similarly named files, searching for one would take all day?

How did you look through your files with the Finder in chapter 5? The files are displayed in a Finder window, and one of the features of every Finder window is a search box. With that in mind, what happens if you put the name of the file into the search box of the window you see in Time Machine?

Try it. Go back into Time Machine and this time, just type "About Stacks.pdf" into the search field. What happens? (When you have a lot of files, you may have to wait a few seconds for anything to appear.)

From here, you can restore the file just as you did earlier.

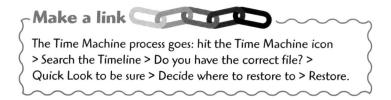

Make a link

The Time Machine process goes: hit the Time Machine icon > Search the Timeline > Do you have the correct file? > Quick Look to be sure > Decide where to restore to > Restore.

Control time

Because Time Machine is so simple, there aren't many things about it you can change. For example, do you want to have backups happen sooner, or later, than every hour? Sorry, you're out of luck.

Run a backup manually

One thing you can do is **run a backup manually**. Remember the Time Machine icon you looked at earlier in this chapter—the one that can display the status of your backup? It also has a menu item that lets you start a backup immediately.

1. Click the Time Machine icon in the Menu Bar.

2. Click the **Back Up Now** menu item.

Exclude folders from a backup

What else might you want to control? What if you wanted to save space on your Time Machine drive by not including some folders when you back up? Say you edit video and you move large files onto your Mac's internal hard drive, then copy them back to an external drive when you're done. If you use your Mac to change the files frequently, but don't store them on your Mac, allowing Time Machine to back them up every time they change while they're on your Mac's drive would fill up your Time Machine drive fast.

So you need a way to tell Time Machine not to backup these files. How do you think you'd do that?

1. Open the **Time Machine preference pane**, either from the icon in the Menu Bar (you saw how earlier), or via System Preferences.

2. Click the **Options** button. What do you see?

3. Click the plus (+) button to add a folder to be excluded. A navigation window appears.

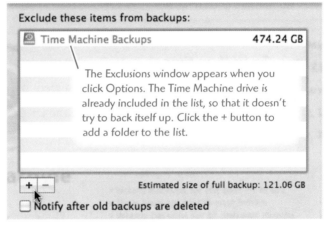

Exclude these items from backups:

Time Machine Backups   474.24 GB

The Exclusions window appears when you click Options. The Time Machine drive is already included in the list, so that it doesn't try to back itself up. Click the + button to add a folder to the list.

+ −   Estimated size of full backup: 121.06 GB

☐ Notify after old backups are deleted

4. Find the folder you want to exclude from the backup and select it, then click **Exclude**.

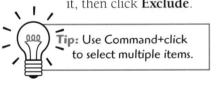

Tip: Use Command+click to select multiple items.

5. Click **Done**.

From the Time Machine preference pane, you can also **turn off automatic backups** by sliding the switch to the Off position. And, as you've already seen, the **Select Disk** button lets you choose a specific disk for your backups.

- -

Take a break

It's time to give your brain a break. Go for a walk or write down your shopping list. Just about anything other than reading this book is what your brain needs at this moment. When you're ready, come back and start with the review.

Review

Set up Time Machine

↻ How often does Time Machine make backups? Circle the correct interval.

Every hour   Every month

Every week   Every year

↻ When your Time Machine drive fills up, Time Machine asks how you'd like to handle this. What are your options when this happens?

1. Do nothing and by default ....

....

2. ....

Go back in time

↻ How do you get to the cool restore screen in Time Machine?

↻ The timeline down the right side of the restore screen lets you

....

↻ How do you search for a file in Time Machine?

....

↻ Press the .... button to quickly check a file to see if it's the one you really want to restore. This feature is called ....

Control time

↻ To manually start a Time Machine backup, click ...... > ....

↻ How do you tell Time Machine to exclude certain files or folders from backups?

....

↻ Can you turn Time Machine off? If so, how do you do it?

....

How did you do?

Did you forget anything? It's hard to remember it all. Go ahead and re-read the sections covering what you overlooked. Your brain might need a bit more time to absorb all the information.

Experiment

Suppose you have a document that you've changed multiple times over several weeks. It might be a text to-do list, a draft blog post, or a presentation for work. The file name may never change, but its contents sure do.

If you're not sure when the version you need was saved, and the file appears at multiple points in time, how do you know which is the exact one you're looking for?

The secret is in the large back/forward buttons to the right of Time Machine's Finder windows in the recovery screen. When you select a file in a folder and click the back button, you'll jump back to the previous time that file was backed up.

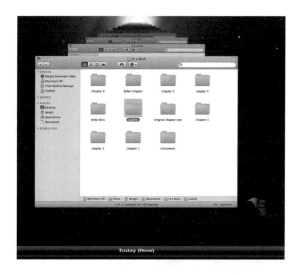

This experiment will take anything from a few days to a few weeks to complete, but it will show you the power of this feature.

1. Create a file and store it in the Documents folder. It can be anything, from a photo to a word processing document to a video file.

2. Every other day, make some change to the file. If you want the experiment to last longer, do it at random intervals over a period of a few weeks.

3. After you've got several saved versions of the file, try using the back/forward buttons to find a specific version, and using Quick Look to make sure it's the right one.

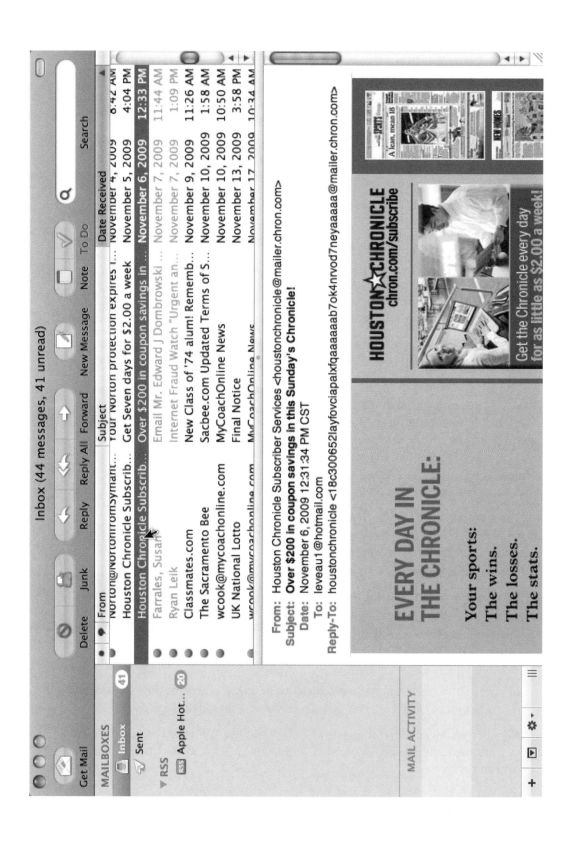

7 Do more with your e-mail

Do you have more than one e-mail address? Keeping up with all your accounts in Windows can be a chore; checking some in your e-mail software, others on the Web. Maybe you used the built-in e-mail program. Were you frustrated by its lack of features? Did it have a spam filter? Did it integrate with your calendar application?

No Problem!

Your new Mac comes to the rescue with one of the best e-mail programs on any platform. Known simply as Mail, it can handle many types of e-mail, including the latest version of Microsoft Exchange, AOL and Yahoo! Plus. Mail also has excellent spam filtering and cool integration with iCal, the Mac OS X's calendar application.

In this chapter, you'll learn how to:

⇨ Set up a Mail account.

⇨ Import your e-mail from your Windows PC.

⇨ Receive, compose and send e-mail.

⇨ Organize your e-mail.

⇨ Filter spam.

Create your account

Mail works with most common types of accounts:

→ **POP3** or **POP**, an older type of mail system that's still used by a lot of Internet service providers and some webmail services.

→ **IMAP**, a more advanced service also used by ISPs, webmail and many businesses.

→ **Exchange IMAP**, a type of IMAP available to companies running Microsoft's Exchange servers.

→ **Exchange 2007**, the latest version of Microsoft's e-mail server. Unfortunately, this is the only version of Exchange that Mail currently supports.

Do you have one main e-mail account that you rely on more than others? Let's set up that one.

1. Click on the **Mail icon** in the Dock.

   The Welcome to Mail window appears.

2. Fill in your name, e-mail address and e-mail account password in the appropriate fields, then click Continue. The Account Summary window appears.

3. Study the information in the summary, and if it's correct, click **Create**.

   Once you're done, Mail's main window, with your account in it, opens.

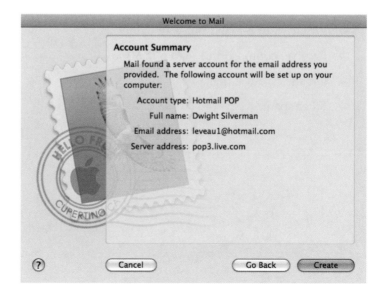

Welcome to Mail

Account Summary

Mail found a server account for the email address you provided. The following account will be set up on your computer:

Account type: Hotmail POP

Full name: Dwight Silverman

Email address: leveau1@hotmail.com

Server address: pop3.live.com

Cancel   Go Back   Create

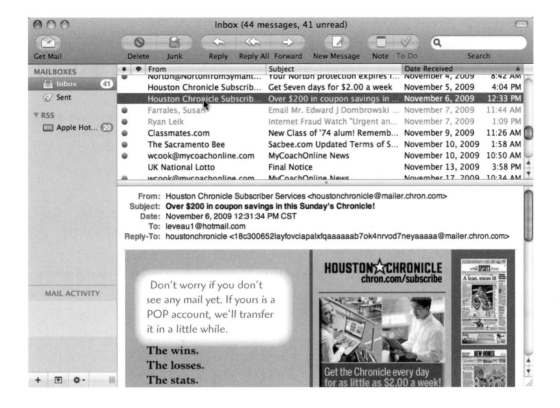

Something went wrong!

What if your setup process didn't result in a working e-mail account? If Mail can't auto-configure your account, it comes directly to the Accounts window, where you can make changes manually.

The most common mistake when setting up an existing mail account in new e-mail software is mistyping your password, or e-mail address. Double-check that those are correct.

When you've double-checked the e-mail address and password are correct, check the main window again. Do you see an Inbox for the new account?

Tip: Because the password field is obscured it's easier than you think to mistype a password. Type your password into a word processor (TextEdit, found in the Applications folder, will do), then copy and paste it into the password field in Mail's Accounts window to ensure you're entering the password correctly.

If you don't see an Inbox, you can input the following items:

→ The name of the **incoming server**. This is the server that collects your e-mail and sends it to your computer.

→ The name of the **outgoing server**, that's the server that handles the mail you send.

→ Whether either server uses any security features. They may use a **specific port** (indicated by a number) or use some form of **encryption** to keep your data safe, such as SSL.

> Don't be surprised if the names of the incoming and outgoing servers are the same, particularly if your mail provider uses Exchange.

You might find the information you need in the setup area in your Windows e-mail software or you may have received a message from your e-mail provider with these details. If not, contact your provider.

If you're still having problems, check the help area on your e-mail provider's website.

Add another account

Mail can recognize and auto-configure itself for some of the most popular e-mail services, including Google's Gmail, AOL, Yahoo! Plus (the paid version) and more. In most cases, these three steps are all you need to set up accounts from any of these providers.

Do you have more accounts you want to add?

1. Click **Mail** in the Menu Bar then click **Preferences**. The Mail Preferences window appears.

2. Click the **Accounts** tab at the top. Click the plus (+) button in the lower left-hand corner of the window. The familiar Add Account window appears.

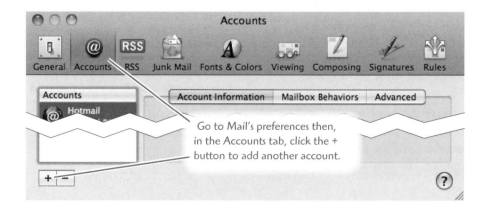

Go to Mail's preferences then, in the Accounts tab, click the + button to add another account.

3. Repeat the steps you went through for the first account to set up the new account. When you're done, if everything went according to plan, you'll be back at the Accounts page, where you'll see your new account in the left-hand column.

Close the ptreferences window, and you'll see the new account with its own Inbox in Mail. If you don't see it, click the arrow next to the main Inbox. Click the Inbox to see your mail for that account.

Transfer your e-mail

You've transferred your documents and other files from your Windows PC to your Mac in chapter 4, but you didn't transfer your e-mail, so let's do that now.

If you have a POP3 account that's set to delete messages from the server once they're on your machine or you have mail stored on your PC, you need to grab the e-mail from your Windows PC and move it over.

Unfortunately, there's no simple way to get the e-mail stored on your Windows PC onto your Mac. Conceptually, it seems simple.

> **Note:** If your mail provider uses IMAP, Exchange IMAP or Exchange 2007, your e-mail is stored on the incoming server. Once you've set up your account in Mail, you immediately have access to your e-mail. So you're in luck: you can skip this section and move to page 94.

> **Tip:** Got POP e-mail? Many providers offer both IMAP and POP. If you're using POP, see if you can switch to IMAP. It will make life much easier (even though you'll still have to grab your old mail now, you'd never have to do it again if you used IMAP instead).

→ Export the mail into a format that the Mac can read.

→ Copy the file or files to a folder on your Mac.

→ Import them into Mail on the Mac.

The problem is that Apple's Mail application can't import files used by Microsoft's e-mail programs, and these are the most common programs used by Windows users. This is particularly true of Windows Mail in Vista, and Windows Live Mail, its downloadable successor for Windows 7. In fact, there's really no simple way to transfer stored e-mail in bulk from these two programs.

If you don't have to move a lot of e-mail, you can forward individual e-mails to yourself from your Windows e-mail programs, then download them into Mail. But this isn't ideal because this method loses the original sender's details.

If your PC uses Windows XP with Outlook Express as its mail program, you can use Mozilla's Thunderbird mail program as a go-between. It automatically imports from Outlook Express when you install it on your Windows PC and the mailbox files it creates can be imported by Mail.

Tip: Remember the Apple Store's One-on-One service that moves your files from a PC to your Mac? That includes e-mail. It may cost you money, but it *will* save you time.

Export your mail		
Outlook Express	1. **Download Thunderbird** (free) from www.mozillamessaging.com/thunderbird/ and **install** it on your Windows PC. 2. Run Thunderbird, and it will ask if you want to **import** your e-mail from Outlook Express. Click OK. 3. Make sure you have hidden files/folders set as visible, then follow this path in Windows Explorer: My Computer > C drive > Documents and Settings > YOUR LOGIN NAME > Application Data > Thunderbird 4. Once you're in the Thunderbird folder, open the folder with the **.default** extension, and copy the Mail folder to your Mac's desktop just like you did with your documents in chapter 4.	
Outlook	**Best method** If you have e-mail stored in Outlook, spend $10 on **O2M**, an excellent program that will copy your mail and folder structure into the .MBOX files that Mail uses. It will save your files in a folder, which you can copy over to your Mac. O2M will also convert your contacts and address book. Get O2M at www.littlemachines.com.	**Alternative method** **Thunderbird**, the free Mozilla e-mail program, will work with Outlook as well. Follow the steps detailed in the Outlook Express column.
Windows Mail / Live Mail	**Method 1** **Create a Gmail account** at www.gmail.com and send the e-mail from your Windows PC to your new Gmail account. Turn on **IMAP** in Gmail's settings, then set up the Gmail account in Mail. (This will take a long time if you have a lot of messages.) You can even set your Gmail account to grab messages from a Windows Mail or Windows Live Mail account automatically so they'll appear in Mail, too.	**Method 2** Create a **new folder** on your Windows desktop, then drag individual messages you want to save from the e-mail program into the folder. This creates a file for each mail with a .EML extension. Copy this folder to your Mac's desktop. This method is s-l-o-w, as you'll have to open each e-mail individually in the next step. If you can live without the date sent and sender details, or if you have a lot of e-mails to import, try method 1.

Import your mail		
Outlook Express	1. Launch **Mail** on your Mac. 2. In the Menu Bar, click **File > Import Mailboxes**. Select **Thunderbird**, then click Continue. 3. Navigate to your desktop and click on the folder containing the mail you copied from your PC. 4. Click **Choose** to get a list of mail folders to import. Select the ones you want, then click Continue. Your mail will be imported into a folder in Mail called **Import**. From there, you can sort it into folders as you'll see a little later in this chapter.	
Outlook	If you're using Thunderbird, follow the Import Your Mail steps for Outlook Express. If you're using O2M: 1. Launch **Mail** on your Mac. 2. In the Menu Bar, click **File > Import Mailboxes**. Select **Files in mbox format** from the list of import types then click Continue. 3. Navigate to your desktop and click on the folder you copied from your PC. 4. Click **Choose** to get a list of mail folders to import. Select the ones you want, then click Continue. Your mail will be imported into a folder in Mail called **Import**.	
Windows Mail / Live Mail	**Method 1** 1. Add your new Gmail account in the same way you'd add a new account to Mail. 2. The e-mail you uploaded to Gmail will be pulled into Mail, where you can sort it into folders. Or, leave it in the Gmail account if you like. Since you turned on IMAP, you can get at e-mail in this account on the road, at home, in the office, and so on.	**Method 2** The .eml files in the folder you copied *can't* be imported into Mail, but you *can* read each e-mail using Mail. 1. Move the copied folder to your Documents folder. 2. Double-click on any of the e-mails there to read, reply or forward them.

Now that you've got your accounts set up and your old e-mail moved over, you can start using Mail.

Don't worry about your contacts and address book for now, we'll deal with those in chapter 8.

Get (all or just some) new e-mail

Mail looks and—on the surface—behaves like most other e-mail programs. The left-hand column shows the mailboxes and folders for your e-mail, the top-center pane shows header details about each e-mail, and the viewing pane lets you see what's in each item.

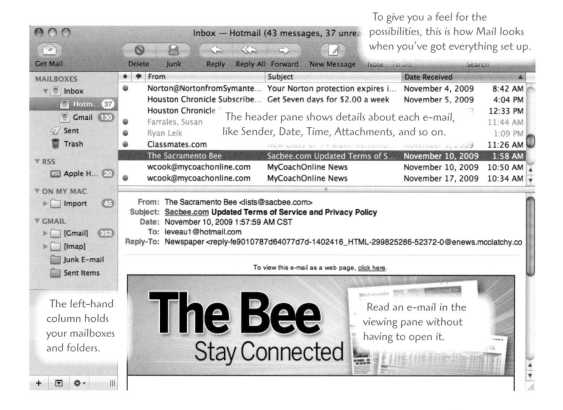

To give you a feel for the possibilities, this is how Mail looks when you've got everything set up.

The header pane shows details about each e-mail, like Sender, Date, Time, Attachments, and so on.

The left-hand column holds your mailboxes and folders.

Read an e-mail in the viewing pane without having to open it.

Mail checks for new items in all your accounts every five minutes by default. Click the **Get Mail** button on the toolbar to check for new e-mail manually.

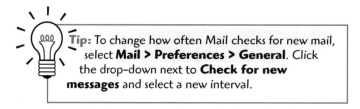

Tip: To change how often Mail checks for new mail, select **Mail > Preferences > General**. Click the drop-down next to **Check for new messages** and select a new interval.

Mail helps you do more than just read your e-mail

Play with it

Reading and composing mail is very similar to the way you did it in your Windows-based e-mail software. For example, how would you select an e-mail to read in your Windows program? Try the same techniques here. Click on an item in the headers pane to see it in the viewing pane, or double-click it to open it in its own window.

Read e-mail in the viewing pane, or double-click to open it in a new window.

But there are some things you can do while reading e-mail on the Mac that you probably couldn't do on your Windows program, and they're pretty cool.

Find an e-mail in your Inbox that has a **street address** in it. Hover the cursor over it. What do you see? Click the drop-down arrow that's appeared to the right of the address. (How well this works depends on how properly formed the address is. Mail may not always recognize an address as a result.)

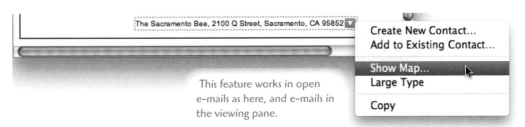

This feature works in open e-mails as here, and e-mails in the viewing pane.

What do you think will happen when you click **Show Map** in the pop-up menu? Try it and see if you were right. Mail also knows that you might want to show the address in bigger type, add the address to your Address Book, or simply copy it to the clipboard so you can paste it elsewhere.

Now find an e-mail that contains a time or **date reference**. It could be a specific date, or even something as casual as "tomorrow." Hover your cursor over the date or the word, then click the drop-down.

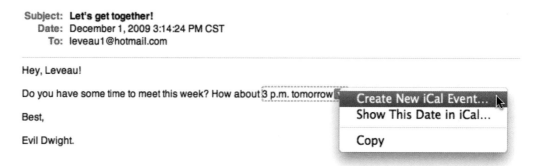

Mail knows that "3 p.m. tomorrow" means "3 p.m. on the next calendar day." Better yet, when you click the drop-down you can click **Create New iCal Event...** to add an item to iCal, the Mac's calendar program. That creates an iCal entry on the spot without having to open the other application and set up the event there.

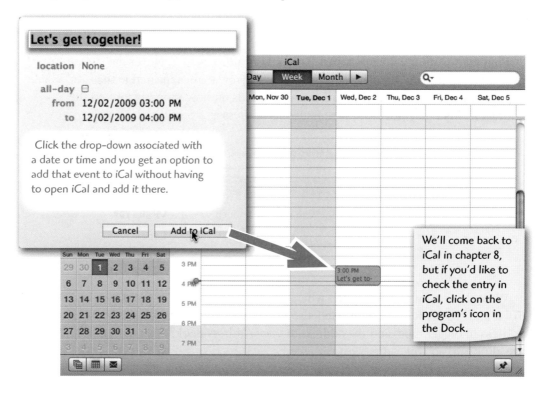

Images show up automatically in the reading pane, but what about other kinds of attachments? Find an e-mail with an attachment other than an image—like a Word document or a PDF. Rather than saving the attachment, then launching another application to view it, you can use **Quick Look**. Just click the Quick Look button up in the header.

From: dwight silverman
Subject: **My cat**
Date: December 1, 2009 4:34:55 PM CST
To: evildwight@gmail.com
▶ 🔗 1 Attachment, 196 KB (Save ▾) (Quick Look)

Dude,

You've gotta see this trick my cat can do with its eyes!

Use the Quick Look button to view an attachment right from Mail without having to open another application.

Mail has another trick up its sleeve. Click **New Message** in the middle of the toolbar to begin writing an e-mail. Mail's composition window lets you do all the things you can with other e-mail programs—adjust the font size and type, use boldface and color in your text, and apply stationery. Write some text in your e-mail, then try the buttons running across the toolbar.

There's one button that's unique to Mail: **Photo Browser**. Given the name, what do you think this does?

It's actually a small window into another Mac OS X program, iPhoto, which you'll explore in chapter 11. Click the Photo Browser button. Find the image you want in the Photo Browser, then drag it into your e-mail to attach it.

You can adjust the font size, attach files, use stationery, even drag and drop photos via iPhoto, once you've moved pictures into it in chapter 11.

Make a link

▶ Dates and times belong in iCal and street addresses show in Google Maps in Safari.

▶ Take a Quick Look at attachments you receive or Browse your Photos to manage attachments you want to send.

Send e-mail through an alternate mail server

When you're ready to send your e-mail, you can either hit the Send button to send the e-mail using the main account and outgoing mail server that account's associated with, or you can send it from another address, or use an alternate e-mail server.

See the two drop-downs underneath the Subject field in the composition window? Click the right-hand one to **choose an SMTP** to send the e-mail using an alternate server.

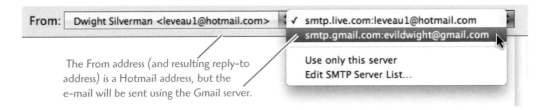

The From address (and resulting reply–to address) is a Hotmail address, but the e-mail will be sent using the Gmail server.

So if your ISP's mail server is down and you can't get new mail, you can at least still send e-mail using an alternate provider. When you're finally ready to send your missive, click the, uh, Send button.

Organize your e-mail

Moving all your e-mail to a new place is certainly a hassle, but it's also an opportunity to get yourself organized, get rid of junk, and bring a little order to your e-mail.

You can change the way you view messages in Mail in a couple of ways. Let's start with the way e-mail is displayed in the headers pane.

Normally, you see your list of e-mail items in linear fashion, one after the other. You can change the order by clicking on the column titles at the top of the pane (From, Subject, Date Received, and so on). That's pretty much the way it was in your Windows program, right?

Play with it

Do you have all the column titles you want? **Change the column titles** by right-clicking or Control+clicking on any one of them. From the menu that appears, select the ones you want, and deselect those you don't.

Group e-mails by thread

You e-mail a friend, she replies, you reply to her, and so on. Wouldn't it be great if you could gather those conversations under one heading? Grouping your e-mail based on conversation is called **Threading**. (It's also found in Outlook in Windows.)

Click **View > Organize by Thread** to sort your e-mail based on similar subject lines and senders. Click on one of the combined threads to see a list of messages in this thread in the viewing pane.

E-mails in this thread have been grouped together in the viewing pane. Click the arrow to the left of the highlighted e-mail to expand the thread in the header pane.

Click on the arrow to the left of the highlighted item to expand the thread in the header pane (and show all the message headers), and display the most recent message in the thread in the viewing pane below.

You can also view your e-mail by account, or all in one Inbox.

1. In the left-hand column click on **Inbox**. You'll see e-mail from *all* your accounts in the header pane.

2. If you have multiple accounts and only want to see the mail in *one* account, click on the arrow next to Inbox. Separate Inboxes for each account appear.

3. Click on any one of them to see just the e-mail for that account in the header pane.

Create and group mailboxes

The other place to organize your e-mail is in the left-hand column. As you'd expect, you can add new folders to sort and store e-mail. And there are even features that will do this for you.

To **create a new folder**, click **Mailbox** in the Menu Bar, then **New Mailbox**. Give the new mailbox a name and click OK. Now you can drag items into this folder, or set rules to route items there automatically.

Let's say you want to route mail from your boss into one folder so you don't have to spot her messages in the glut you get every day. You could create a folder and manually move messages into it, but what if you miss one that's important? Wouldn't it be great if Mail could sift through your e-mail and grab certain messages for you?

The easiest way to collate messages from one person or group of people is to create a **Smart Mailbox**. This is a standing search that automatically finds mails in your Inbox that match the search criteria and displays the matching mails in a special folder. As the name implies, they're smart, making complex mail-sorting tasks easier.

1. Click the plus (+) button at the bottom of the left-hand pane.

2. Choose **New Smart Mailbox** from the menu that appears. The Smart Mailbox dialog slides out.

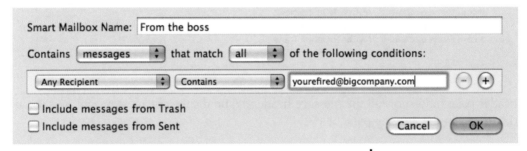

3. Give the Smart Mailbox a name, then **set the conditions** that will cause e-mail to show up in the Smart Mailbox. You can base the conditions on messages or to-do items; recipient names or e-mail addresses; text found in a message; the mail's priority; whether it has an attachment, and more.

4. When you're done, click OK and the Smart Mailbox will appear in your left-hand column in Mail.

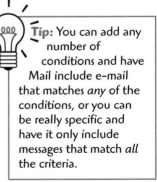

Tip: You can add any number of conditions and have Mail include e-mail that matches *any* of the conditions, or you can be really specific and have it only include messages that match *all* the criteria.

That's a start, but your boss isn't the only one at your company who sends you e-mail. If you create Smart Mailboxes for all your colleagues, that's almost as hard to manage as sifting through the mail mountain. What you need is a way to keep the Smart Mailboxes together.

Mail offers **Smart Mailbox Folders**, which let you cluster Smart Mailboxes together. Remember how you can view each Inbox, or see them all in a global view? Well, you can have a similar setup for your Smart Mailboxes, too.

1. Create several Smart Mailboxes.

2. Click Mailbox > **New Smart Mailbox Folder**.

3. Give the folder a name, then click OK.

4. The folder appears in your left-hand column. Drag the Smart Mailboxes you want to include into the Smart Mailbox Folder.

5. Click the arrow to the left of the folder to see the Smart Mailboxes inside it.

    Once you have e-mail flowing into the Smart Mailboxes, you can view each one separately, or see them all together by clicking on the Smart Mailbox Folder itself.

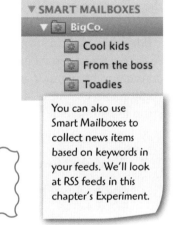

You can also use Smart Mailboxes to collect news items based on keywords in your feeds. We'll look at RSS feeds in this chapter's Experiment.

Make a link

▶ Smart Mailboxes aren't really mailboxes, but search results.

▶ Smart Mailbox folders group your Smart Mailboxes.

Train Mail to kill spam

What about spam? Nobody likes receiving unsolicited commercial e-mail. Mail's spam feature has been working since you started downloading mail into your account. Take another look at your header pane. Do any of the messages in it have lighter text than the others? Why do you think that is?

●	Zune	Your free mp3 credits are ab...	Oct 12, 2009	1:33 PM	
	MICROSOFT *ZUNE	Confirmation of cancellation...	Oct 15, 2009	12:24 AM 📎 5	
●	Norton	Toshiba PC – Important Prot...	Oct 18, 2009	7:11 AM	
●	Mark Spiner	Online Assistant Needed	Oct 19, 2009	10:57 AM 📎 1	
●	Nurmala Moyden	Ray White Insurance	Oct 19, 2(		
	Mrs.Betty Lawson	CHECK ATTACHMENT FOR T...	Oct 20, 2		
●	Mr. Tran Quy	Write Me Back.	Oct 20, 2		

These items have brown colored text.

Mail thinks those lighter items might be spam. Are all the mails marked as spam really unwanted messages? Do all of the dark colored e-mails look as though they're not spam?

Mail's spam filters don't always get it right immediately, so you'll have to train them about what you consider to be spam. Do you see the **Junk button** in the toolbar? Found it? Okay, now click on a spam-colored item in the header list. What happens to the Junk button?

If you see something that's not marked as spam but *should* be, select it in the header list and hit the **Junk** button. If you see an item that's marked as spam that *shouldn't* be, click it, and the button changes to **Not Junk**. Click the button to indicate you don't think the mail is spam.

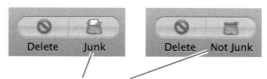

The Junk/Not Junk button is contextual. It displays the opposite of Mail's guess about an e-mail's spam status. So you can click it to change the e-mail's status and train Mail to recognize Junk vs. Not Junk more accurately.

Mail opts to leave suspect items in the Inbox while Mail's in Junk training mode. As you designate some items as Junk and others as Not Junk, Mail learns what you consider to be spam. It gets better at automatically flagging spam messages. When you're comfortable with how Mail's handling these duties, you can have it move suspected spam to a Junk folder automatically. Here's how:

1. Click on **Mail** in the Menu Bar, then **Preferences**. Click the **Junk Mail** tab.

2. Select the **Move it to the Junk mailbox** option.

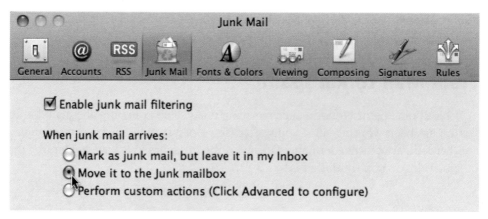

A warning appears to let you know that, if you have spam set to be automatically deleted from the Junk folder after a certain period, you may not get a chance to check it before it's removed. If you haven't changed these settings, you can click Move.

Now look in your Inbox. Where'd all the spam-colored e-mail headers go? Check the new Junk folder in the left-hand column periodically to make sure Mail hasn't mismarked something as spam, and use the Not Junk button to move it back to your Inbox.

Make a link

Spam e-mails are colored brown in Mail (unless you decide they're Not Junk).

Play with it

Control how Mail handles spam

Take another look at the Junk Mail preferences. By default Mail won't designate as Junk e-mail that's addressed to your full name; e-mail coming from people to whom you've sent e-mail; or any e-mail from anyone in your Address Book. You can check or uncheck this to fine-tune the spam filter's behavior.

Want to get even more precise? Select **Perform custom actions**, and the **Advanced** button becomes active at the bottom of the window. Click the Advanced button to get even more options to fine-tune your spam settings.

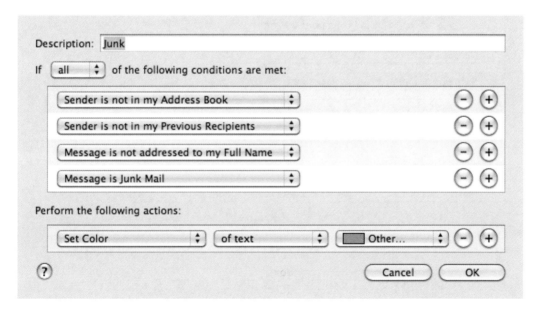

These settings are a lot like the Smart Folders conditions. Spend some time playing around with these options until you have settings that work best for you. You can always go back to the Move it to the Junk mailbox option if you decide custom actions are more than you need.

Set some rules

You can also filter spam as well as other kinds of messages, using the Mail's Rules feature. **Rules** are found in many e-mail programs—including Outlook and Windows Live Mail—so you may already know how to work with rules.

The setup is very similar to the advanced spam controls you've just been playing with. You can filter into specific folders—not just Junk—and even designate filtered items by color.

1. Click **Mail > Preferences > Rules** tab.

2. Click **Add Rules**.

3. Set the **parameters** you want. Click the plus (+) buttons to add more rules.

4. Click **OK** when you're done.

Any rules you set up are run automatically on every new e-mail that arrives, but what if you want to run them manually on a specific e-mail item? Right-click (or Control+click) on its header and choose **Apply Rules**.

Take a break

Your brain needs time to sift through what you just learned about getting, reading, composing, organizing and sending mail. Time to take a break. We're nearly at the end of the chapter. All that's left is the review and the experiment. So, walk away and give your brain something else to focus on for just a little while.

Review

Create your account

↺ What four types of e-mail accounts does Mail support?

1. ....

2. ....

3. ....

4. ....

↺ To set up an additional e-mail account, go to .... > ....

Receive and read e-mail

↺ Mail checks for new messages every .... To change this, go to .... > .... > ....

↺ Hover your cursor over a street address in Mail to get a drop-down that lets you .... of that address?

↺ Hover your cursor over a date or time reference to get the option to

....

↺ To view an attachment without having to open the application it's associated with, click the .... button.

Continues, flip the page

105

Write and send e-mail

↻ There are two ways to attach an image to an e-mail:

1. Click the .... button, browse to the file's location, select an image and drag it to the e-mail you're composing.

2. Click .... and browse to the image's location, select the image and hit the .... button.

↻ The option to send an e-mail with a different "From" address than the account you're using can be found on the ....

Organize your mail

↻ Right-click to change the .... in the headers pane.

↻ To create a new mail folder, go to .... > ....

↻ To create a new Smart Mailbox, go to .... > ....

↻ To group related Smart Mailboxes you'd use a ....
....

Kill spam

↻ Why might you *not* want Mail to automatically move e-mail into the Junk folder?

....

↻ What does the Not Junk button do? When do you see it?

....

↻ How do Rules differ from automatic spam filtering? How are they similar?

....

How did you do

Did you forget anything? It's hard to remember it all. Go ahead and re-read the sections covering what you overlooked. Your brain might need a bit more time to absorb all the information.

Experiment

If you've been using the Web for any length of time, you probably know about RSS feeds, but if not: they're a simple way to have text, images, audio, and even video come to you, rather than going out on the Web to find them.

Chances are, you've used RSS feeds, whether you know it or not. Ever customized a Google or Yahoo home page? They use RSS feeds to provide the news headlines from various sources. And many blogs offer an RSS feed of their posts.

Mail, like many e-mail programs, can manage your RSS feeds. Go to File > Add RSS Feeds… Click on Specify the URL for a feed. Enter the web address for the feed you'd like to add and click Add.

When you subscribe to feeds in Mail, the resulting items look like e-mail, complete with headers and message bodies, only they are news items rather than mail from your friends.

Once you've set up a few RSS feeds in Mail, use Smart Mailboxes to capture stories with specific keywords. For example, you might want to search for stories with the word "Stock Exchange" in the body if you're interested in finance.

You can also subscribe to RSS feeds in Mail using Safari, the Mac's web browser. We'll cover that in chapter 10.

Note: Don't know where to get RSS feeds? You can start out with feeds from National Public Radio www.npr.org/rss/ and the New York Times www.nytimes.com/rss.

Right-click on the name of the feed and choose Copy Link.

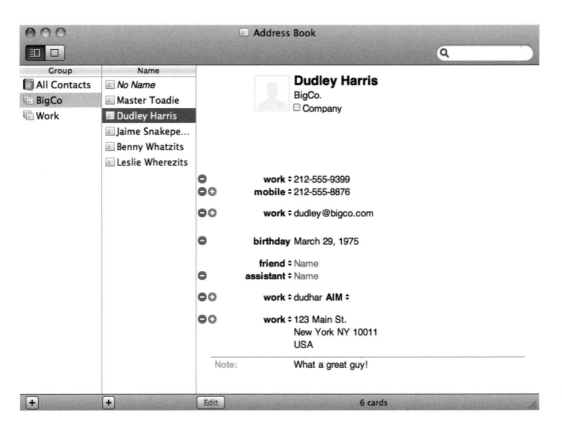

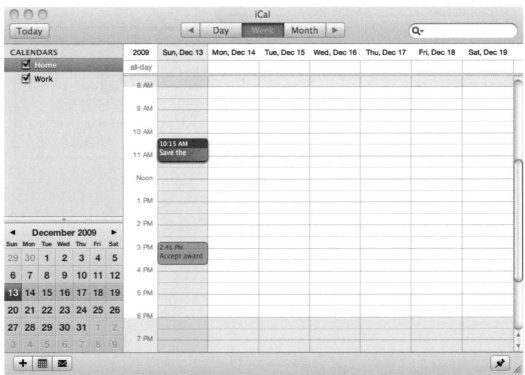

8 Manage your life with Address Book and iCal

Each of the last three versions of Windows had a different approach to managing your contacts and events. Unless you were willing to buy a program like Outlook, you may have been winging it because you didn't have the tools at your disposal to organize your events and contacts.

No Problem!

Your new Mac comes with easy-to-use but powerful contacts and calendar applications. In chapter 7, you got a glimpse of iCal and the way it integrates with Mail. In this chapter, you'll learn what you need to get the people and events in your life in order. With Address Book and iCal you can:

⇨ Import your contacts from Gmail, Yahoo or your PC.

⇨ Sort your contacts into groups.

⇨ Add new contacts, either manually or from Mail.

⇨ Add new calendar items (both standalone and recurring) and get reminders about events.

⇨ Sync your calendar items with other calendar services.

⇨ Organize your calendars into groups.

Import your contacts from a Windows PC

Like your e-mail, you'll need to import your contacts from your Windows PC to **Address Book** on your Mac. Importing contacts is easier than importing e-mail, though the basic process is similar:

1. **Export** your Windows contacts to a format your Mac can read.

2. **Copy** the formatted file or files to your Mac.

3. **Import** the contacts into Address Book.

	Export your contacts
Outlook Express	1. Open the **Address Book** in Windows XP. **Highlight** the contacts you want to export. 2. Click **File > Export > Other Address Book**. Select **Text File (Comma Separated Values)**. Click the **Export** button. 3. Enter a name in the **Save exported file as** field. Click the **Browse** button and navigate to the location where you'll save the file. The desktop's fine for this. 4. Click **Next**, then choose the fields you want to export, such as address, phone number, and so on. Click **Finish**. 5. **Copy** the resulting file (which will have a .CSV extension) to your Mac.
Outlook	As recommended in chapter 7, spend $10 on O2M, which will copy your contacts from Outlook as well as your mail. It will give you the option to export and save your files in a folder, which you can then copy over to your Mac. The steps are identical to exporting your mail in the previous chapter. Get O2M at www.littlemachines.com. Alternatively, you can use Outlook's **Export** function which follows similar steps to export your contacts as Outlook Express.
Windows Vista / Windows 7	1. Click the **Start** button, then type **Contacts** in the **search** box and hit Enter. 2. In the Contacts folder, **Highlight** the contacts you want to export. Click the **Export** button on the toolbar (if you don't see it, set the window at full screen). 3. Choose **Commas Separate Values** and click **Export**. 4. Enter a name for the file and click **Browse** to find a place to put the file—the desktop's fine. Click **Save**, then click **Next**. 5. Choose the fields you want to include and click **Finish**. 6. Find the **file** with the **.CSV extension** and **copy it to your Mac**.

	Import your contacts
Outlook Express, Outlook, Windows Vista / Windows 7	**1.** Launch **Address Book** on the Mac. In the **Menu Bar**, click **File > Import**. If you're using O2M, you'll want to choose the **Files in mbox format** from the list of import types. **2.** Select the **.CSV** file you copied over. You'll get the chance to scroll through the contacts before they're imported. **3.** Click OK when everything looks good.

Add contacts from Gmail or Yahoo

If you use a web-based service, such as Gmail or Yahoo, to keep your contacts organized, the Mac's Address Book can import these, too, and it can stay synchronized with them. When you add a contact to either of these web services, the information will be stored on your Mac, and vice versa.

Because these services are web-based, there's no need to export or import anything. You add the web services right from Address Book itself, so let's take a look at the Address Book. Launch it from the Dock.

To synchronize with Gmail or Yahoo contact information so you can work with those addresses in Mail:

1. Click **Address Book** in the Menu Bar, then **Preferences**, and then the **Accounts** tab.

2. **Select the service** you'd like to synchronize with. The process is similar for Yahoo and Google's Gmail.

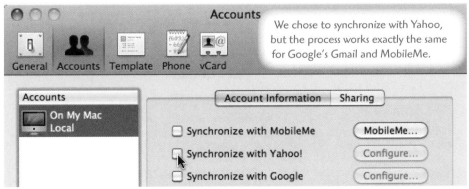

We chose to synchronize with Yahoo, but the process works exactly the same for Google's Gmail and MobileMe.

3. Click the **Configure** button, then click **Agree** to accept the license agreement.

4. Enter your **web service's sign in and password**, and click **OK**. Your contacts are imported into your Mac's Address Book.

Now, when you add a contact to the Address Book, it will automatically be added to the contacts stored on your web service's contact list, and vice versa.

Make a link

Address Book > Preferences let you **Sync** contacts from a **web service**.

Add contacts to Address Book

If you've been using Outlook Express on Windows XP, or Outlook on any Windows computer, Address Book's layout should look familiar. Even if you're used to managing your contacts with a web service, Address Book looks similar to a lot of the Mac's other applications.

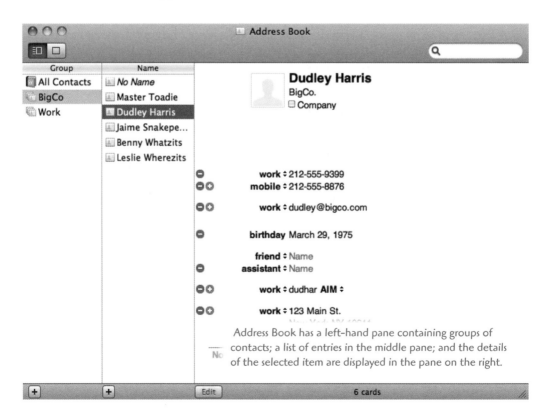

Address Book has a left-hand pane containing groups of contacts; a list of entries in the middle pane; and the details of the selected item are displayed in the pane on the right.

Let's **add an entry**.

1. Click the **plus (+) button** below the list of names in the middle pane, and a blank contact form appears.

2. Fill out the form with the appropriate items.

As you fill in certain items, see how the icons next to the fields change? Click the red delete (-) icon next to a field to remove it, or click the green plus (+) icon next to a field to add another field below it.

Don't need a particular field? Click the delete icon next to a field to remove it.

Use the plus icon to add more fields.

> **Note:** Click the AIM drop-down item to access a list of different instant-messaging (IM) services supported by iChat, the Mac's IM software. If you know a contact's IM handle, enter it here.

3. To add a photo of your contact, double-click the box to the left of the name you entered. Click the **Choose** button to pick an image.

4. When you're done, click the **Edit** button at the bottom to *stop* editing.

> **Tip:** You can also add contacts from Mail. Select an e-mail, then click Messages > Add Sender to Address Book. Or try Shift+Command+Y. You can also right-click an address in the address field to add it.

Group your contacts

If you have a lot of contacts, you may want to organize them into **groups**. Let's start a new group and then populate it.

1. Click the **plus (+) button** under the Groups column on the left-hand side.

2. Enter a **Name** for your group, something like "Work" for a group containing your colleagues' contact details, then hit the Return key.

3. Click on the **All Contacts** group in the left-hand column.

4. Find a contact in the **Name** column that fits the group you just created. If you chose Work, **drag** the name of someone at your company and **drop** it on the new group in the left-hand column.

Drag and drop a contact from the All Contacts list to your new list.

   Repeat this step to add further contacts to the group.

5. Click the **Work** group to see the names you've placed there.

Send e-mail to a group

Groups can be handy for organizational purposes, but they're also great for sending an e-mail to an entire group.

1. Launch **Mail**, then click the **New Message** button.

2. In the **To** field:

   a. **type the group's name**;

      or

   b. click the **Address Book** button; and

      1. double-click the group name;

         or

      2. drag the name into the To field from the Address Book window.

3. Write your e-mail, then click the **Send** button.

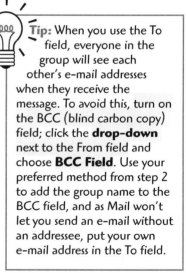

Tip: When you use the To field, everyone in the group will see each other's e-mail addresses when they receive the message. To avoid this, turn on the BCC (blind carbon copy) field; click the **drop-down** next to the From field and choose **BCC Field**. Use your preferred method from step 2 to add the group name to the BCC field, and as Mail won't let you send an e-mail without an addressee, put your own e-mail address in the To field.

Make a link

Create a **Group** of contacts and send the group members e-mail addressed only to the group name, Mail does the rest.

Play with it

What are your preferences?

Want to change how names are displayed? The Address Book doesn't let you go wild, but there are a few things you can do.

1. Click Address Book > **Preferences** > General.

2. Now you can change the sort order by first or last names.

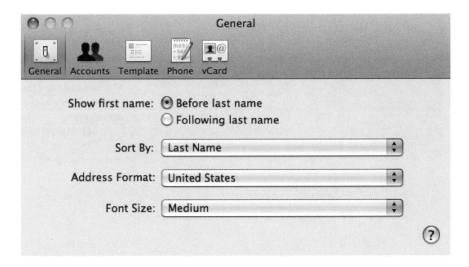

You can also **change the font size** in the **General** tab of the Address Book's preferences.

List contacts by Company

Either create a new card, or edit an existing contact's details (select a name, click the Edit button under the pane), and check the box next to **Company** under the contact's name in the contact card to list the contact by the name of their organization instead of their own name.

Add your own contact card

Add a card to Address Book that contains **your own contact information**. You'll see why you need it in a moment or two.

Now that you have your friends, family and coworkers organized, let's tackle your schedule with iCal.

Add events to iCal

In chapter 7, you got a quick glimpse of **iCal**, Apple's calendar application, when you clicked on date or time references in e-mails. That's just one way to get events into iCal, but the most common way is to add events to the application directly. Launch iCal from the Dock.

By default, iCal shows you the **week view**.

Use the **toolbar buttons** to select alternate views.

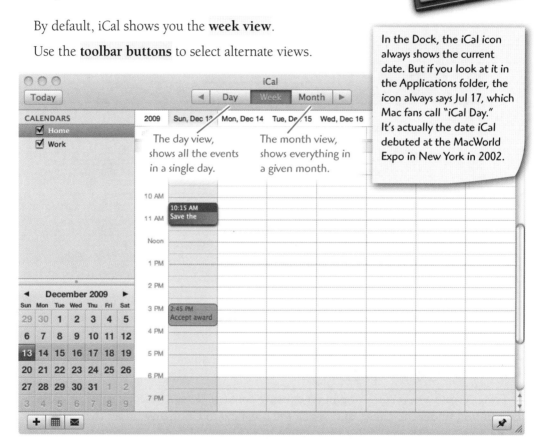

> In the Dock, the iCal icon always shows the current date. But if you look at it in the Applications folder, the icon always says Jul 17, which Mac fans call "iCal Day." It's actually the date iCal debuted at the MacWorld Expo in New York in 2002.

The day view, shows all the events in a single day.

The month view, shows everything in a given month.

How do you think you'd move to the previous or following day/week/month? To move back and forth in time, click the **arrows** on either side of the view buttons to move to the **next** or **previous** day, week, or month.

You can add entries from any of these views, but let's start at the week view, because it's the default. If you're in a hurry, you can drop in an item quickly and flesh it out later. So, say you want to schedule a meeting with the boss at 3 p.m. on a Tuesday. Looking at the week view, how do you think you'd start?

1. **To add an entry:**

   a. **Double-click** the 3 p.m. area on Tuesday.

   b. You can also **right-click** an area and choose **New Event** from the pop-up menu.

   c. Or, you can press **Command+N**.

2. Enter a name for your event, and hit Return.

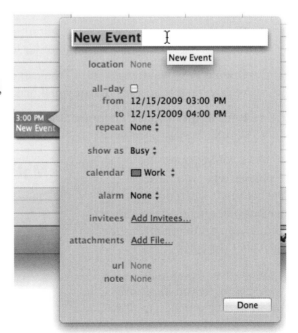

2009	Sun, Dec 13	Mon, Dec 14	Tue, Dec 15	Wed,
all-day				
8 AM				
9 AM				
10 AM				
11 AM			10:15 AM Save the	
Noon				
1 PM				
2 PM				
3 PM			2:45 PM Accept	3:00 PM Meeting with
4 PM				

Edit an event

You've got an event scheduled, but what if you want to add more information than just a name and a time? To **edit** an entry, **double-click** it, or press **Command+E**.

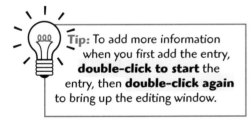

Tip: To add more information when you first add the entry, **double-click to start** the entry, then **double-click again** to bring up the editing window.

The **editing window** lets you add all kinds of information:

→ **How long** the event lasts, by clicking the from and to fields.

→ **Which calendar** it's added to (iCal starts out with Work and Home calendars, but you can add more).

New Event

location	None
all-day	☐
from	12/15/2009 03:00 PM
to	12/15/2009 04:00 PM
repeat	None ⏦
show as	Busy ⏦
calendar	▦ Work ⏦
alarm	None ⏦
invitees	Add Invitees...
attachments	Add File...
url	None
note	None

Done

→ **When and how iCal will alert you** that an event is coming up.

→ You can **attach a file**, associated web address or **add notes** about the event (like teleconference details or which room the meeting's going to be held in).

→ You can also use this window to **invite other people** to the meeting by clicking on the "**Add invitees**" link. Enter the e-mail addresses of the people you want to invite, and they'll be sent an invitation via Mail.

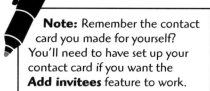

Note: Remember the contact card you made for yourself? You'll need to have set up your contact card if you want the **Add invitees** feature to work.

Play with it

Have you ever forgotten an important event that you meant to attend? **iCal has an alarm feature** that can alert you to an event in a variety of ways. Double-click an item to edit it, then click the Alarm drop-down. You have several choices:

→ **None**: you won't be alerted at all.

→ **Message**: a message opens on your desktop alerting you to the upcoming event.

→ **Message with Sound**: same as the above, but your computer also plays a sound.

→ **E-mail**: you can be sent an e-mail alerting you to the event. You need to have an Address Book card for yourself in order for this feature to work.

→ **Open a File**: want to get fancy? You can open a file at the prescribed time. It can be anything, from a document you'll need for a meeting, to a song file, to a video.

→ **Run Script**: if you're into programming, you can use Apple's scripting language to set off a variety of actions.

Once you've chosen the reminder type, you have the chance to set when the reminder will appear, ranging from minutes before (you set the number), to days after the event.

You can set up as many of these alarms as you like, both before and after the event. Play around with them and see what works best for you.

Make a link

There are four ways to create a new event in iCal:

1. Use the **iCal** event scheduler in Mail.
2. **Double-click** a date or time.
3. **Right-click** a date or time.
4. Press **Command+N**.

Editing's easy, too; double-click to start an entry, double-click it again to add more detail. To edit existing entries **double-click** an entry, or select an entry and press **Command+E**.

Never miss an event again; set an iCal alarm!

Add a calendar

iCal starts out with two calendars: **Work** and **Home**. But what if you belong to a group that wants you to keep track of its events? Or maybe you want to keep separate calendars for each member of your family. Can you add your own calendars?

1. Click the **plus (+) button** at the bottom-left of the main iCal display. An **Untitled calendar** appears in the left-hand column.

2. Give the calendar a name and hit Return. The new calendar's checkbox is a different color from those of Work and Home.

3. Add an entry using your favorite method. See how the color of the entry matches the color of the calendar it belongs to?

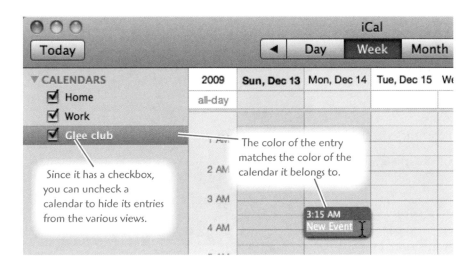

Since it has a checkbox, you can uncheck a calendar to hide its entries from the various views.

The color of the entry matches the color of the calendar it belongs to.

Add a calendar from a web service

Can you import **calendars from web services** like Google or Yahoo? Just as you can synchronize your contacts with those services, you can also synchronize existing calendars with them, too. The process is similar:

1. With iCal open, click iCal in the Menu Bar, then Preferences > **Accounts**.

2. Click the **plus (+) button** at the bottom of the Accounts window, and the **Add an Account drop-down** appears.

3. Click the **Account type** drop-down and choose your service. We chose to add a Google calendar.

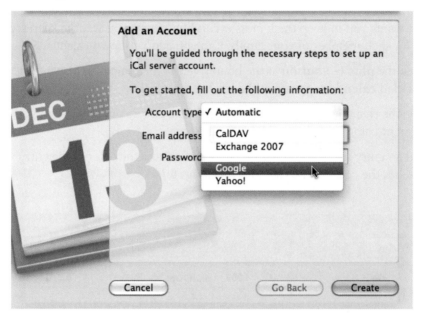

4. Enter the e-mail address and password for the service.

5. Click **Create**, then close the preferences.

The new calendar appears in iCal's left-hand pane. Click on it to see events stored there.

When you add an event in the Google calendar via the Web, it will show up here, and vice versa.

You can add as many calendars as you like, but that could get a little chaotic, so Apple has a feature that helps you organize your calendars.

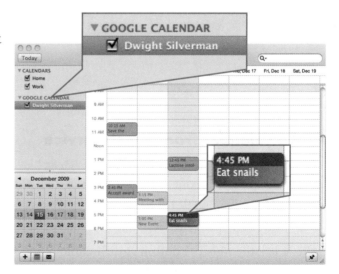

Calendar groups

Remember how Mail lets you create folders to store mailboxes? You can do the same here with calendars. Say you have a big family, and each member has a calendar. You can group all of the calendars into a folder, where you can see all their events at a glance.

1. Click **File** in the Menu Bar, and then **New Calendar Group**. An untitled group appears in the left-hand column.

2. Give the group a name and hit Return.

3. **Drag** the calendars you want to add to the group into the folder.

Add some events to each individual calendar in the group, and then click the folder. What do you see in the main calendar pane? Now click a different calendar not in the group. What happens?

Now that you know how to create entries and organize your calendars, spend some time getting your events set up, complete with alarms and invitations.

Make a link

Hit the plus (+) button in the main iCal window to add a calendar. To add a calendar from a web service, it's Preferences > Accounts > plus (+) button to add the service.

Take a break

It's time to give your brain a break. Take some time away from this book and your Mac to focus on something other than contacts and events. Grab a drink, or go for a walk. You could even do a few sit-ups if you felt like it. It doesn't matter what you do, just make sure it's something other than thinking about Address Book and iCal. Your brain will thank you for it by working on it in the background while you actively *don't* think about it! When you're ready, come back and start with the review.

Review

Import contacts from a PC

↻ What are the basic steps for transferring your contacts regardless of the contact management program you used on your PC?

1. ....

2. ....

3. ....

Add contacts from Gmail and Yahoo

↻ To synchronize Address Book with a web service, you click
.... then click the .... tab and add your details.

Add contacts to the Address Book

↻ Click the .... to start adding a contact.

↻ If a contact has more than one email address, you click the
.... next to the .... on their card.

↻ How do you add a photo of a contact to their contact card?

....

....

↻ List the three ways you can add a contact to the Address Book from an e-mail message in Mail:

1. ....

2. ....

3. ....

↻ How do you create a group in the Address Book?

↻ List the three ways you can send an e-mail message to an Address Book group from Mail:

1. ....

2. ....

3. ....

Add events to iCal

↺ .... view is the default view in iCal. You can also view calendars in .... view and .... view.

↺ List the four ways you can add events to iCal:

1. ....

2. ....

3. ....

4. ....

↺ How do you add extra information to an event?

....

↺ How do you set up an event alarm?

....

Add more calendars

↺ Click the .... to add more calendars to iCal.

↺ To synchronize calendars from web services like Yahoo and Google, you click .... then click the .... tab and add the calendar details.

Calendar groups

↺ How do you show or hide calendars and groups?

....

How did you do?

Did you forget anything? It's hard to remember it all. Go ahead and re-read the sections covering what you overlooked. Your brain might need a bit more time to absorb all the information. Be sure to make strong and vivid links to the information.

Experiment

Add a contact's birthday to their contact card

One of the Address Book's optional fields to add to a contact card is the Birthday field. This is a really neat way to seem like you remembered your boss's birthday when in fact, you don't have to do anything but add it to the contact card and… Well, let's do that first and you'll see what happens next.

1. Make sure you're in Address Book, then in the Menu Bar click Card > Add Field > Birthday.

2. Enter the contact's birthday. You need to enter it in MM/DD/YYYY format for the clever part to happen in the next step.

3. Switch back to iCal, open the Preferences menu and choose the General tab.

4. Click the box next to Show Birthdays Calendar, and then close the Preferences window.

5. Take a look at the main iCal window. What do you see?

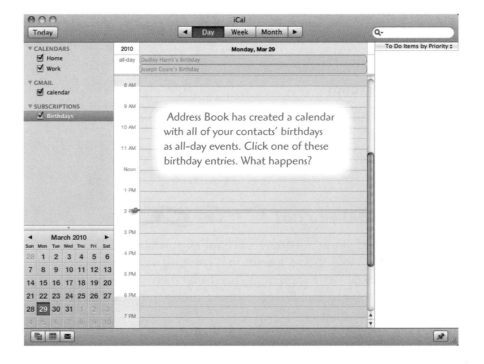

Address Book has created a calendar with all of your contacts' birthdays as all-day events. Click one of these birthday entries. What happens?

Change a calendar's color

1. Select the calendar in the Calendars list and choose Edit > Get Info.

2. Choose a new color from the pop-up menu in the top-right corner of the Info window.

If you need the color to match a sports team or corporate branding and none of the default colors are right, you can customize a calendar's color. At step 2, choose Other.

The Colors window opens showing a color wheel. You may be able to find the right color on the wheel, but if you're having trouble, click the magnifying glass icon, and then move the cursor around the wheel.

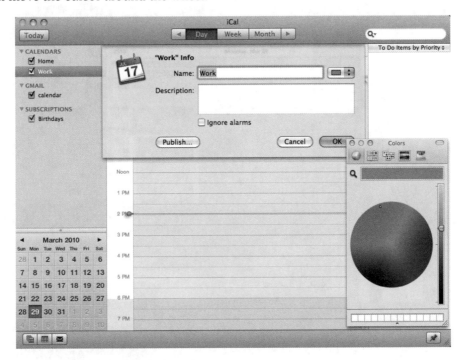

Alternatively, you could try the other color tabs:

→ Color Sliders: this has various color or grayscale sliders.

→ Colors Palettes: Apple shows up by default, but click the drop-down to see others like Web Safe Colors.

→ Image Palettes: shows a spectrum and a dot that you can drag over the spectrum to mix the right color.

→ Crayons: shows a bunch of pre-mixed crayon colors.

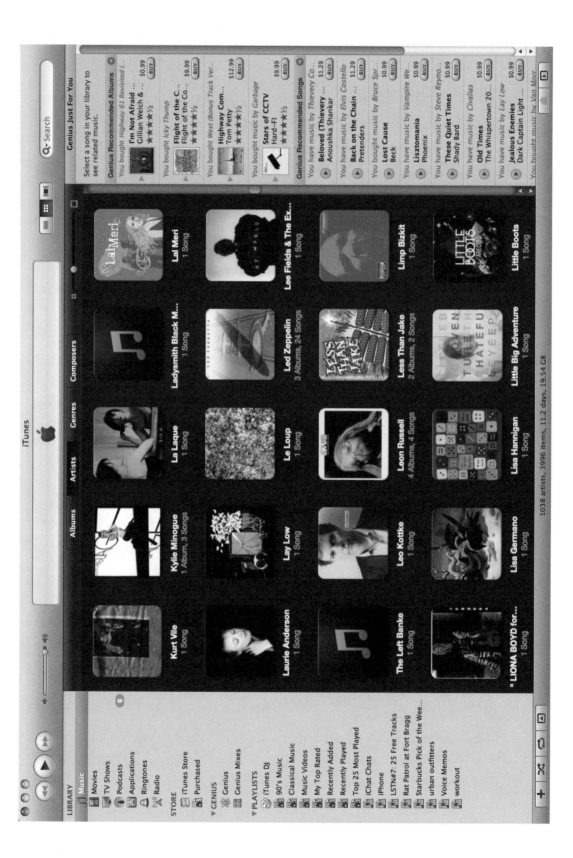

9 Manage music and more with iTunes

You've got music. A lot of it. Is it already in digital format and transferred to your new Mac? What if your music is still in CD format, can you convert those songs to digital files? Either way, you need a way to organize, categorize, and catalog all that music. It's a big job, and you need some software that's up to the task.

No Problem!

iTunes is Apple's all-in-one tool for music. It does all the above, and then some. The chances are good you've used it before because iTunes is available for both Windows and Macintosh computers, and it's required for syncing up an iPod, an iPad, or an iPhone.

On the Mac, what can iTunes do for you? Pretty much everything it does on the PC:

⇨ Import your music as digital files or from CDs.

⇨ Create audio CDs.

⇨ Buy music, video, and applications from the iTunes Store.

⇨ Organize your music in many different ways.

⇨ Help you build Playlists, or even craft lists for you.

⇨ Sync your iPod and manage apps on your iPhone.

One big difference: you'll find iTunes on the Mac runs faster and is more stable. It also integrates with other Mac OS X programs, as you'll discover in future chapters.

Is iTunes for Mac like iTunes for Windows?

If you're familiar with iTunes for Windows, you'll have very little problem navigating the Mac version. On the surface, they look almost identical.

Here's the grid view of the artists' list in the Windows version of iTunes 9.

And here's the same view in iTunes for Mac.

Both have the same design:

→ A **left-hand column** for navigating iTunes' various features—your music, movies, podcasts, TV shows, applications, and radio; the iTunes Store and the media you've purchased there; and your Playlists.

→ A **central pane** that shows your media in a variety of views, the iTunes Store or your Playlists.

> The central area changes depending on what you've clicked on the left.

→ A **right-hand column** devoted to content chosen by the Genius feature. The Genius suggests music and videos based on what you've selected.

→ A **toolbar** across the top to stop, start, and advance through media. You can also search and change the way you view your library from here.

Nearly all the differences between the Windows and Mac versions have to do with where menu items traditionally live on Macs vs. PCs. You already know about some of them. For example, if you want to access the iTunes Preferences on your PC, you do that via the Edit menu. You know where the Mac keeps the Preferences for every application, so the leap from PC to Mac isn't too much of a stretch, the rest of the differences are similar to this one.

	Windows	**Mac**
Menus	Above the player controls	In the Menu Bar
Preferences	Edit menu	iTunes menu
Equalizer	View menu	Window menu
Check for Updates	Help menu	iTunes menu

The bottom line: if you know how to use iTunes in Windows, you'll know how to use it on your new Mac.

Import your music

In chapter 4, you transferred all your files from a PC to your new Mac and organized the files by moving them into the appropriate folders. Did you put your music files into the Music folder inside your Home folder? That's the logical place for them, and for this exercise, we'll presume that's where your music is stored.

> If you didn't already transfer your music files, do that now, then come back here.

Launch **iTunes**, which is in the **Dock** by default.

When you launch iTunes, you'll first have to click through the setup screens. After agreeing to the obligatory license agreement, iTunes pops up screens asking questions:

1. **Internet Audio**: Do you want to use iTunes to listen to audio streamed over the Internet? For now check Yes and then Next. You can always change the default player for Internet radio in the future.

2. **Find Music Files**: If you put your music into the Music folder inside the Home folder, your best move is to choose Yes and click Next. iTunes will look for your files there and add them automatically to its library. If your music is stored elsewhere, choose No and then Next.

3. **Download Album Artwork**: iTunes can download album art for individual songs and albums. If you used iTunes for Windows, you've seen this before. This screen is only for information, and includes instructions for adding artwork manually.

   > If iTunes can't find art for a song or album a placeholder image of a musical note will be displayed instead.

4. Click Done to finish the setup.

When you click Done, iTunes begins to search your Music folder for music files. This could take some time depending on how much music you have stored. When it's complete, you'll see a Welcome to iTunes screen that will let you watch videos describing the software's features.

Leave the Show this window when iTunes opens box checked (so you can check out the tutorials next time iTunes opens), and close the Welcome window.

There's your music. iTunes initially displays your songs in what it calls the **Grid View**.

Play with it

If you're new to iTunes, select a song, then use the **controls** in the top left of the **toolbar** to **play** a song, and **move** to the previous or next item.

Would you prefer a **dark background** in Grid View? Click iTunes > Preferences > **General** tab. Click the drop-down menu next to Grid View and choose **Dark**, and then OK.

Play and pause a song and move to the next or previous item with the controls in the top left of the toolbar.

Import music manually

Did you put your music into a folder other than the Music folder? Is your music stored on an external hard drive, or a server on your home network? In these cases, you'll need to get your music into iTunes manually.

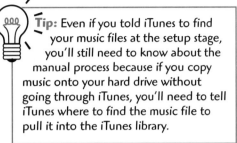

Tip: Even if you told iTunes to find your music files at the setup stage, you'll still need to know about the manual process because if you copy music onto your hard drive without going through iTunes, you'll need to tell iTunes where to find the music file to pull it into the iTunes library.

1. Click **File > Add to Library**. A Finder window appears.

2. **Navigate** to the folder where you stored your music.

3. Click the folder that contains the music you want to add.

4. Click **Choose**.

iTunes goes through the same procedure it does for the automatic process, and at the end shows you your music in the Grid View.

Convert CDs to digital music

iTunes can **import CDs**, converting the songs to digital audio files and adding them to its library.

1. With iTunes launched, **insert a CD** into your Mac's optical drive. The disk appears on your desktop and a pop-up window appears to ask if you'd like to import the CD into your iTunes library.

   a. Click **Yes** and iTunes will **import (or "rip")** the songs from the CD onto your hard drive.

   b. Click **No** and you can still use iTunes to **play** the CD *without* ripping the songs (you can always choose to rip the songs later).

2. When iTunes is done importing, click the **Music** item under **Library** in the left-hand column to see the music you've imported.

Note: iTunes rips from CDs to AAC format. Not every device or media player can work with these kinds of files. If you'd prefer to use the MP3 format, click iTunes > Preferences > General > Import Settings. Change the Import Using drop-down to MP3 Encoder.

Change your view

By default, iTunes displays your library in **Grid View**, with thumbnails showing album art. Look at the iTunes toolbar. Do you see something that looks similar to a Finder window? There's a set of three buttons to the right that let you change the way things look.

Click on each one. How does the view of your library change? In the **List View**, try clicking on the column headers—see how the list sorts differently? This is like the list views in both Windows Explorer and the Mac's Finder.

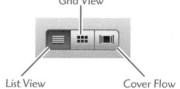

Grid View

List View   Cover Flow

You can tweak the List View even more by turning on the **Column Browser**.

1. Click **View > Column Browser > Show Column Browser** (or hit Command+B). The Column Browser shows up on the left side of the list.

Artists	▶	Name	Time	Artist ▲	Album
All (339 Artists)		☑ God Is Going to Get Sick of Me	3:27	Aberdeen City	The Freezing Atla
Compilations		☑ Addicted	3:41	Ace Young	Ace Young (Bonu
Aberdeen City		☑ Addict	3:41	Ace Young	Ace Young (Bonu
Ace Young		☑ Road	3:45	Aerosmith	Honkin' On Bobo
Aerosmith		☑ Shame	2:15	Aerosmith	Honkin' On Bobo
After Midnight Project		☑ Eyesigh	3:10	Aerosmith	Honkin' On Bobo
Aiden		☑ Baby, Please Don't Go	3:24	Aerosmith	Honkin' On Bobo
Algebra Blessett		☑ Never Loved a Girl	3:12	Aerosmith	Honkin' On Bobo

List View with the Column Browser on the left.

2. Click View > **Column Browser** to choose where you want the browser to appear. To move it to the top of the list, select On Top.

See how the Column Browser changes when it's at the top of the list window? Click around in the columns and watch what happens to the list below. How might this be useful in finding and organizing your music and video?

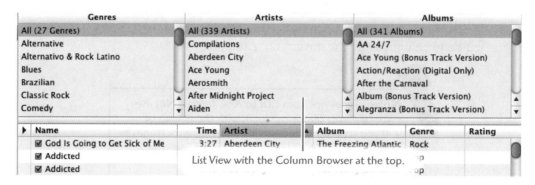

Genres	Artists	Albums
All (27 Genres)	All (339 Artists)	All (341 Albums)
Alternative	Compilations	AA 24/7
Alternativo & Rock Latino	Aberdeen City	Ace Young (Bonus Track Version)
Blues	Ace Young	Action/Reaction (Digital Only)
Brazilian	Aerosmith	After the Carnaval
Classic Rock	After Midnight Project	Album (Bonus Track Version)
Comedy	Aiden	Aleganza (Bonus Track Version)

▶	Name	Time	Artist ▲	Album	Genre	Rating
	☑ God Is Going to Get Sick of Me	3:27	Aberdeen City	The Freezing Atlantic	Rock	
	☑ Addicted					
	☑ Addicted					

List View with the Column Browser at the top.

In **Cover Flow** view, click the forward or back arrows to move through your album artwork one album at a time, or use the slider to browse faster. Double-click an album or song's cover art to start playing it.

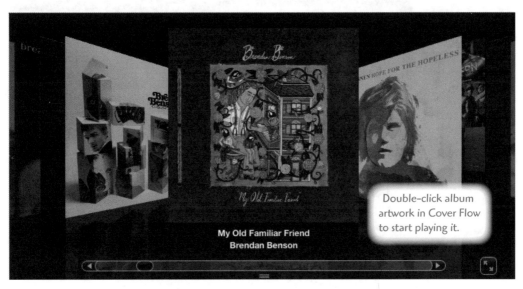

Double-click album artwork in Cover Flow to start playing it.

My Old Familiar Friend
Brendan Benson

Buy music and video from the iTunes Store

Purchasing music and video from the **iTunes Store** requires an account, and you'll need to provide a credit card number. If you had an account with the Windows version of iTunes, it *will* work with the Mac version; just click **iTunes Store** in the left column, then click the **Sign In** button on the right side of the middle pane, and enter your credentials.

If you don't have an account, you'll need to create one. (You can still play with the iTunes Store, even without an account—just skip the Sign In process—though of course without an account you won't be able to buy things.)

1. Click Sign In then choose Create New Account then Continue.

2. Check the box next to I have read and agree to the iTunes Terms and Conditions, and click Continue.

3. Fill out the series of forms that appear, including one that will take your credit card information.

> The forms use a secure connection to Apple, so your information is protected.

Once you're logged into iTunes, you'll be able to buy music and video, as well as apps if you have an iPhone, iPad, or iPod Touch.

The online store is organized just like a movies/music store, with sections devoted to different genres of video and music.

Click the row of black buttons at the top of the middle pane to browse through more categories.

Play with it

Use the search field on the right side of the toolbar to search for the names of artists, songs, albums, movies, TV shows, or apps. Say you want to find the Nine Inch Nails song *Closer*. If you type closer into the search box, what do you see?

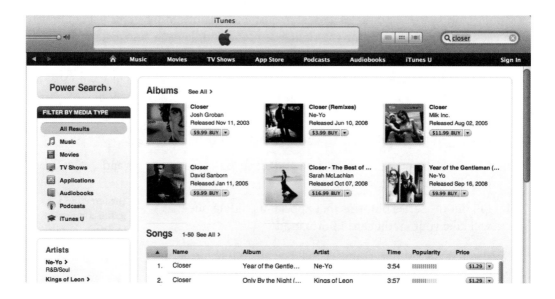

iTunes' results show any media that includes that word, so you'll get movies, albums and songs that match. Can you see the song you're looking for in the list?

Next to items you can purchase is a button with a price on it. Songs are usually either 99 cents or $1.29. Click the button to make your purchase. You may be asked for your password again, even though you're signed in, as a security measure.

You can buy whole albums, which vary in price (most are around $10), movies to own or rent, music videos, and TV shows.

Buy music from other online stores

If you're using iTunes as the way you manage music on your Mac, are you stuck only buying through the iTunes Store?

iTunes can play several different audio formats, including AAC, MP3s, AIFF, WAV and more. So you can buy music from other services, and add it to your iTunes library. You just need to make sure you purchase them in a format that iTunes can play and you can import the music into your iTunes library manually.

One competitor has made it easy. `www.amazonmp3.com`, which is part of the Amazon.com retail site, has a downloader that lets you buy music from its website, then moves the files into your iTunes library. In some cases, songs and albums cost less than on the iTunes Store, and they're in the MP3 format, which can be used in any player.

Stay organized with Playlists

Remember how you used the folders in Mail to organize your e-mail? iTunes **Playlists** are similar. They let you sort songs into collections that make sense to you. And just as Mail has Smart Mailboxes, iTunes has **Smart Playlists** that update automatically.

The gear icon means these are Smart Playlists.

Smart Playlists are structured just like Smart Mailboxes, using conditions to search your library and collect items that match the conditions you set. You can use them to create Playlists based on artists, albums, genres, composers and on when something was added to your library.

There are several Smart Playlists set up for you already. Can you tell by their names what they do?

Play with it

Let's see how the **Recently Added** Smart Playlist works. Select it and click **File > Edit Smart Playlist**.

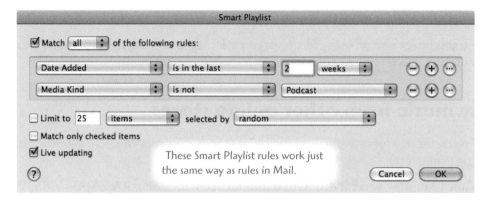

To **set up a new Smart Playlist**. Click **File > New Smart Playlist**. Then configure it based on the rules you want. Try making different choices in the drop-down menus, mixing and matching them. What kind of list appears? If you have a lot of songs, it can get quite interesting!

Did you see the **New Playlist** option in the File menu? Simple **Playlists** let you build collections of songs manually. Click **File > New Playlist**, then name the new Playlist that appears in the left-hand column.

Just drag songs from your library into the Playlist to add them. You can also drag whole albums and even all the works of a particular artist into a list.

To remove a song from a Playlist just **highlight it and hit the Delete key** on your keyboard. Don't worry, the song is only removed from the Playlist, it stays in your library and on your hard drive.

And just as you could create folders to organize your mailboxes in Mail, there are folders for Playlists, too. Click File, **New Playlist Folder**, then name the folder. Just drag appropriate Playlists into your new Playlist Folder.

Make a link

Playlists and Smart Playlists both show subsets of your library. Playlists' contents don't change once you've set them up, though Smart Playlists' contents change according to the criteria you set. You can group Playlists into Playlist Folders.

Your personal Genius

The **Genius** can automatically assemble a list of songs that sound great together. The Genius can also recommend music for you to buy, based on your existing tastes. Click the Genius item in the left-hand column, and information about the feature appears.

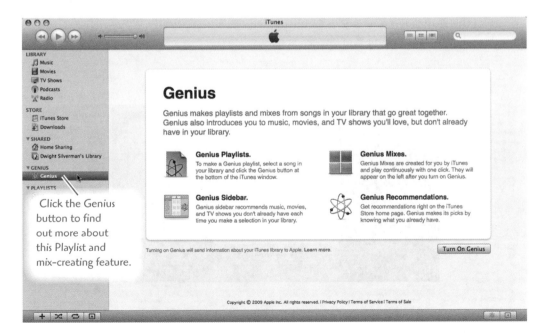

Click the Genius button to find out more about this Playlist and mix-creating feature.

Click the **Turn On Genius** button. You'll be asked to sign in to your Apple account, which is necessary because iTunes sends information about the songs you have to Apple. (If you don't have an Apple account, you can create one here.) You're also asked to approve a Terms of Service agreement for the Genius feature.

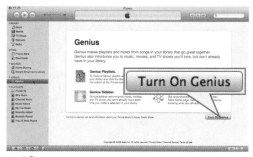

Once you've done this, information about your music is sent to Apple. After a short while, information used to build Genius Playlists is sent back to your computer from Apple—you can watch in the small display in the top of the iTunes window as the information is sent to Apple, then retrieved. When it's complete, you can begin using the Genius feature.

Note: Apple says information about your songs is sent anonymously to its servers. The music you have in your library is *not* associated with your identity, according to the Terms of Service. Click the Learn more link just to the left of the Turn On Genius button to get the full explanation.

Play with it

How does the Genius work with the music you already have? **Select** any song in your library. Click the icon that looks like an **atom** in the lower right-hand corner of the iTunes window and a Genius Playlist is automatically built based around the song you chose.

The list is largely genre- and era-based, but you'll often find some surprises in the list. If you like a particular Genius Playlist, click the **Save Playlist** button in the upper right-hand corner of the middle pane and it will be added to the left column as a Playlist.

Note: Not every song is capable of seeding a Genius Playlist. Very obscure and very new music often won't work. You can try resending information about your library to Apple by clicking **Store > Update Genius**.

Genius Mixes

Genius Mixes are even simpler. Click Genius Mixes in the left column, and 12 mixes are built from music in your library. Each mix focuses on a specific genre, which is indicated by the album art. Hover your cursor over each mix and look at the bottom of the iTunes window. What happens?

Indie Rock & Lo-Fi Mix
Based on: Pixies, The Raconteurs, The Shins, & others.

Click the play button on any mix to start playing that collection. Genius Mixes are like a "black box." You won't know what the next song is until you hear it. This is like listening to a radio station, and it's a great way to explore rarely played gems in your music collection.

Play around with these two approaches to listening to you music with the Genius. Which do you prefer?

Finally, the Genius will also recommend music to buy based on songs you select. Click any song in your library, and look at the right-hand column. What do you see there?

Click the small arrow icon to preview a song, or purchase it with the Buy button.

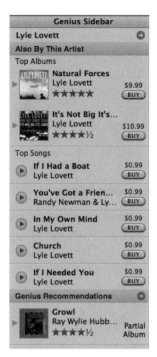

Make a link

Genius searches Apple's database of people with similar music tastes to create surprising and interesting mixes from your existing library, or to recommend new music.

Take your music with you

As much fun as iTunes is, you can't stay parked in front of your Mac to listen to your music. You have to go outside sometimes and, Apple produces a bunch of products that let you take your music with you when you do.

Connect a previously connected device to iTunes

If you used an **iPod, iPad, or iPhone** with the Windows version of iTunes you'll be happy to know that the synchronization process works just the same way on the Mac.

Because you're using it on a different computer, you'll need to fiddle with some settings. iTunes sees your iPod, iPad, or iPhone as a new device, but because it's been used with a Windows version of iTunes, you need to go through a couple of steps to sync it to your Mac.

Let's sync an iPod, though the steps are the same for Apple's other portable music devices. Make sure you've imported your music into iTunes before you start.

1. Launch iTunes.

2. Connect the iPod to your Mac using the provided USB cable. A window opens warning that the device has already been synced to another iTunes library. You have a couple of choices. You can:

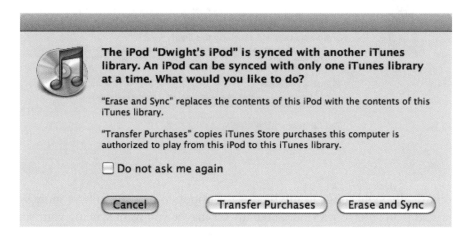

The iPod "Dwight's iPod" is synced with another iTunes library. An iPod can be synced with only one iTunes library at a time. What would you like to do?

"Erase and Sync" replaces the contents of this iPod with the contents of this iTunes library.

"Transfer Purchases" copies iTunes Store purchases this computer is authorized to play from this iPod to this iTunes library.

☐ Do not ask me again

(Cancel)   (Transfer Purchases)   (Erase and Sync)

→ **Transfer purchases** from iTunes on your iPod to the library on your Mac. If your purchased songs were on your PC as well as your iPod, and you moved them across to the Mac along with all your other stuff, you can ignore this option. (If you choose it, the songs are copied to your library and the synchronization process stops.)

→ **Erase and Sync** is the option you want if the songs on your iPod are already in the iTunes library on your Mac. Your iPod will be erased, and songs from your library will be synced to it. If you have any purchased songs that aren't already in your library, they'll be copied to your Mac first.

3. For now, click **Erase and Sync**. You'll learn about manually syncing later.

When the synchronization process is complete, your music will be on your iPod, and any purchased songs not in your library will have been copied there.

Connect a new device to iTunes

What if yours is a brand new iPod that you've never connected to another PC or Mac before? What happens then?

When you plug in a new iPod, you're asked to make a few decisions.

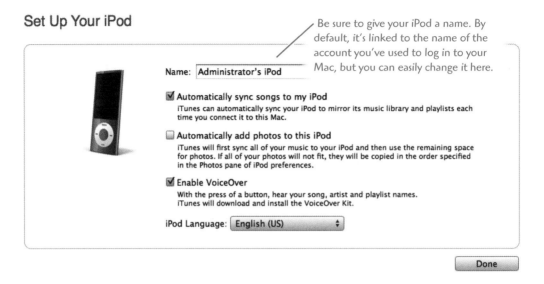

Set Up Your iPod

Be sure to give your iPod a name. By default, it's linked to the name of the account you've used to log in to your Mac, but you can easily change it here.

Name: Administrator's iPod

☑ Automatically sync songs to my iPod
iTunes can automatically sync your iPod to mirror its music library and playlists each time you connect it to this Mac.

☐ Automatically add photos to this iPod
iTunes will first sync all of your music to your iPod and then use the remaining space for photos. If all of your photos will not fit, they will be copied in the order specified in the Photos pane of iPod preferences.

☑ Enable VoiceOver
With the press of a button, hear your song, artist and playlist names. iTunes will download and install the VoiceOver Kit.

iPod Language: English (US)

Done

Automatically sync songs to my iPod is the option to pick if you have more space on your iPod than your songs would take up. Or maybe you want syncing your songs to be as simple as possible? Check this box. When you connect your iPod, it will be synced without you doing anything else.

Automatically add photos to this iPod does for photos what the previous selection did for music.

Enable VoiceOver lets newer iPods speak the name of the song and artist currently playing to you.

Made the choices you want? Click **Done**.

The syncing process begins, and if you hadn't yet installed the VoiceOver software, it will be installed for you.

- -

Take a break

Phew! Now that you're up to speed with iTunes, give your brain a break. Go do something else for a while. Got a magazine to read? Need to check your e-mail? Want to go for a walk with your newly synchronized iPod? Do that now and we'll see you back here in 10.

Review

What's where in iTunes for Mac?

↺ What are the primary menu differences between iTunes for Windows and Mac? Where do you find these features? Fill in the blanks.

	Mac
Menus	In the .... Bar
Preferences	.... menu
Equalizer	.... menu
Check for Updates	.... menu

Import your music

↺ Can iTunes play Internet Audio? Yes/No

↺ To import music manually into iTunes, click File > ....

....

↺ Name the three the different ways you can view your music in iTunes:

1. .... view

2. .... view

3. ....

Convert CDs to digital music

↺ iTunes uses the .... audio format by default when ripping songs from CDs. How do you change it?

....

Buy music and video

↺ How do you search for music, video and apps in the iTunes Store?

....

↺ If you buy music from other sources will it work with iTunes? Check one and put the reason why in the blank.

☐ Yes ....

☐ No ....

☐ It depends ....

Continues, flip the page

Stay organized with Playlists

↻ How do Smart Playlists work?

....

....

↻ How can you tell a Smart Playlist from a regular one?

....

↻ To create a Smart Playlist, you hit .... > New Smart Playlist.
To edit a Smart Playlist, you hit File > ....

↻ How do you add songs to a Playlist?

....

Your personal Genius

↻ What's the difference between a Genius Playlist and Genius Mixes?

....

....

Take your music with you

↻ Can you sync an iPod with your iTunes on your Mac if it's previously
synced with iTunes on a Windows PC? Yes/No

How did you do?

Did you forget anything? It's hard to remember
it all. Go ahead and re-read the sections covering
what you overlooked. Your brain might need a bit
more time to absorb all the information.

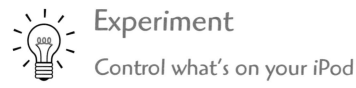

Experiment

Control what's on your iPod

So far you've seen how to use iTunes' automatic feature to manage how your music and video are transferred to your iPod. But what if you want to be more selective? Do you have a music or video collection that's too big for your iPod's capacity? Or maybe you only want to take certain songs with you.

Sure, you can choose to sync all your music and videos to your iPod, or just the ones you want, with Playlists. But you can get even more specific than that.

Connect your iPod to your Mac and make sure iTunes is running. Click the iPod icon in the left-hand column, and then click the Music tab in the center pane. What do you see?

These three windows—Playlists, Artists and Genres—give you almost limitless control over what you sync to your iPod. And there are similar screens for the TV Shows and Movies tabs.

Take some time to experiment with various combinations of Playlists, Artists and Genres. By checking and unchecking different boxes in each window—including the various Genius Mixes—you can craft interesting combinations of tunes every time.

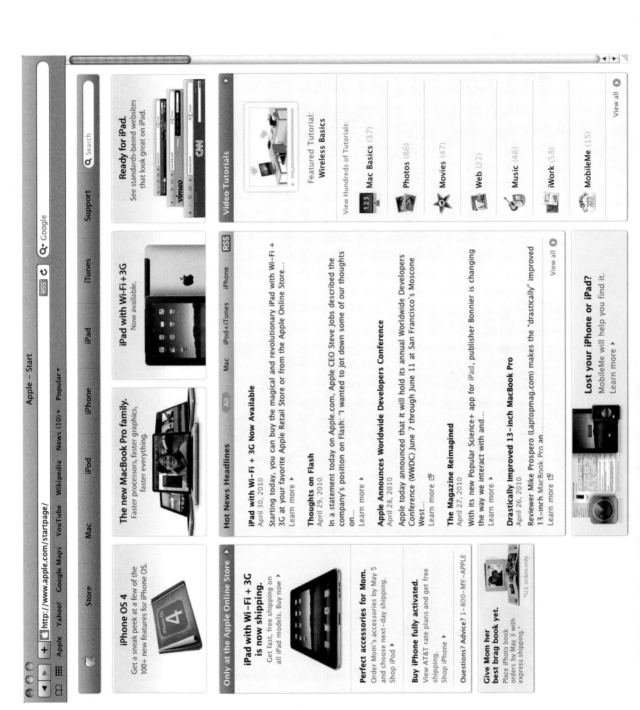

10 Surf with Safari

From reading news, to shopping, to planning a trip, to making restaurant reservations, to keeping track of friends and family, the Web is where it's at. Managing your online activities can either be a hassle or a pleasure, depending on the quality of the tools at your disposal. If you remember what life was like with Internet Explorer on Windows, then you probably know all about the hassle.

No Problem!

Fortunately, on the Mac, you've got Safari, Apple's fast and powerful web browser. Wait, that's not exactly right, because Safari is a *lot* more than just another browser. It's a useful all-in-one tool for the Web, giving you multiple tools to organize and manage your online life with ease. In Safari, you've got:

⇨ One of the fastest and easiest-to-use browsers.

⇨ Visual components for keeping up with favorite sites.

⇨ A secure browser that allows for private surfing.

⇨ A way to grab just what you need, and no more, from web pages.

Customize Safari

You've already used the Mac's web browser a few times in previous chapters, so launch Safari but this time take a look at its toolbar. How is it different from Internet Explorer, or whatever browser you used in Windows?

What's missing from the toolbar? Safari's default design is minimalist; it lacks many of the buttons you might expect to find, but don't be fooled! You can do many things with the little that you see. Let's explore Safari's toolbar. What does each item do?

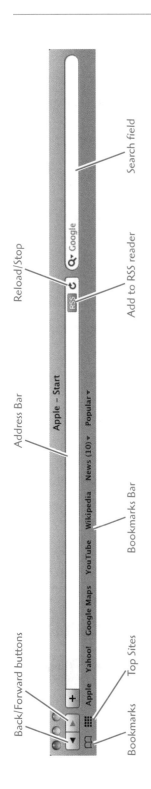

Search field

Reload/Stop

Add to RSS reader

Address Bar

Apple – Start

News (10) ▾ Popular ▾

Bookmarks Bar

Wikipedia

YouTube

Google Maps

Yahoo!

Back/Forward buttons

Apple

Top Sites

Bookmarks

Back/Forward buttons. Just as you would with Internet Explorer or Firefox, use these buttons to move between web pages you've viewed in Safari.

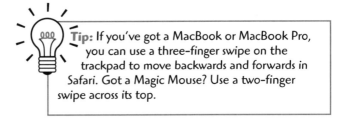

Tip: If you've got a MacBook or MacBook Pro, you can use a three-finger swipe on the trackpad to move backwards and forwards in Safari. Got a Magic Mouse? Use a two-finger swipe across its top.

Bookmarks shows your bookmarks and history. We'll come back to using the Mac's Cover Flow to see them a little later in the chapter.

Top Sites displays a "wall" of thumbnails showing the sites you visit most often.

Bookmarks Bar. As with other browsers, this bar lets you bring frequently used bookmarks front and center.

Address Bar. Enter the web address you want to visit here and hit return.

Add to RSS reader. Click this button to add a website's RSS feed to Safari's built-in feed reader.

> RSS stands for Really Simple Syndication, and it's a quick way for updates on websites to come to you, rather than checking them constantly to see what's new.

Reload/Stop. Click the circular arrow icon to reload the current page. While it's reloading, the icon changes to an X, which you can click to halt the process.

Search field. Use this to search using Google (and only Google; you can't change search engines in the Mac version of Safari).

The toolbar is clean and simple, but what if you want a Home page button, or a Print button?

Play with it

Customize Safari by adding buttons to the toolbar. Click **View** in the Menu Bar, and then **Customize Toolbar** (or right-click the toolbar and choose Customize Toolbar). You'll get a collection of buttons you can add.

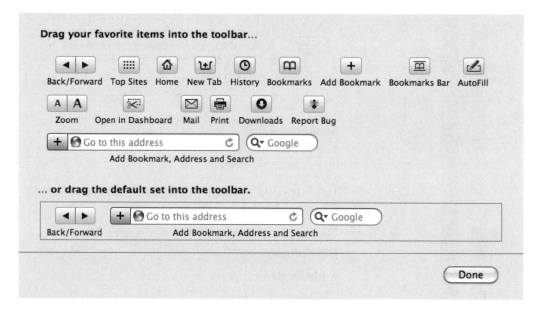

See any icons you'd like to add? Drag them to the toolbar and drop them into place. To remove an icon, just drag it off the toolbar.

For now, make sure you drag the **Home**, **New Tab**, and **Open in Dashboard** buttons to your toolbar. They'll make other steps in this chapter easier and you can always remove them when you're done with the chapter.

Here's how your toolbar should look with the new buttons you just added.

When you're finished, click Done.

What's Safari doing?

Out of the box, Safari also lacks many of the "bars" that are found on Internet Explorer. They are available; you just have to turn them on. For example, Internet Explorer has an area at the bottom of the browser called the Status Bar that shows you when a web page is loading, when a file is downloading, and so on.

To turn on Safari's **Status Bar**:

View	History	Bookmarks	W
Hide Bookmarks Bar	⇧⌘B		
Show Status Bar	⌘/		
Show Tab Bar	⇧⌘T		
Hide Toolbar	⌘|		
Customize Toolbar...			
Stop	⌘.		
Reload Page	⌘R		
Actual Size	⌘0		
Zoom In	⌘+		
Zoom Out	⌘−		
Zoom Text Only			
View Source	⌥⌘U		
Text Encoding	▶		

1. Click on the **View** item in the Menu bar.

2. Click **Show Status Bar**. Reload the current page, or load a new one to see the Status Bar in action at the bottom of Safari's window.

Safari also has tabbed browsing, similar to Firefox and Internet Explorer versions 7 and 8. In case you came to the Mac from Internet Explorer 6, which doesn't have this feature, tabs are a way to view multiple web pages in one browser window, each held in its own tab.

Click the **New Tab button** you added to the toolbar. What happens?

Play with it

Want to turn a tab into a separate Safari window? Just drag the tab out of the window that's currently holding it.

You can turn on the **Tab Bar**, which always shows at least one tab.

1. Click **View** in the Menu bar.

2. Click **Show Tab Bar**, and check the area below the Bookmarks Bar in your new window.

> **Note:** The Tab Bar will always appear when there are two or more tabs present.
>
> To hide any of the bars you just turned on, or any of the others listed in the View menu, just click the "Hide..." option that appears when a bar is active.

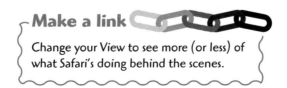

Make a link

Change your View to see more (or less) of what Safari's doing behind the scenes.

Choose your Home page

By default, Safari uses Apple's Start page as its Home page. Do you have some other web page you'd prefer to use? Changing your **Home page** is easy:

1. In Safari, go to the page you'd like to set as your Home page.

   To start with a blank page, just remove anything that's in the Address Bar.

2. Click the **Safari > Preferences > General** tab.

3. Click the button below the Home page field that says **Set to Current Page**.

Your Home page is now set to the page you set up before diving into the Preferences.

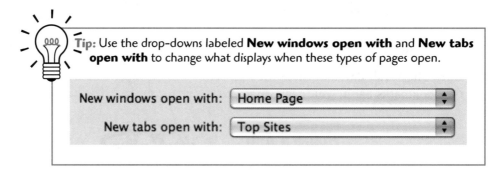

Tip: Use the drop-downs labeled **New windows open with** and **New tabs open with** to change what displays when these types of pages open.

Organize the Web

Safari makes it easy to keep track of the pages you rely on and visit regularly because it provides several slick, visual ways to keep up with your favorite sites.

All browsers keep track of the web pages you visit in their History. Safari also uses your History to keep an eye on how often you visit a site, and organizes your most visited sites in a separate area called **Top Sites**.

Remember the Top Sites icon ▦ from your tour of the toolbar? Click it now.

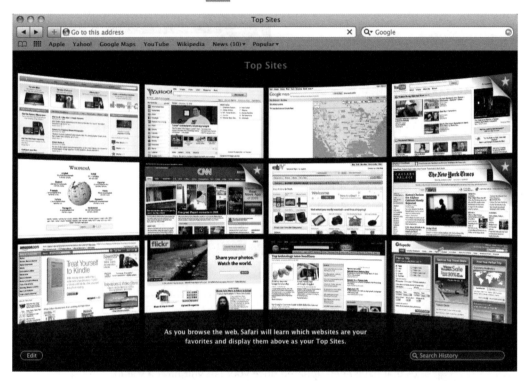

The Top Sites wall of thumbnails starts out with popular sites such as Yahoo!, CNN, the New York Times, Wikipedia and more. But as you surf the Web with Safari, the pages on your wall change, reflecting the sites you visit most.

Make a link

Top Sites is *like* a visual Bookmarks Bar. Click a thumbnail to visit the site.

Can you **manually add a page** to the Top Sites wall? Go to a website you like that isn't yet on your Top Sites wall, then click and drag the icon to the left of its address in the Address Bar onto the Top Sites icon.

Would you like to see **more pages** on Top Sites? Click the **Edit** button in the lower left-hand corner of the Top Sites wall, and then look at the lower right-hand corner of the window. See the **Small | Medium | Large** buttons?

Click Small to reduce the size of the thumbnails, and give you more of them. What would happen if you clicked Large? Give it a try.

Small gives you 24 thumbnails; Medium, 12; and Large, 6 thumbnails.

While you're in Edit mode, look at the **icons** that appear on each of the thumbnails.

The **X** icon **deletes** the page from the Top Sites wall, while the **thumbtack** icon **pins** it permanently in place, giving you another way to add a site to the Top Sites wall. You can also shuffle the thumbnails' order in edit mode.

Do you tend to visit the same sites over and over again? Would it benefit you to use the Top Sites icon instead of the Home page icon?

> **Note:** The thumbnails you see in Top Sites are live. They refresh to show the sites as they are now whenever you go to the Top Sites wall. That's why, if a site requires you to sign in, you'll see its login page.
>
> Sites that have been updated since your last visit have a star in the top right of the thumbnail.

Take charge of your bookmarks and history

Safari can save the names and locations of web pages you want to remember. These are called **Bookmarks** in Safari (as well as in Firefox and Google's Chrome); they're called Favorites in Internet Explorer.

Make a link

Bookmark your *favorite* sites in Safari.

1. There are several ways to **add a Bookmark in Safari**:

   a. When you're on a page you want to remember, click the **plus** icon to the left of the address in the Address Bar.

   b. Click **Bookmarks > Add Bookmark** in the menu.

   c. Hit **Command+D**.

2. Regardless of the method you use, a window appears that lets you rename the bookmark and decide where it should go.

3. Rename the bookmark, if desired, and choose a folder in which to save it.

4. Click **Add** when you're done.

   You can rename a bookmark and choose where to save it. You'll find out how to add items to the list in a moment.

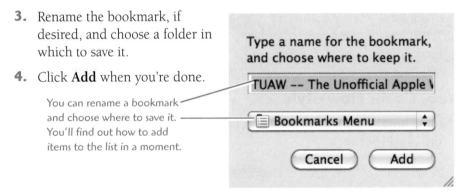

Type a name for the bookmark, and choose where to keep it.

TUAW -- The Unofficial Apple \

Bookmarks Menu

Cancel   Add

Do you have some favorite sites you'd like to add? Go ahead and bookmark them, using the different methods listed above. Which one do you prefer?

Import Favorites into Safari

Would you rather not manually enter all your favorite sites? You can export your Internet Explorer Favorites from your PC and then import them into Safari. The details vary depending on what version of Internet Explorer you're using, but the process is essentially this:

1. In Internet Explorer (IE), click **File > Import and Export...**

2. In **IE6**, click **Export Favorites**, and then **Next**. In **IE7 and 8**, click **Export to a File**, then **Next**, and then **select Favorites**. Hit **Next** again.

3. Choose which folders and/or favorites you want to export. *Choose the topmost "Favorites" folder to get everything.*

4. In all versions of IE, you can now choose where the file goes. By default, it goes in the Documents or My Documents folder. Click **Export**.

5. Take the resulting **bookmark.htm** file and copy it across your network to your Mac, or save it to a flash drive. However you move it, place it on your Mac's desktop.

6. Open **Safari**, and click **File > Import Bookmarks**.

7. Navigate to the saved `bookmark.htm` file, select it, and click the Import button. Safari will save the bookmarks in a dated folder titled "Imported." You can then use the Bookmarks and History feature, which you'll learn about next, to sort them.

> **Tip:** Firefox will also export its bookmarks for you to import into Safari.
>
> 1. In Firefox 3.6 or later, click the **Bookmarks** menu item then **Organize Bookmarks**. The Library containing your bookmarks and history appears.
>
> 2. Click the **Import and Backup** dropdown, and choose Export HTML.
>
> 3. Save the `bookmarks.html` file to your Windows desktop, then follow from Step 5 in the Internet Explorer instructions.

Your Web, Cover Flow-style

Click the **Bookmarks icon** on the toolbar. The Bookmarks page opens by default to show your browsing History.

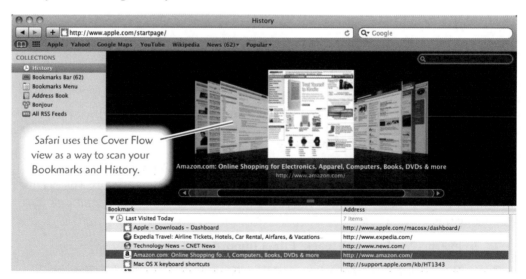

Safari uses the Cover Flow view as a way to scan your Bookmarks and History.

Just like you can in the Finder and iTunes, you can scroll horizontally through the sites you've visited, or use the List View below to find a page. Click a page in the Cover Flow window to go to it, or double-click it in the pane below.

To view your bookmarks instead, look in the left-hand column.

Under the Collections heading, the **Bookmarks Menu** shows you bookmarks you see when you click the **Bookmarks item** in the Menu Bar. The **Bookmarks Bar** shows the **Bookmarks** that appear in Safari's **toolbar**.

Remember how Mail and iTunes let you add folders for organizing your e-mail or music? You have the same ability here in Safari.

1. Click **Bookmarks** in the Menu Bar.

2. Select **Add Bookmark Folder**. Or you could do what you've always done; click the plus (+) button in the left-hand corner.

3. Name the folder in the left-hand column.

4. Drag bookmarks into the folder from the List View on the right.

Both the Bookmarks and the History items in the Menu Bar have different ways of displaying web pages you want to find. Spend some time clicking through them to see the various items. When might you want to use these menu items rather than the Bookmarks and History manager?

Browse privately

Your browser records the sites you've visited, and those sites may also leave small text files, called cookies, on your computer to record your visit. It's not nefarious; it's just the way browsers and the Internet work.

Go ahead and give it a try. Check Safari's History to see the most recent sites you've visited. All the sites you've visited so far are listed there.

But there are times when you really don't want your browser keeping track of where you go. For example, during the holidays, you may use the web to look for or buy presents for family members. Do you really want them poking around in Safari's History feature to see where you've been?

Safari's **Private Browsing** feature lets you surf the Web, but leave no tracks on your computer as you do. When you have Private Browsing turned on, Safari doesn't include the sites you visit in its History. Safari will delete a record of any downloads (though the file will remain in your Downloads folder). And any changes made to cookies on your Mac are only temporary, and revert back when you turn off Private Browsing.

Note: Private Browsing does *not* render you anonymous on the Internet. Websites can still see your Internet Protocol (IP) address and identify your browser type. Private Browsing only masks actions *on your own Mac.*

To **turn on Private Browsing**:

1. With Safari running, click **Safari** in the Menu Bar, then select **Private Browsing**. A dialog box appears asking if you want to turn on Private Browsing.

2. Click OK to clear the dialog box and turn on Private Browsing.

Do you see anything different about Safari? The browser doesn't change—there's no visible clue that Private Browsing is turned on. The only way to tell is to click Safari in the Menu Bar, and you'll see that Private Browsing now has a checkmark next to it.

Visit two or three sites, and then check the History again. Are the sites that you just visited saved in the History?

There are two ways to **turn off Private Browsing**:

1. Since you have to decide to turn it on, Private Browsing is **turned off when you quit Safari**.

2. Click **Safari** in the Menu Bar, then **select Private Browsing again**. This time the checkmark will disappear.

What happens if you forgot to use Private Browsing, but still want to hide your tracks on the computer? In this case, you can reset Safari:

1. Click **Safari > Reset Safari**. A dialog box appears that lets you select different aspects of your browsing record to reset, or delete.

2. **Uncheck** the items you *don't* want to reset.

3. Click the **Reset** button.

This is similar to the Delete Browsing History feature of Internet Explorer.

Save Web Clips to the Dashboard

You may visit a lot of web pages, but do you revisit the same areas on a page, looking for specific information? If that's the case, Safari has a feature you're going to love. It's called **Web Clips**, and it's just what the name implies—it lets you "clip" an area on a web page for repeated viewing. The clips are stored and viewed in another feature called the **Dashboard**.

The Mac OS X **Dashboard** is a collection of small applications that each do just one thing. Among others, there's a program that shows you a clock, another that's a calculator, and another that gives you the local weather. These little programs are called **widgets**.

Make a link

Did you come to the Mac from Windows 7 or Vista? Widgets are very similar to Windows' Gadgets feature.

Want to see the Dashboard? There are several ways to bring it up:

1. Hit the **F4** key on your Mac's keyboard—it's the key with the gas-gauge icon on it.

2. Hold down the **Fn** key, and hit the **F12** key. (Primarily designed for older Mac keyboards that don't have a Dashboard key.)

3. Click the **Dashboard icon** on the Dock.

We'll come back to the Dashboard in a little while so for now, click on any space between the widgets to close the Dashboard.

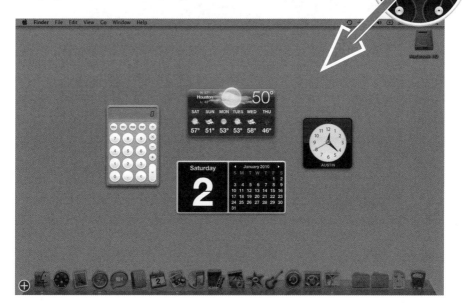

Create a Web Clip

Say you want to keep an eye on the weather radar for your city.

1. Launch Safari and enter www.weather.com in the Address Bar and hit Return to view Weather.com's radar maps.

2. In the search field near the top of the web page, enter your city, state, and ZIP code. Hit Return.

3. Click the **Radar Map** link.

4. Scroll down so the Radar Map is about in the middle of the page.

5. Click the **Open in Dashboard icon** in Safari's toolbar.

You added this icon to the Safari toolbar earlier in this chapter.

💡 **Tip:** If you didn't add the Open in Dashboard icon to the Safari toolbar, you can click **File > Open in Dashboard**.

6. Safari usually does a pretty good job of guessing the area you want to clip. The Radar Map should be highlighted, and the rest of the page grayed out.

If Safari doesn't get it right, move your cursor over the page without clicking anything. Click on the correct area when it's highlighted.

If Safari can't guess, click anywhere on the page and you'll get a highlight box you can drag into place and properly size.

7. When the area you want to clip is correctly framed, **click the Add button** in the upper right-hand corner of the page.

8. Dashboard launches, and the new Web Clip loads.

Arrange your widgets to make room for the Web Clip by just dragging them around.

Play with it

Let's personalize your widgets. Chances are the weather widget isn't set to your locale. How do you think you'd change it?

Move your mouse cursor over the weather widget. Click the small "i" that appears in the lower right-hand corner of the widget to bring up a settings panel.

Enter your city/state or ZIP code. Click Done when you're finished.

You may not see your city in some of the widgets' lists. Just pick the city nearest you.

In the US, the weather widget may start out showing the weather in Cupertino, CA, where Apple has its HQ. In the UK, it shows London.

Add more widgets

Want to add more widgets? Click the plus (+) icon at the bottom-left of your screen—and you'll see a collection of new widgets you can add and customize.

See one that looks interesting? Just click it. After it's appeared, drag it where you want it. When you're done placing and configuring widgets, click the X in the bottom left-hand corner of your screen to finish up.

Click the plus icon in the Dashboard to add more widgets.

| Widgets | Address Book | Business | Calculator | Dictionary |

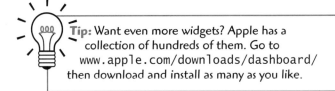

Tip: Want even more widgets? Apple has a collection of hundreds of them. Go to www.apple.com/downloads/dashboard/ then download and install as many as you like.

Take a break

It's that time again. Lucky you. It's time to take a break. You may be tempted to keep forging ahead, but fight the urge. Studies show that your retention of new material will actually increase if you walk away now and then to give your learning muscles a much deserved break. So, go take a break, if for no other reason than the science made you do it.

Review

Customize Safari

↻ To customize Safari's toolbar you click .... > .... , then drag icons onto or off the toolbar.

↻ To change Safari's Home page you ....

Organize the Web

↻ The .... icon deletes a page from the Top Sites wall and the thumbtack icon .... to the Top Sites wall.

↻ Name two of the three different ways you can bookmark a page in Safari:

1. ....

2. ....

Browse privately

↻ When Private Browsing is on, Safari doesn't ....

....

↻ To turn on Safari's Private Browsing, click .... >

....

↻ How do you delete private information from Safari?

Save Web Clips to the Dashboard

↻ What feature does the Dashboard resemble in Windows 7 and Vista?

↻ How do you access the Dashboard?

↻ To make part of a page into a Web Clip, click the .... icon or choose .... > ....

↻ What do you do if Safari doesn't properly guess what part of the page you want to become a Web Clip?

....

↻ To complete the clipping process you need to click the .... button.

Experiment

Go undercover with Safari

Safari's a great web browser, but let's face it, it doesn't have as many users as Internet Explorer or Firefox. And because of that you may run into websites where pages don't look or behave as you expect them to.

For example: A lot of home-banking sites require that you use Internet Explorer to conduct transactions. While you may have used IE on your old Windows PC, you're on a Mac now, and you don't have access to IE... Or do you?

Safari may not be the most-used browser around, but it's one of the few that can mimic other browsers, thanks to a hidden Develop menu you can easily turn on.

1. Click **Safari > Preferences** then click on the **Advanced tab**.

2. Check the box at the bottom of the window labeled **Show Develop menu in menu bar** then close the Preferences window.

    ☑ Show Develop menu in menu bar

    Click on the new Develop item on the Menu Bar. Select the User Agent item to see a list of many different kinds of browsers—including three versions of Internet Explorer—that Safari can impersonate.

Spend some time surfing the Web, and when you land on a page, use the User Agent feature to change Safari's behavior to match one of the browsers on the list. If you have a favorite site that says it requires Internet Explorer, give it a try with Safari's User Agent set as one of the IE versions.

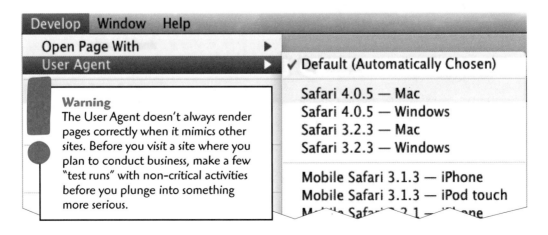

Develop	Window	Help

Open Page With ▶
User Agent ▶ ✓ Default (Automatically Chosen)

Warning
The User Agent doesn't always render pages correctly when it mimics other sites. Before you visit a site where you plan to conduct business, make a few "test runs" with non-critical activities before you plunge into something more serious.

Safari 4.0.5 — Mac
Safari 4.0.5 — Windows
Safari 3.2.3 — Mac
Safari 3.2.3 — Windows

Mobile Safari 3.1.3 — iPhone
Mobile Safari 3.1.3 — iPod touch
Mobile Safari 3.1 — iPhone

Subscribe to RSS feeds

Remember in chapter 7's experiment, when you learned about Mail's ability to organize and read RSS feeds? Safari makes it easy to subscribe to RSS feeds that you can view in Mail or Safari.

Let's say you want to subscribe to CNet's News.com, the tech news site. When you go to www.news.com, you'll see the RSS icon appear in the address bar.

Click on the RSS icon to see a list of the stories included in the RSS feed. How do you think you'd subscribe to them, so they flow into your Mail app?

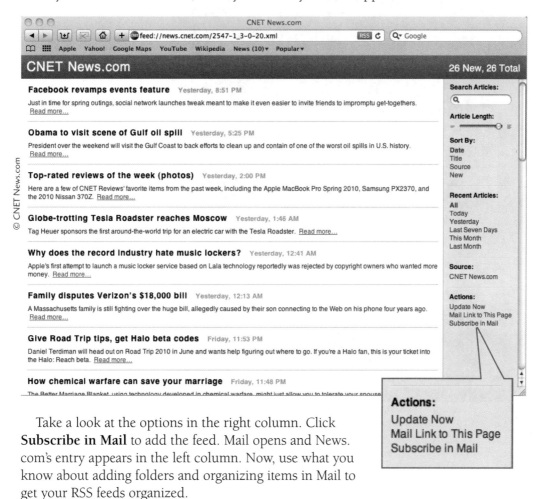

Take a look at the options in the right column. Click **Subscribe in Mail** to add the feed. Mail opens and News.com's entry appears in the left column. Now, use what you know about adding folders and organizing items in Mail to get your RSS feeds organized.

11 Organize and manage your pictures in iPhoto

Taking pictures with a digital camera or a cell phone is so easy and so inexpensive that you do it often. So you've got photos . . . lots and lots of photos, and you need a way to organize, edit, and share them.

But how? Can you do all this without buying several different and possibly expensive programs?

No Problem!

Your new Mac comes with iPhoto, one of the best applications Apple has designed. It makes organizing, editing, and sharing your photos drop-dead simple. At the same time, it's remarkably powerful. You can do things with it that will amaze both you and the people you share your photos with. iPhoto makes it a snap to:

⇨ Organize your pictures by date, place and people.

⇨ Fix and enhance your photos.

⇨ Share pictures with others via social networks and the Web.

⇨ Create slide shows, calendars and even books.

iPhoto is part of the iLife suite that comes with every new Mac, and also includes iMovie, iDVD, iWeb, and GarageBand. If you've got a pre-owned Mac that doesn't have iLife on it, you can buy it at www.apple.com/ilife.

167

Import and organize photos

In chapter 5, when you copied your data from your Windows PC to your Mac's hard drive you moved your photos into the Pictures folder. That's a start, but before you can start using iPhoto, you have to load your pictures into it.

Do you remember how you manually imported music into iTunes? Then you already know how to import photos into iPhoto. The process is similar in both applications.

Launch iPhoto from the Dock.

You'll get a welcome screen similar to the one that introduced iTunes.

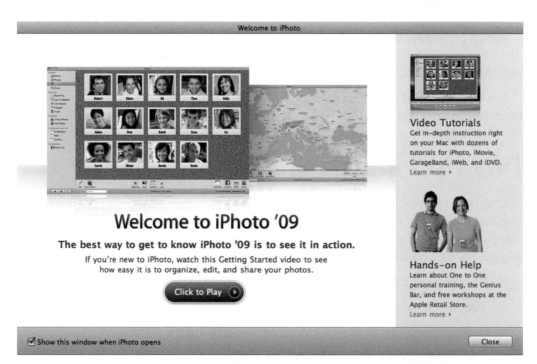

And just like the iTunes welcome screen, the iPhoto screen includes video tutorials you might want to watch. For now, make sure the checkbox in the lower left-hand corner of the window is checked so the screen will appear again the next time you run iPhoto, then click Close.

iPhoto wants to know if you want it to open automatically when you connect your camera to your Mac. If you think you'll **primarily use iPhoto to manage your pictures**, go ahead and check **Yes**. If you're **not sure**, you can click **Decide Later** and you'll get the same dialog next time you launch iPhoto.

Note: There's more than one way to work with photos, and there's also more than one way to get them off your digital camera and onto your Mac. iPhoto is certainly handy, but your Mac comes with an application called Image Capture (you can find it in the Applications folder) that pulls images from devices like cameras and scanners without putting them in your iPhoto library.

Or perhaps your digital camera has its own software for managing photos. You may want to use this if you liked the way it worked in Windows (though there's no guarantee the Mac version will be anything like the Windows version).

Think about how you're going to manage and edit your photos, and that will help you answer the question about whether iPhoto should launch when you plug in your camera.

Finally, iPhoto wants to know if you want to use your camera's built-in GPS feature (if it has one) to tag your photos with the places where they were taken.

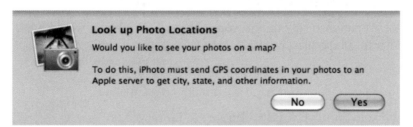

If your camera supports GPS, it can embed location information in the photos it takes. This is most common with cell-phone cameras, though an increasing number of digital cameras can do this, too. If you want iPhoto to use this information to show where you took your photos on a map, click Yes, otherwise, click No.

Do you publish photos to a website or use a photo-sharing site such as Flickr? If so, location coordinates may show up in the photos. If you have privacy concerns, you can turn off the location feature on your camera or cell phone.

Once you've cleared the GPS dialog box, you're brought to the main iPhoto interface.

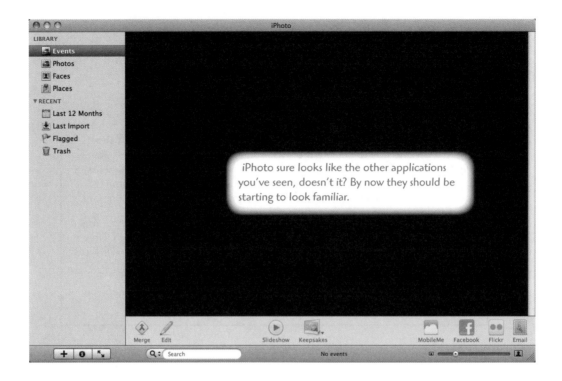

Import photos already stored on your Mac

iPhoto doesn't automatically import your photos. To do that, it would have to scan your computer for photo files, but it doesn't. ——— Why do you think Apple chose not to automate that process?

So you'll need to import your pictures into iPhoto manually.

1. With iPhoto open, click **File > Import to Library. . .**

2. Find the folder that contains your photos and select it.

3. Click **Import**.

Your photos are likely to be in the Pictures folder, but if you chose another folder, select that.

iPhoto begins to import your photos, rushing through them in a speedy slideshow.

When the process is finished, iPhoto displays your pictures in its main window. iPhoto will have organized your photos into **Events**—based on either the dates you took them, or the names of the folders you stored them in.

iPhoto can organize your pictures in other ways. Take a look at the left-hand column, under the Library heading.

LIBRARY

Events

Photos

Faces

Places

→ **Events** groups together photos based on dates or named folders. A representative image is shown.

> What happens when you move your cursor back and forth across an event's thumbnail?

→ **Photos** displays all of your photos, again sorted by date or folder name.

→ **Faces** groups images based on the faces it thinks it sees in each image. We'll come back to this feature.

→ **Places** sorts your photos by location if you enabled GPS tagging earlier. You can also assign map locations to photos manually.

Import photos from your camera

What if you have photos on your camera, how do you get those onto your Mac? To import photos from a camera (or from a camera's memory card):

1a. Connect the camera to your Mac with the USB cable that came with your digital camera.

Or …

1b. If you have a new MacBook, MacBook Pro or iMac, it has a slot for reading SD memory cards. On the notebooks, look on the left side, where your USB connections are, for a slot that's about an inch wide. On an iMac, the slot is on the right side, below the optical drive slot.

Remove the SD card from your camera and insert it in the SD card reader slot.

2. Did you tell iPhoto to launch when you connect a camera? If you did, it will do so when you turn on the camera or insert the SD card. If you didn't choose this option, you'll need to open iPhoto.

> Don't worry, you can leave the photos on the camera or card and import them again with your favorite image manager, but play along now to get a feel for iPhoto.

171

3. iPhoto finds the images on the camera or on the SD card and displays them to you.

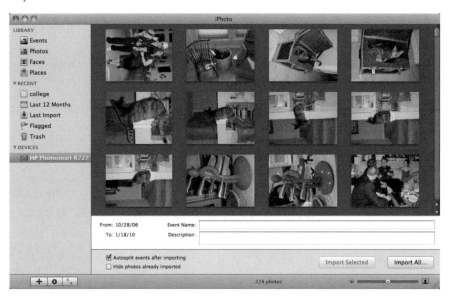

4a. To import *all* the images click the **Import All** button in the lower right-hand corner of the iPhoto window. With the **Autosplit events after importing** box checked by default, iPhoto will organize the images by date.

Or . . .

4b. To import just *some* of the pictures hold down the **Command** key and **select** the pictures you want. Then click the **Import Selected** button.

Make a link

Import All your photos or hold down Command and select to Import Selected photos.

Organize your photos by Events

iPhoto uses the date a photo was taken as the starting point for organizing your photos. Click the Events item in the left-hand column and scroll through the thumbnails in iPhoto for each Event.

If you sorted your photos into folders on your Windows PC, iPhoto uses the name of the folder to name the associated Event. For example, say you took a trip to Yellowstone National Park, and put many of the pictures into a folder called Yellowstone that you imported into iPhoto.

Jun 30, 2007

yellowstone
Jun 30, 2007 - Jul 4, 2007 163

iPhoto considers that folder to be an Event called Yellowstone even though it holds photos from different dates.

If you imported photos from your PC that were already sorted into folders, iPhoto knows that you want these photos grouped and names the Event after the folder name.

Merge and rename Events

Do you have any other photos from the same trip that didn't make it into that folder? Those photos will be sorted by date in the main Events window. Drag those Events onto the Yellowstone Event. iPhoto asks if you want to merge the two. Click **Merge** if that's what you want to do.

Or maybe you'd prefer to give these photos a different name, say Yellowstone 2, if they're from the second week of your vacation. Can you **change the Event name** from a date to a name?

1. Put your cursor over the thumbnail and click the **i icon** that appears in its lower right-hand corner.

2. Highlight the date at the top of the dialog box that appears and **enter the name** you want to use instead.

3. Click Done when you're finished.

Jul 4, 2007

Jul 4, 2007
48 photos

event place

description

Do any of these other features look intriguing? We'll come back to this window shortly.

Create an Event

Can you **create an Event** yourself to put the Yellowstone 2 photos in? Sure:

1. Click the **Photos** item in the left-hand column. This shows you all your pictures.

2. Select the photo you'd like to use to start your Event. (If you want to use more than one photo, select them using Command+click.)

3. Drag the photo or photos onto the **Events** item on the left. A dialog box appears.

4. Click **Create** to generate the event (and check the **Don't Ask Again** box if you don't want to approve this every time).

5. iPhoto takes you right to your new Event when you hit Create. If you used just one photo, the Event is given the name of that file. If you used more than one photo, the Event will be called "untitled event." Either way, click the name to change it.

Warning
Like the dialog box says, a photo can't belong to more than one Event. If you create a new Event, the image will be removed from the old one.

Albums are like Playlists for photos

What if the same picture belongs in several categories? You might have gone to Yellowstone during a specific time frame, but can you also organize your pictures from the trip by, say, some of the attractions there, or by the animals you saw without taking the pictures out of the main Yellowstone Event?

Remember the Playlists in iTunes? iPhoto has a similar feature, called Albums. To add an Album, click **File > New Album**, and it appears in the left-hand column. **Rename it,** then **drag photos** from the main iPhoto window into the Album. iPhoto also has **Smart Albums**, started from the **File** menu, that are automatically populated based on criteria you set.

 **Make a link**

By default, photos are organized by Events that take place on a specific date. Each photo can only be in one Event, but can appear in multiple albums.

Organize your photos by Faces

Grouping photos by the people that appear in them is one of the coolest features in iPhoto, and it's incredibly addictive. Don't start on this unless you've got the time to spend, because once you get started with iPhoto's Faces feature, it's hard to stop!

As the name implies, **Faces** uses facial recognition to organize your photos based on your friends' and family's faces. You show iPhoto a picture of a person's face, and it tries to find others that contain the same face. —— For the most part, Faces works fairly well, and even when it doesn't, the results can be entertaining.

Click the Photos item in the left-hand column to get access to all your pictures, then:

1. Find a photo that has a person in it; someone who appears in many of your pictures. Select the photo and click the **Name** button in the toolbar at the bottom of iPhoto's main window.

2. The photo zooms to fill the main iPhoto window, and a box frames the face. Click the "unnamed" tag under the box, and then enter the person's name.

3. Click **Done**.

4. Click the **Faces** item in the left-hand column, and you'll see the image you chose on a corkboard in the main iPhoto window.

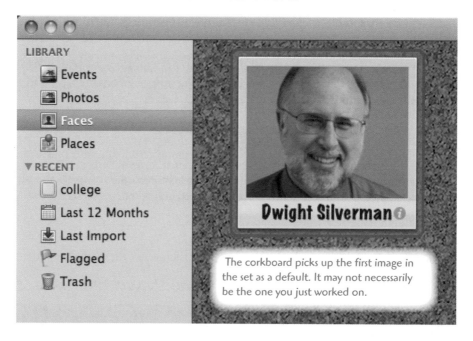

5. **Double-click** on the face to see **other pictures that iPhoto thinks show the same face**.

6. Select a photo, then click the **Confirm Name** button at the bottom of the window. The screen changes to focus on the face in each picture.

7. **Click** once on each picture **if the face is a match**; double-click **if it's not**. Scroll through the photos in the window until you have confirmed (or unconfirmed) each picture.

8. Click Done. You'll be presented with a new batch of photos, because your confirmations have helped iPhoto improve its recognition.

9. Repeat the process until all the faces in all your photos have been confirmed.

You can do this for the people who appear regularly in your photos. As you add new people, click the Faces item on the left to see your corkboard filling up.

Play with it

You've been through all the pictures iPhoto presented as having the matching face, but you *know* there are other pictures that it missed. Can you get iPhoto to recognize the same face in those photos, too? Yes, click a photo and **add that person's name** to it. That will uncover still more photos.

What if you find a picture that contains a person, but iPhoto doesn't know that it has a face in it, can you fix that, too? Click the **Name** button, then **Add Missing Face**. Move the resizable box around the face, then give that person a name.

Finally, play around with animals' faces. While iPhoto's better at recognizing human faces, you can use facial recognition for other species as well.

Make a link

Click a photo and Name the person in it. Once iPhoto's recognized a face, click once to confirm, double-click to unconfirm.

Organize your photos by Places

Click the **Places** item on the left. If you don't have any GPS-tagged photos, you'll see a note telling you how to add locations to your photos, or to import photos with GPS coordinates. If you included photos from a GPS-enabled smartphone or digital camera in your iPhoto import and allowed iPhoto to use GPS data when you set it up, iPhoto has already plotted them on a map.

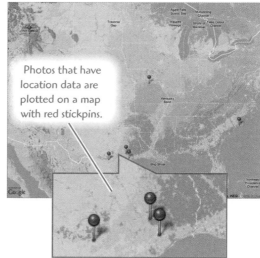

Photos that have location data are plotted on a map with red stickpins.

Map Data ©2009 Google, Tele Atlas, INEGI

Hover your cursor over each pin. What do you see? What happens when you click on the name of the place that appears? Photos that have location data are already organized based on place.

If your photos don't have GPS info, can you still organize them by place? Yes, but you need to add location data to them. Remember how you changed the name of an Event? That window can also be used to place either a single image or an entire Event's worth of photos on a map.

1. Click the **Events** item in the left-hand pane.

2. Find the Event you renamed, ours is called Yellowstone 2, and hover your cursor over its thumbnail. Click the **i icon** in the lower right-hand corner.

3. Click the field marked **event place** and begin typing a location. If iPhoto knows about it, you'll see some search suggestions.

4. If you see a suitable suggestion, select it. The map changes to show the new location.

5. Didn't like any of the search suggestions? Select **Find on map…** to bring up a Google map with more capabilities.

6. From here you can search again, or move the map around and find the location manually. Click the **Drop Pin** button when you find the right spot, then click the **Assign to Event** button.

Assigning a location to a single photo works the same way: hover, click the i, add a location, click Done.

Make a link

Hover, click the **i**, add the **location**, click **Done**.

Take a break

Now that you have your photos better organized, you're ready to make them look better, too, but right now it's time to give your brain a break. The next topics require your full attention and that's best achieved after you've given your brain a rest. Go do something fun for 10 minutes then come on back and tackle the last few topics.

Fix your photos

iPhoto has a great set of tools for tweaking your pictures. Just like the other Mac OS applications you've seen so far, iPhoto is simple on the surface, but lets you dive deeper for more advanced capabilities if you need them.

For the basics, just click on any picture in iPhoto, and look at the bar that appears underneath it. What icons do you see there that might help you improve the photo?

Tip: Don't worry about making changes to an image you may later regret. iPhoto uses **non-destructive editing**, which means you can undo any edits. You can always use the standard **Edit > Undo** to reverse the last change you made. If you make multiple changes in a session and want to undo them all, use **Photos > Revert to Previous**. And if you want to go back to the original version of a photo, just as it came off your camera, use **Photos > Revert to Original**.

The **Rotate** button lets you **rotate an image 90 degrees** at a time. Try it, even though the image you're working with may be oriented properly (just keep clicking until it's back where it was).

The **Edit** button takes you into iPhoto's editor, and that's where the fun begins. Click it with an image selected.

Click the Edit button to access more advanced editing functions.

Make a link

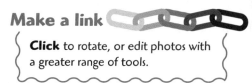

Click to rotate, or edit photos with a greater range of tools.

Play with it

Check out the new buttons that appear on the toolbar under the photo. These are your editing tools. The first six, from left to right, are fairly simple and straightforward, while the last two give you greater flexibility.

Try the tools and write down in the blanks what each one does.

Rotate ....

Crop ....

Straighten ....

Enhance ....

Red-Eye ....

Retouch ....

Effects ....

Adjust ....

When you're finished making the changes and your picture is perfect, click the Done button. And don't forget: you can always go back and undo what you've done.

Export your edited photos

Now that you've tweaked, trimmed and tuned your picture in iPhoto, you may want to give your improved photos to someone else, or take them to a store to have them printed. Use iPhoto's **Export** feature. Select the picture or pictures you'd like to save to new files, then click **File > Export**.

Click **Export** to name the file and select a folder in which to save it on your hard drive.

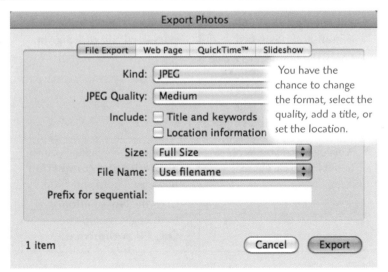

You have the chance to change the format, select the quality, add a title, or set the location.

Share your photos

Once you've got your photos organized and edited so they look their best, it's time to share them with the world. In the digital era, there are several ways to do that: Online, in an animated slideshow and on paper . . . all published from your Mac, of course.

Put your pictures on the Web

The fastest way to share your pictures is to put them on the Web, and iPhoto makes that incredibly easy. There are three ways to do this.

Did you sign up for a MobileMe account? If so, you can also post your pictures to a gallery there.

Post photos to Facebook	Post photos to Flickr	Post photos to MobileMe
1. Select the **Events**, **Photos**, **Faces**, or **Places** and choose the photos you want to upload.		
2. Click the **Facebook button** in the lower right-hand corner of the iPhoto window. A dialog box asks if you want to set up a Facebook connection to iPhoto.	2. Click the **Flickr button** in the lower right-hand corner. A dialog box asking if you want to set up Flickr appears.	2. Click the **MobileMe icon.** A dialog box appears asking if you want to publish the photos to your MobileMe gallery.
3. **Click Set Up.** A Facebook sign-in window appears.	3. **Click Set Up.** You're taken to a Yahoo sign-in page in Safari (Yahoo owns Flickr).	3. Choose who can view the pictures, and enable whether they can be downloaded or added to. Click **Publish** when you're ready. That's it!
4. **Enter your Facebook e-mail and password.** Check the box next to **Keep me logged in to iPhoto Uploader** so you don't have to log in each time you upload photos. Click **Login**.	4. Enter your **Flickr login and password** and click **Signin**.	
5. A dialog asks if you want to publish to Facebook.	5. A page appears asking you to **authorize the connection** between iPhoto and Flickr. Click the **Next** button to the right then click **OK, I'll authorize it**.	

Because MobileMe is Apple's own service, you don't have to jump through the authorization hoops used for Facebook and Flickr.

Post photos to Facebook	Post photos to Flickr	Post photos to MobileMe
6. Click the **Photos Viewable By** drop-down to determine whether everyone, just your friends, or your friends' friends can see the pictures. Click **Publish** to post your photos.	**6.** Now, go back to iPhoto. A dialog is waiting there for you to choose who can see the photos and the size they'll be. The latter only has choices beyond "Web" if you have a Flickr Pro account. Make your choices, then click **Publish**.	
iPhoto uploads your pictures, and then gives you a web address at the top of the window where you can see them in Facebook. Click the address, and there are your photos, already set up in a Facebook gallery.	The photos upload, and as with Facebook, you're given a Flickr web address at the top of iPhoto's window that lets you view your pictures. Click the address to see your photos.	When the upload is complete, iPhoto gives you a URL at the top of its window. Click the address to see the MobileMe gallery you just created.

Now that you've set up links to your online accounts, all you need to do is select the photos to upload and click the button to upload them.

Create a slideshow

iPhoto lets you build a slideshow with music, that you can save as a movie to run on your Mac, or share with others. There are *two* ways to build a slideshow in iPhoto. The first lets you build a quick slideshow for one-time use, the other lets you build a slideshow and save it as a movie.

Quick slideshow

Maybe you've got friends coming over, and want to show off some photos in the background while they visit. You can throw together a quick slideshow and then let it run, without saving it:

1. Select the photos or Events you'd like to use.

2. Click the **Slideshow** button in the toolbar at the bottom of iPhoto's window.

3. Your Mac's screen goes black, and the first image fills the screen. A dialog box lets you choose from several different themes.

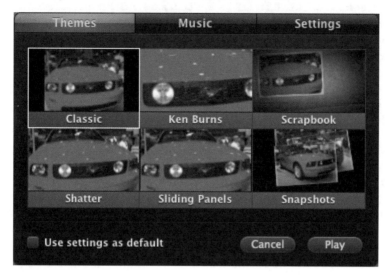

4. Choose a **theme**.

5. Click **Play** if you want the slideshow to begin. It will include sample music designed to fit the theme you chose.

Play with it

Take a good look at the Themes window. See the tabs labeled **Music** and **Settings**? You can do a lot even with this quick-and-dirty method of building a slideshow. iPhoto lets you add your own music from your iTunes library, and change the way the slideshow behaves.

Go ahead and spend some time playing with your music and the slideshow's settings, then come on back to see how to create and save a slideshow.

Saved slideshow

To craft a slideshow, save it and **share** it is easy in iPhoto and the process will be familiar. Remember how you created folders and added content in the Mac applications you've already met? Building a slideshow to share works the same way:

1. Select the photos or Events you'd like to include in the slideshow.

2. Click the plus (+) button in the lower left-hand corner of the iPhoto window. A window slides down from the top of iPhoto.

3. Choose **Slideshow** from the list of things you can create and give your project a name.

4. Click **Create**. The slideshow appears in the left-hand column, and the first slide with the slideshow's title appears in the main window.

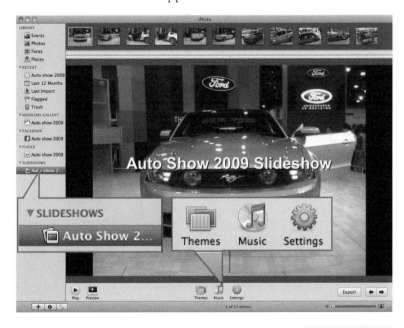

5. Just like you could with your quick slideshow, you can customize your music and what the slideshow does. See the three buttons centered below the main window? They're the same ones from the **Themes** window in the quick slideshow. Click through them to bring up windows that let you make the changes you want.

6. Now, look across the top of the iPhoto window. See the thumbnails? Those are the pictures you've selected for your slideshow. Want to change the order your slideshow's pictures are in? Drag the thumbnails to rearrange the order.

7. When you're ready to see your creation, click the **Preview** button or to see it full screen click **Play** instead.

When you're happy with your slideshow, you'll need to export so you can share it with others:

8. Click the **Export** button in the lower right-hand corner of the iPhoto window. A dialog box appears.

9. From this dialog, you can choose the format for the file, and how big the slideshow's display should be. *You can select more than one size or device type.* Make your choices, and then click **Export**.

You can select more than one checkbox to export your slideshow for different media types.

10. Click OK to store it in the iPhoto Slideshows folder or navigate to a folder of your choice.

The export process begins. Depending on the size of the slideshow and the speed of your computer, this may take a while. Go make a cup of coffee while you wait!

The slideshow will be saved in iTunes (hey, it's a movie after all), or you can go directly to the iPhoto Slideshows folder, inside your Pictures folder. If you chose multiple sizes, you'll see a different file for each one. Watch and enjoy! Or, e-mail the saved file to a friend as an attachment. In chapter 13, you'll learn how to burn the slideshow to a DVD for use in any DVD player or drive.

Make a link

Creating a slideshow to share is just like creating a new album, the only difference is you need to **Export** a slideshow.

Take a break

Congratulations. You're near the end of this chapter. The best thing to do after tackling organizing and editing your photos in iPhoto is to take a break. Go for a walk, or better yet, go grab a snack. Maybe even clean out that junk drawer in the kitchen. Take some time to focus on something else before you come back and try out the review and the experiment.

Review

Import and organize your photos

↺ To import pictures stored on your hard drive into iPhoto, you click .... > Import to ....

↺ Once imported, how does iPhoto initially organize your pictures?

↺ List the four ways iPhoto can organize your pictures:

1. ....

2. ....

3. ....

4. ....

↺ Can you create an iPhoto Event and put photos into it? Yes / No

↺ To start the facial recognition process to organize photos by .... , iPhoto needs you to give it a .... and a ....

Fix your photos

↺ What is non-destructive editing?

....

....

Continues, flip the page

↺ List the three ways you can revert a photo after editing it:

1. ....

2. ....

3. ....

↺ .... removes unwanted areas of a photo.

↺ If the horizon wasn't level you'd need to .... a photo.

↺ How do you remove red-eye from a picture?

↺ What exactly can you adjust with the Adjust tool?

↺ What kind of effects does the Effects button let you apply to a picture?

Share your photos

↺ In .... and .... you can determine who can see your pictures when you share them.

↺ How do you create a quick slideshow for viewing on your Mac?

↺ Click the .... button to create a new slideshow and when you're ready hit the .... button to save it.

How did you do?

Did you forget anything? It's hard to remember it all. Go ahead and re-read the sections covering what you overlooked. Your brain might need a bit more time to absorb all the information.

Experiment

Print your photos

You don't have to just share your photos electronically. Apple has a service that lets you design books, calendars and greeting cards in iPhoto, then have your creations brought to life on high-quality paper.

Although there's a fee for the printing and delivery of them (see `www.apple.com/ilife/iphoto/print-products.html` for pricing), you can still design and explore this feature as a part of iPhoto. You can even take a book you've designed and turn it into a slideshow!

You already know the basics for setting this up. Select the photos or Events you want to use, then click the **Keepsakes** button at the bottom of the iPhoto window, then choose the **Book**, **Calendar**, or **Card** button.

In each case, you'll get the chance to choose a design for the published product. For example, the Book option lets you choose from hardcover, softcover, and wirebound editions, and what size you want the book to be. Then you can select themes that dictate how the design will look.

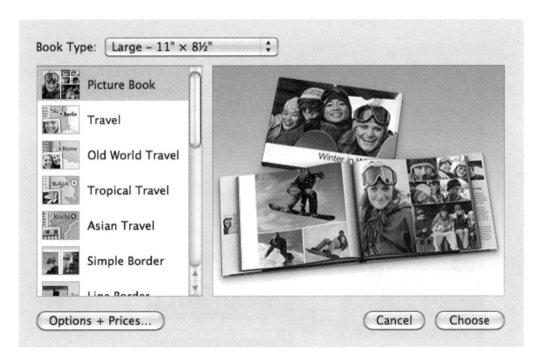

Next you need to drag your photos onto the various pages of the book, or click the **Autoflow** button to automatically place the pictures you've chosen into position (though once they're placed, you can still rearrange your pictures).

Spend some time working with the various print features. You can alter the backgrounds, change the layout and add or remove pages. Click the **Settings** button, and you can even dictate which fonts appear on which pages.

If you like what you see and want a physical copy, click the **Buy** button in the lower right-hand corner of iPhoto when you're working in Books, Calendars, or Cards.

Organize your photos with keywords

Take what you learned from working with other Mac programs and apply them to building some Smart Albums.

One way to create a Smart Album is to assign keywords to your photos. These can be really useful if you take lots of photos of, say, the beach and you want to be able to find a photo of a specific moment quickly.

View	Window	Help
Titles		⇧⌘T
Rating		⇧⌘R
Keywords		⇧⌘K
Event Titles		⇧⌘F
Hidden Photos		⇧⌘H
Sort Photos		▸
Show in Toolbar		▸
Full Screen		⌥⌘F
Always Show Toolbar		
Thumbnails		▸

There are two ways to add keywords to a photo:

1. In the main iPhoto window, or in a specific Event, click **View > Keywords**.

    Move your cursor over a photo and **add keywords** appears below it. Click on the add keywords text and type a keyword into the empty field.

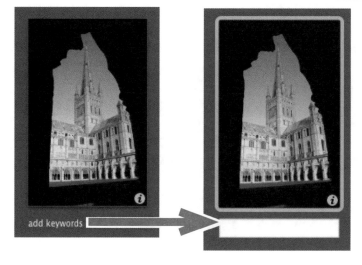

When you're done adding keywords, choose View > Keywords again.

2. Or you can add keywords from the Keywords window. Click **Window >
Show Keywords**.

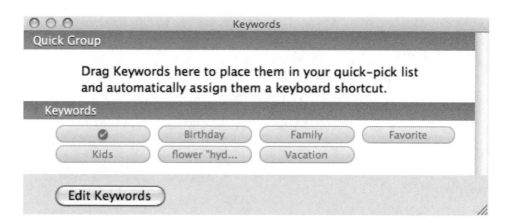

Click one or more keywords to assign them to a photo. To deselect a keyword or a
checkmark, just click it again.

If you need to edit the list first, click the Edit Keywords button and add keywords.
When you're done, click OK.

12 You can be a GarageBand rock star

Do you have a burning, inner desire to make music? You'd also like to get better at crafting tunes, but music lessons are expensive and hard to make time for.

Or maybe you've got *Louie Louie* down cold on that used guitar you bought at the flea market. You may even have a few original songs you've picked out. But before you can share your talent and creativity with the world you need to record and enhance your music.

No Problem!

Lucky you. Every brand new Mac comes with GarageBand. This powerful software is essentially a sophisticated recording studio on your hard drive, as well as a gateway to improving your musical skills.

GarageBand is unique to the Mac universe, nothing like it comes included on Windows PCs, but don't worry—although it's powerful, it's also intuitive, so buckle up and get ready to ROCK!

With GarageBand, you can:

⇨ Control—and even play along with—an automated band.

⇨ Take music lessons, including some from popular musicians.

⇨ Build songs with software instruments and loops.

⇨ Record yourself singing or playing instruments.

Enter the Garage

As you've learned, Apple's programs usually work at two levels. The basic level lets you do just what you need in a simple way, or you can drill down to more sophisticated capabilities. GarageBand epitomizes that philosophy.

In this chapter, we'll focus on the more accessible parts of GarageBand, and give you enough of a taste of its more serious capabilities to begin learning on your own.

Launch GarageBand via its icon in the Dock.

GarageBand launches with a welcome screen similar to those that kick off other Apple iLife programs. Leave the **Show this window when GarageBand opens** box checked. And click Close to clear the box.

Note: Many of the features in GarageBand work with instruments connected to your Mac. Although newer electronic keyboards have USB connections, most musical instruments don't have a built-in way to do this.

Acoustic instruments and voice can be recorded via a microphone plugged into the mic or combined input/output jack on your Mac. Apple has a support document on its website that provides details about adapters and other products that help with a connection, and links on where to find them. Visit http://support.apple.com/kb/HT2508.

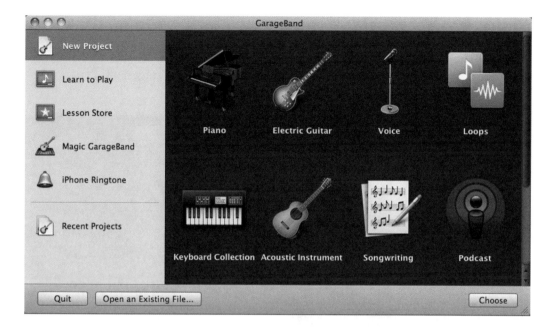

The New Project window is your starting point in GarageBand. As with other Mac programs, the left-hand column is your starting navigation area. Click on each item there and look at the pane on the right when you do.

Here's what each item does:

→ **New Project** starts something new in GarageBand, beginning with different instruments—piano, electric or acoustic guitar, even your voice. You can combine or add **Apple Loops**, which are pre-recorded musical building blocks. You can also write a song, record a podcast or create a soundtrack for use with iMovie.

→ **Learn to Play** with beginning music lessons for guitar or piano. More lessons in this group are available to download for free.

→ **Lesson Store** is the place to download more advanced lessons taught by such stars as Sting, Rush, Norah Jones, John Fogarty, Fall Out Boy and more. They cost about $5 each.

→ **Magic GarageBand** makes your Mac play songs in different genres: blues, rock, country, roots, funk, reggae. You can tweak the instruments to see the effect. Or even plug in and play along with the "band."

→ **iPhone Ringtone** lets you make ringtones for your iPhone.

→ **Recent Projects** shows projects you've started so you can reopen them.

Make Magic music

Magic GarageBand is an animated overlay for the musical engine that powers the application, and it's a great way to get started. Click the **Magic GarageBand** item on the left side. What's your favorite musical style in the list?

Listen to the **Previews** of the various styles and when you find a song you like, **double-click the icon**.

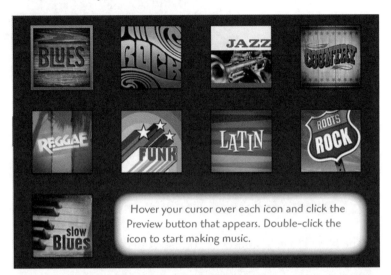

Hover your cursor over each icon and click the Preview button that appears. Double-click the icon to start making music.

A new screen opens to reveal a stage with instruments. Front and center is **My Instrument**, which in this case is a grand piano. What happens when you hover your cursor over the other instruments?

For this exercise, we've got the Blues!

To get a feel for how Magic GarageBand works, click the **Play** button in the middle of the bottom toolbar. Look carefully at the area just above the toolbar—what do you see?

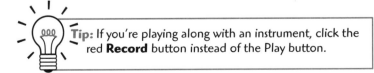

Tip: If you're playing along with an instrument, click the red **Record** button instead of the Play button.

The slider, called the **playhead**, moves along and shows you where you are in the song. You'll see the playhead in other areas of GarageBand.

Here, three verses are the milestones in the slider.

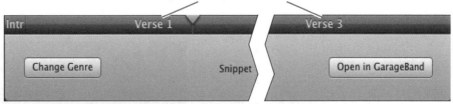

While the song's playing, click the Guitar; different types of guitars become available in the toolbar below. The same is true for the other instruments— clicking on the drum kit will get you different types of drums, and so on.

Play with it

Here's where it gets fun. What happens if you **choose a different type of guitar**, *then play the song over again*? Try changing the keyboard. How does the song change? If you make enough changes, the song will sound dramatically different.

How different? Try this: click on an empty area of the stage. See the two buttons that appear beneath it?

Click the **Shuffle Instruments** button, then click **Play**. Now, **try clicking the button** *while the song is playing.* Do it a few times. After a while, the song may not even be recognizable when compared to the original.

Now, click the **Start Over** button, and then the **Reset** button in the window that appears to return to your starting point.

Listen to individual instruments

Do you want to hear what each instrument sounds like while the song is playing? In Magic GarageBand, you can isolate the tracks for individual instruments with a single click.

1. Click an instrument you'd like to hear. The name of the instrument appears underneath its picture onstage.

2. Now, click the **small arrow to the left** of the instrument name. Additional controls appear lower down in the dialog.

3. Click the Play button on the Magic GarageBand toolbar. The song begins to play.

4. Now look again at the controls under the instrument you've selected. See the icon that looks like a set of **headphones**? Click it. What happens to the music you're hearing?

   All the other instruments are muted, and you only hear the instrument you've selected. Would you like to reverse it, and hear what the song sounds like without your instrument?

5. Click the speaker button, and your instrument is muted. Or, use the slider control to reduce or increase the volume of your instrument.

Make a link

Magic instruments can be varied to alter the sound of a song, or even shuffled while the song plays.

Take some music lessons

If you've ever wanted to learn the basics of playing a common instrument, or if you can play and want to get better, GarageBand's got you covered. The application comes with its own set of music lessons. If you know nothing at all about playing, there are **introductory lessons for guitar and piano**.

Tip: If you're more accomplished, there are advanced lessons, including some you can purchase featuring big-name musicians.

How basic are the introductory lessons? The instructor tells you how to hold the guitar, and how to sit while playing a piano.

To see the lessons, open GarageBand and, in the **New Project** window, select **Learn to Play**.

There's an introductory lesson for guitar and one for piano. You can play along with the instructor by connecting your instrument to your Mac, or by using a microphone.

Let's try the piano lesson.

1. Double-click the **Intro to Piano lesson**. If you've got a keyboard connected, you'll be told that "The number of MIDI outputs has changed." If you don't have a keyboard connected, you'll be told that "GarageBand has detected that you do not have a musical keyboard attached." Either way, click OK to continue.

    The lesson begins.

Remember the playhead that appeared above the toolbar when you were watching the songs play in Magic GarageBand? Here it is again, indicating where you are in the lesson. Click on any topic to jump right to it.

2. Move your cursor into the lesson area in the top half of the screen, and you'll see a choice of **Learn** or **Play**. The lesson starts out in Learn mode. Click Play to play along with the instructor.

3. To help you keep time, click the **metronome icon** in the toolbar. The slider to the right lets you control the metronome's tempo.

4. Click the **Settings** button in the upper right-hand corner to change the way notes and chords are displayed during the lesson. You can also change the language the instructor is speaking and add subtitles.

5. When you're done, click the **Change Lesson** button in the lower left-hand corner of the window. You'll return to the New Project window.

Have you mastered the initial lessons, or were they a little too basic for you? Both the guitar and piano have eight more **free lessons** you can download. Click the **Lesson Store** item to see them. Click the Download button to grab one, then double-click it to begin the lesson.

In the Lesson Store window, click the **Artist Lessons** tab.

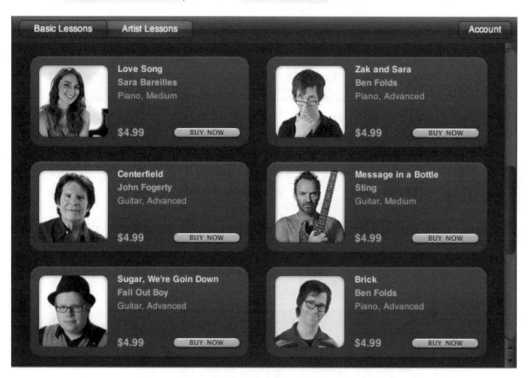

These are lessons from famous musicians, for both piano and guitar, and ranging in difficulty from easy to advanced. They're $5 each and you'll need an iTunes account to purchase them.

As with the free lessons, the musician shows you how to play the song, then you get the chance to play along.

You can click the **Mixer** button in the upper right-hand corner of the screen to bring up a series of volume controls you can use to mute the parts you don't want to hear, and boost the volume on those you want to keep.

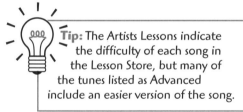

Tip: The Artists Lessons indicate the difficulty of each song in the Lesson Store, but many of the tunes listed as Advanced include an easier version of the song.

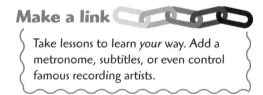

Make a link

Take lessons to learn *your* way. Add a metronome, subtitles, or even control famous recording artists.

Get Loopy with GarageBand

When professional musicians go into the studio, they often record guitar, bass, drums, strings, and so on individually onto their own track. The tracks are tweaked; effects are added, or maybe the volume of one track is boosted over another, before they're combined to create the finished song.

GarageBand lets you record your own tracks, then supplement them with effects and pre-recorded tracks from a wealth of different instruments.

Let's build a song from scratch. You don't even need an instrument of your own to do it (though if you have one, by all means bring it to the party). Begin at the **New Project** window. For now, we'll use the **Piano**.

1. **Double-click** the **Piano** icon. A dialog box opens.

> **New Project from Template**
>
> Save As: My Song
>
> Where: GarageBand
>
> Tempo:
> Signature: 4 / 4   120 bpm
> Key: C   major
>
> Cancel   Create

2. The dialog lets you give your project a name, as well as change the time signature, the tempo, and the key. Unless you have particular settings in mind, you can leave these alone for this exercise. Just give your song a name and click **Create**. The main GarageBand window appears.

The column on the left contains the **track headers**, which let you control the characteristics of each track. Where have you seen the headphone and speaker icons before? Based on what you've seen previously, what do you think they do?

The middle pane is the **timeline**, where you'll see visual representations of each track. It's empty right now because *that's the track where you'd record the instrument plugged into your Mac*. This is called the **Master Track** because it controls the key, tempo, and time signature of the song.

On the right is the **loop browser**, where you can sample pre-recorded loops before dragging them into the timeline.

3. In the loop browser click Rock/Blues (you could choose any of the genres, but we'll focus on this one for now).

4. Scroll through the list of loops in the bottom half of the browser. Those with a blue sound wave icon are real recorded instruments and the loops with green musical note icons are software instruments. Either can be added as loops. Click on them to hear them.

Tip: The loops with no icons are optional loops that you can either download from the Internet, or pull off the iLife DVD. Click on the loops for instructions on adding them to your hard drive. They'll take up about 1.2 GB of space.

Play with it

GarageBand comes with dozens of **software instruments**, which are different sounds that are generated when you play a connected instrument. Do you have a USB piano keyboard? Connect it to your Mac, then tell GarageBand to generate the sound of a guitar when you play the keyboard. In this way, your USB keyboard can play every instrument in the band!

If you don't have an instrument, GarageBand's got a clever workaround. Your Mac's computer keyboard can double as a musical one.

Click **Window > Musical Typing** (or **Shift+Command+K**).

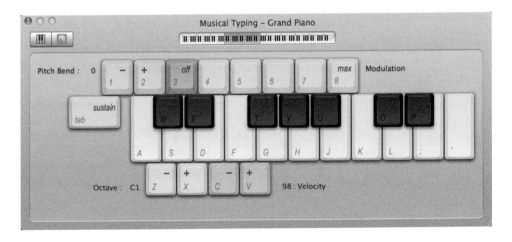

The map at the very top of the Musical Typing keyboard shows you where your fingers would be on a full-sized piano keyboard. Click along the map to move the location, or use the Z or X keys to move up or down an octave.

See the two small buttons in the upper-left corner of the Musical Typing window? Click the one that looks like a few piano keys, the window morphs into an onscreen piano keyboard you can play with your mouse.

5. Have you found a loop you like? For now, drag Blues Guitar 02 from the loop browser into the area just below the Grand Piano track and release.

6. Click the Play button in the toolbar down below to hear the loop.

7. If you're building a song and the loop is too short, you'll want it to continue for a while. Place your cursor on the upper right-hand corner of the track in the timeline, so that the cursor turns into a curved arrow.

Click and hold the cursor and drag it to the right. The ruler at the top of the timeline shows you the length of the track in seconds. Drag the track to be as long as you'd like and release.

8. Let's add a rhythm section. To add drums, click **Kits**. Find a drumbeat you like and drag it into place, and then drag the right edge so that it matches the length of your previous track.

That's a lot like the column view in Finder. Click on the item in the left-most column to drill for more choices. This view will make it easier to find the instruments you want.

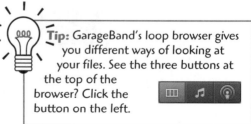

Tip: GarageBand's loop browser gives you different ways of looking at your files. See the three buttons at the top of the browser? Click the button on the left.

9. Continue to add other instruments until you have a complete "band." To have the song **repeat** after it's done playing, click the **recycle icon** in the toolbar, to the right of the Play button.

10. Once you have your song just the way you want it, click **File > Save**.

Make a link

Start a **New Project**, **Browse** the **Loops** and drag them to the timeline. Loops can be *lengthened* or *shortened*. And when you're done, the whole song can be **recycled**.

Play along with the GarageBand

Remember the Grand Piano track at the top when you started? It's blank right now; the instruments you added are below it in the timeline. If you have a keyboard or a guitar you can connect to your Mac, or an acoustic instrument that you can record via a mic, you can add your instrument to the song you just created.

There are *two* **record buttons** you need to hit to begin recording. In the **Grand Piano track header**, click the circular **record button** to the right of the piano icon. It should turn red.

The Grand Piano track is now ready to accept your input. When you're ready to record, hit the red **record** button in the **lower toolbar of GarageBand**, or just tap the **R** key on the keyboard. The track you're recording turns red, and you can begin playing. A metronome helps you keep time.

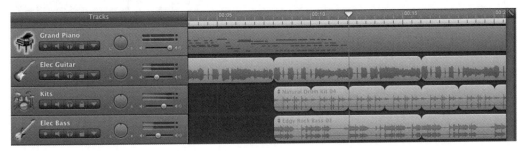

If you've got the recycle button set, the song will loop back and you can keep playing. Each time you start recording from the beginning is a **take**.

When you're done, hit the space bar to stop the recording. Did you let the song loop a couple of times with the recycle button on while recording? If so, you'll see a number on a yellow button at the start of the recorded track. Click the number to choose which track to use.

Make a link

Add your own instrument to the **Grand Piano** track, but remember to click record *twice*.

Play with it

GarageBand includes a rudimentary audio editor that lets you enhance selected parts of a track, or cut/copy/paste pieces of it. Click the icon that shows a pair of scissors in the lower left-hand corner of the GarageBand window. The editor fills the bottom of the window.

Use the controls on the left to tweak the pitch, tuning and timing. Highlight areas of the track you'd like to edit, then cut/copy/paste just like you would in a word processor.

Once you've chosen your take, save the song again. And now you're ready to share it.

Click **Share > Send Song to iTunes** to put it in your iTunes library.

Sorry, this doesn't upload it to the iTunes Store.

Or click **Share > Export Song to Disk** to convert it to an AAC or MP3 file, which you can e-mail to your friends. And **Share > Burn Song to a CD** will do just that.

There's (too much) more!

As you can see, GarageBand is simple on the surface, and very complex down below. There's too much to go into for this book, but you've learned enough now to start playing and exploring on your own.

If you're serious about music and other types of recording and you want to learn about everything GarageBand can do, grab a copy of *iLife '09 Portable Genius* (Wiley, 2009) by Gary Hart-Davis to get the most out of GarageBand.

- -

Take a break

Becoming a GarageBand rock star is a tough job. Now's a good time to take a break to let your brain sift through all this new material before you forge ahead to tackle another topic. When you return, there's a great challenge waiting for you to reinforce your new Rock Star status.

Review

Enter the Garage

↻ If you want to play along and record music in GarageBand you'll need
.... or ....

↻ To preview the musical styles available in Magic GarageBand you
....

↻ Can you play along with your own instrument in Magic GarageBand?
Yes / No

↻ What does the playhead do?

....

....

↻ How do you change instruments in Magic GarageBand?

....

....

↻ To randomly select different instruments while a song plays in Magic
GarageBand, click on the .... of the stage, then click the
.... button.

Take some music lessons

↻ How do you get to the two introductory lessons?

↻ How do you activate the metronome?

Get loopy with GarageBand

↻ What is a software instrument?

....

....

↻ How do you play a software instrument?

....

....

○ The Save As… dialog box lets you save the:

1. .... signature.

2. ....

3. ....

○ What are the three primary components of GarageBand's main window?

1. ....

2. ....

3. ....

○ The Master Track controls the ....

○ To extend the time a loop plays you ....

....

....

○ To make a song repeat or "loop" after it's played through once, click the .... button.

○ What two buttons do you have to hit to record your own instrument as a track?

1. ....

2. ....

○ What are "takes"? How do you access them?

....

....

○ How do you bring up the audio editor?

....

....

How did you do?

Did you forget anything? It's hard to remember it all. Go ahead and re-read the sections covering what you overlooked. Your brain might need a bit more time to absorb all the information.

Take some time to re-read your links, or if you didn't remember them, consider creating a new link that's bigger, sillier, scarier, more extreme, anything to make it more memorable.

Experiment

Play along with Nine Inch Nails

Although GarageBand comes with plenty of musical content to explore, wouldn't it be fun to play along with some of your favorite artists, or even use GarageBand to remix and tweak their works?

A handful of musicians have released some of their songs as GarageBand-compatible files, and invite fans to download them and even change them. The popular techno band Nine Inch Nails offers dozens of songs you can download and remix. In fact, the band invites fans to upload remixes back to the site, and has even published some of them on a CD.

Even if you're not a fan of NiN's music, these songs are fun to play with and can teach you a lot about GarageBand's capabilities.

To begin, log in at `http://remix.nin.com`. You'll need to register for an account, but it's free. Click the Mix link at the top, then on the Download Multi-tracks link.

There are a lot of files here, and all of them will work in GarageBand, but the ones labeled RAW will require more work. To start, download a few songs that have GarageBand-specific files. Click the words GarageBand to download them. They'll open automatically on your Mac as a folder. Double-click the guitar icon to launch the song in GarageBand.

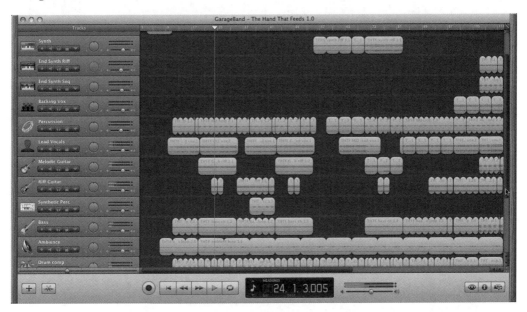

Click the Play button to watch the song play. You can see each instrument's part. Using the track headers, you can have each instrument go "solo" to hear what it's up to.

Now, use what you've learned about GarageBand to add loops, change which tracks are emphasized, or even add your own instrument to the mix.

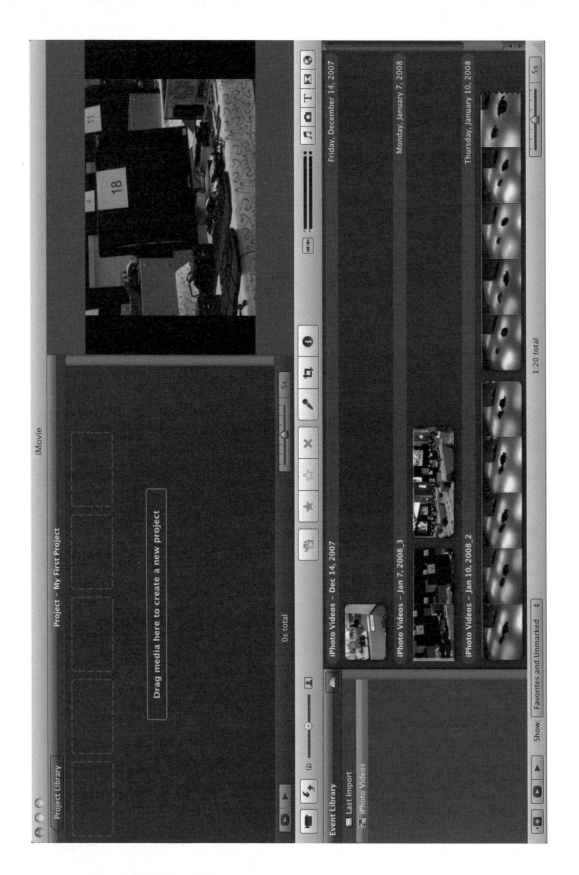

13 Lights! Camera! iMovie!

Have you already written your acceptance speech for "Best Picture?" Maybe not, because as good as they are, you know your videos could stand a little enhancing. But video-editing software is pricey and complex, so what's a budding filmmaker to do?

No Problem!

iMovie is iLife's video importing and editing application. iMovie makes it very easy to do some sophisticated things with the movies you take, even if you've got some experience with video editing. iMovie is so powerful and versatile that you may not need any other program.

With iMovie you can:

⇨ Import and organize video.

⇨ Create movies from your video.

⇨ Enhance your video with themes and transitions.

⇨ Share your movies with others.

⇨ Burn DVDs with iDVD.

Roll the iMovie titles

iMovie is part of the iLife suite that also includes iPhoto and GarageBand. Because video is a different beast than music and still photos, iMovie looks and behaves a little differently than the other Mac programs you're now familiar with.

Let's launch iMovie and check it out. Its icon is another one that's already in the Dock.

iMovie immediately has a question for you.

iPhoto Video Thumbnails

iMovie needs to generate thumbnails for the videos in your iPhoto library. This process may take several minutes.

You can postpone this operation by clicking Later, but your iPhoto videos will be unavailable until the next time you restart iMovie.

Later   Now

iMovie wants to look at your iPhoto library to see if any videos are stored there. If it finds any, iMovie gives each a video thumbnail in its own library. Even if you don't think there are any videos in the library, go ahead and **click the Now button**.

There's the familiar welcome screen common to the iLife applications, with the main intro video and links to more video tutorials.

Do you want to watch the intro? Go ahead, we'll wait for you. When you're done, click the Close button and take a look at iMovie's various parts.

Note: You don't have to do it right now, but if you don't let iMovie check your iPhoto library, you'll be pestered to do this each time you launch iMovie and you won't be able to use the videos in the iPhoto library until you do. So just go ahead and click the Now button to give yourself peace and quiet down the road.

There are four panes in iMovie's layout. Here's what each one does:

→ The **Project Browser** pane, in the upper left-hand corner, is where you work with **video**, **photos** and **audio** to build your movie. All these pieces together are called a **project**.

→ In the *upper right-hand* corner, the **Viewer** lets you watch movies or clips.

→ The **Event Browser** in the *lower right-hand* corner of the iMovie window holds the thumbnails for your videos. These will be the building blocks for any movies you make.

→ The *lower left-hand* corner is the **Event Library** where you organize the Events that are comprised of your video clips.

> If you let iMovie look for videos in your iPhoto folder and it found any videos, do you see the thumbnails in the lower right-hand window?
>
> If you didn't have any videos in your iPhoto library, or if you opted not to let iMovie do its search, the Event Browser will be empty.

> Wait a second. What's an "event" in iMovie? Remember Events from iPhoto? The same concept applies here.

These panes all work together when you build your movie projects. Expect to spend a lot of time in the Event and Project Libraries. But first, of course, you'll have to have some video to work with.

Import video from your Mac

Did you have video on your Windows PC? Did you copy it over to your Mac in chapter 4? Let's go get it!

1. In iMovie's Menu Bar, click **File > Import > Movies**. You'll get a dialog box explaining about video size.

    Choose the size you want based on the type of video you're importing and your available hard drive space (you can change this later), and click OK. A navigation window appears.

2. Video copied from your PC should be sitting in the Movies folder inside your Home folder, otherwise navigate to the folder where you stored your video.

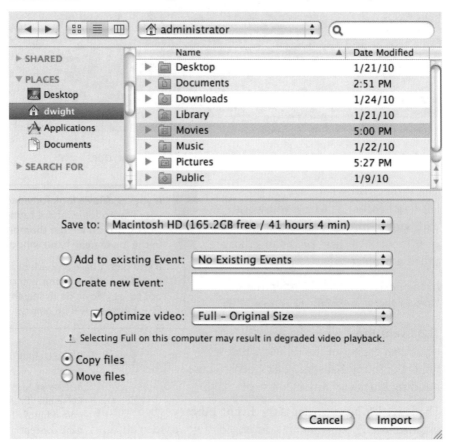

3. If you have a lot of video, it can take up a lot of space. The bottom half of the Import window offers help with space management and organization.

→ **Save to:** lets you choose the drive you'll use to store your iMovie library. The default is your Mac's internal hard drive. Do you have an external drive (other than your Time Machine drive)? Saving video there might save space, though external hard drives are usually slower than internal ones.

→ **Add to existing event/Create new event**: adds your imported video to an event, or creates a new one with a name you choose. If you do nothing, by default iMovie will create a single, date-based event.

→ **Optimize video:** lets you reduce your movies' file sizes by choosing a new resolution from the drop-down menu. You can import your video at full size, but if you want to save space, this is a good option.

→ **Copy/Move files**: Copy lets you keep copies of your raw files in the original folder, while Move brings all the files into iMovie's library.

4. Once you've made your choices, click **Import**.

5. iMovie asks if you want to import the entire directory. Click OK.

iMovie copies (or moves) your video into its library, optimizing video if you left that option checked. It may take a while to complete the process if you have a lot of video.

When it's done take a look at the Event Browser.

There are dozens, hundreds or even thousands of thumbnails. *Each thumbnail represents five seconds of video.*

In the Event Browser, move your cursor across the compiled thumbnails, which are called **filmstrips**. What happens in the Viewer? Move your cursor slowly, then try moving it quickly. The preview lets you look at video clips so you can find just the part you want to add to a project.

> **Tip:** If you've got a lot of video, the number of five-second clips may be overwhelming. Fortunately, you can change the length each thumbnail represents. See the slider in the lower right-hand corner of the main iMovie window?
>
> Drag the slider to the *right* to *increase* the amount of time for each thumbnail. The longer the thumbnail's duration, the fewer of them there will be. Drag the slider to the *left* to see *less* time for each thumbnail.

Import video from a camera

It's as easy to import the video from your camcorder into iMovie as it was to get pictures from your digital camera into iPhoto.

1. Launch iMovie.

2. Turn on your video recorder. If your recorder has an *Export* or *PC* setting, which lets it talk to your Mac, put it in that mode now. Not all cameras do, so check the manual to see whether it's necessary.

3. Connect the camera to your Mac using either a USB or Firewire cable.

> **Note:** Not all Macs have Firewire ports, but **all Macs have USB ports**. If you have a Firewire camcorder but no Firewire port on your Mac, you may need to buy a Firewire-to-USB adapter.

4. Look at the toolbar running across the center of iMovie. See the first button on the left, which looks like a movie camera? That's the **Camera Import** button, go ahead and click it. The Import Movie window opens.

Some cameras make the Import Movie window open automatically when you attach them to your Mac.

218

5. You can import some or all of what's stored on the recorder. For now, let's import some, but here's how you import both ways.

   a. To import *all* your video, click the **Import** button. You're done.

   b. To *select which video clips to import*, set the Automatic/Manual switch in the lower left-hand corner of the window to **Manual**.

6. Thumbnails of the movies on your camera each have a checkbox below. Check the boxes to mark videos you want to import.

7. When you've selected the videos you want to import, click the button marked **Import Checked**. The same navigation window opens that you saw when you imported video from your Mac's hard drive.

8. Make any space management choices, like you did before, and then click **Import**.

Note: If you have a digital *tape* camcorder, the import process is a little different. You still need to connect the camera to your Mac and press the **Import Movie** button, but the window that appears when you do looks and works a little differently.

There's a frame from the current video on the tape, and below that buttons to play, fast-forward and rewind the tape.

6. You have a choice when you're importing video:

   a. Set the Automatic/ Manual switch to **Automatic** to *import all your videos automatically*;

   b. Use **Manual** to **choose** where you want to import from using the play buttons.

7. Then click Import, and iMovie will begin pulling in your video.

Your video imports into iMovie. This may take a while, particularly if you have a lot of video or if you're using a tape-based camera. When it's completed, you'll see the thumbnails in the Event Browser.

Import video from a webcam

If yours is an iMac or one of Apple's notebook computers, you've got a built-in webcam. Apple calls its webcam iSight. You can use this for video chatting (which you'll learn about in chapter 16), but you can also use your iSight camera to capture live videos with iMovie.

1. Make sure there's no external camera connected to your Mac and click the **Import Movie** button. The Import Movie window opens.

2. Click the **Capture** button, and a dialog box drops down.

3. Name your event, or choose to add the video to an existing event. Click the box next to **Analyze for stabilization after import** if you think the video you're about to capture might be shaky.

4. Click the **Capture** button again to begin saving video directly to your hard drive.

5. Click **Done** when you're finished. The video appears in your Event Browser.

Make a link

File > Import Movies from your hard drive.

▶ Connect your digital video recorder and **Automatically > Import All** your videos, or **Manually** choose where to > **Import...** from.

▶ Connect your tape video recorder and **Automatically > Import All** your videos, or **Manually** choose where to **Import Checked**.

▶ **Import Movie > Capture** to use your webcam to capture video.

Organize your video

Keeping track of all your video can be complicated, but iMovie uses Events the same way iPhoto uses them to help you stay on top of your collection. The Event Library is similar to the left-hand column in other Mac applications.

Play with it

Take some time to get your video clips in order. Having them organized makes building movies in iMovie much easier.

→ **To create a new event** click **File > New Event** in iMovie's Menu Bar. Give the event a name, but note that it will be set with today's date.

→ **To combine events into one**, drag the event you want to add onto the event you want to add it to.

→ **To split a single event into two**, click the event, **find the point where you'd like to split the event** in the Event Browser and **right-click** (or Control-click) and choose **Split Event Before Selected Clip**. The event will be split at the point you chose.

→ **To change how you view events, click View**, then choose from several different views:

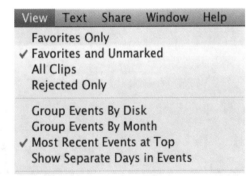

→ by month

→ by the hard drive the events are stored on

→ most recent events first

→ by events recorded on specific days.

Make a movie

Did you use Windows Movie Maker to edit and create movies on your Windows PC? If so, you'll recognize many of the concepts and processes in iMovie. Clips are dragged-and-dropped, edited, and pieced together in projects.

If you've never worked with a program like iMovie before, here's a simple way to think about it: it's a lot like writing a sentence. You stack the clips (your words) in your project (the sentence), and the way the words hang together determines the quality of your sentence.

Your first project

Do you have multiple clips from some special event in your collection of video, moments you've been meaning to piece together into something special? Using what you learned in the previous section about organizing your video, why don't you locate video clips in the Event Library you want to combine?

For now, we'll focus on the basics, but as you've seen with other Macintosh applications, you can start simple and call on more complex tools later.

1. If you've been playing around and dropped some video in the Project window, you'll need to clear it to start fresh. Click **File > New Project**, or press **Command+K**. You'll get a dialog box that lets you select themes and other enhancements. Just cancel it; we'll come back to that later.

    The project window in the upper left-hand corner should look like this:

2. Select the event that contains the clips you want to use from the **Event Library**. The clips associated with that event show up in the Event Browser.

Select a clip in the Event Library and it shows up in the Event Browser.

3. Find a clip in the **Event Browser** that you want to use. Click once at the start of the clip to select it.

Use the handles on the left and right edges of the box to expand the clip in either direction to get just the video you want to use.

The yellow box represents five seconds of video. Use the handles on either edge to expand the length of the clip.

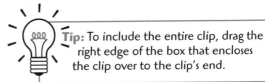

Tip: To include the entire clip, drag the right edge of the box that encloses the clip over to the clip's end.

4. To add the clip to your project, hit the **E key**, or **drag and drop** the clip into place.

Look at the clip you just added in the Event Browser. See the orange line under it? That indicates you've already added the clip to your project.

Repeat steps 3 and 4 until you've added all the clips you want to the project.

5. If you want to rearrange the clips in the project, drag and drop them where you want them.

Watch your movie by clicking either of the two play buttons at the bottom of the Project window.

Tip: These buttons also appear in the Event Library, giving you a choice as to how you watch clips in Events as well.

The button on the left shows you the movie in fullscreen glory, while the button on the right plays the movie in the Viewer.

Note: Don't worry about losing your projects if you step away from your Mac or have to close iMovie. You don't need to save them because iMovie keeps track of the changes you've made.

To find projects you've worked on, click the Project Library button above the Project window. The Project Library looks like the Event Library, except that it's populated by projects.

Make a link

Go to the **Library**, **Browse** the **Events**, then **drag, drag, drag**! **Drag** and drop to add clips to your project, **drag** the handles to choose the clip length, **drag** and drop the clips to rearrange them.

Add themes and transitions

iMovie lets you dress up your movie in two ways. You can apply preselected themes offered by Apple, or you can add some tweaks manually.

Let's start with Apple's themes. There aren't many, unfortunately, but you can probably find one that fits the tone of your production among the five available.

1. Right-click anywhere on the clips in the Project window and choose **Project Properties...** from the menu that appears. The Project Properties window drops down. From here you can choose some key options.

   → **Aspect ratio** is the rectangular shape of your video. Standard (4:3) is the shape of a traditional TV set, as well as Apple's iPad; iPhone (3:2) is the size for an iPhone or iPod Touch screen; widescreen (16:9 or 16:10) is the shape of a high-end TV and some computer monitors (including iMacs).

      Note: Choose the aspect ratio based on the device the video will play on, *not* the ratio generated by your camcorder. iMovie will compensate for the difference.

   → **Theme**: This lets you choose from Photo Album, Bulletin Board, Comic Book, Scrapbook, and Filmstrip themes, as well as None.

→ **Automatically add**: If you select a theme, this option changes to a simple checkbox that says: **Automatically add transitions and titles**. If checked, transitions and title fonts are preselected for the theme. If you choose **None** as a theme, check this box and select a transition option, to control how iMovie handles shifting from one clip to another.

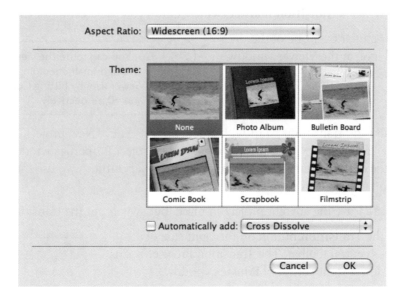

For now, go ahead and select one of the themes, and then click OK. (You can go back and change a theme later if you don't like it.)

2. Click either of the Play buttons under the Project window to see the result now that iMovie has added the theme to your movie.

Play with it

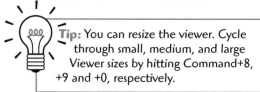

Of course, if you don't care for any of the themes that come with iMovie, or you want more control over the transitions between scenes, that's no problem! Let's take a look at what iMovie did when it added the theme. In the Project window, look carefully at the area between scenes. Do you see the icon that looks like two boxes overlapping each other? ▣ That's a **transition marker**, which shows you the location of transitions.

Move your cursor over one of the markers and look at the Viewer window. iMovie shows you what the transition will look like when you play the movie.

Tip: You can resize the viewer. Cycle through small, medium, and large Viewer sizes by hitting Command+8, +9 and +0, respectively.

To manually add transitions, start with a new project (File > New project or Command+K) and select None as your theme in the Project Properties window. Or you can change the current theme in the **Transition Browser**. Either way, use the browser to drag-and-drop transitions where you want them.

For now, let's leave the current project in place, but switch out the transitions.

1. Click the **Transition** button on the right side of iMovie's central toolbar. The Transition Browser opens in the lower right corner of iMovie's window.

2. Since you applied a theme, click the **Theme** button in the upper left and choose **None** from the window that appears. Click OK.

3. Move your cursor across the transition thumbnails to preview what they'll look like when applied to your movie.

4. When you find one you like, *drag and drop* it into the spaces *between scenes* in your project.

5. When you're done, close the Transition Browser and click one of the play buttons to see how your project looks with your new, hand-picked transitions.

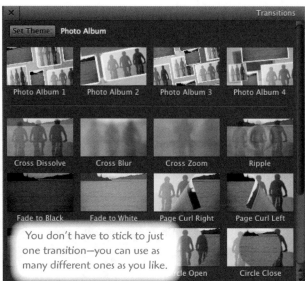

You don't have to stick to just one transition—you can use as many different ones as you like.

Tip: If you like the themes, but still want more control over transitions, start with a preset theme and replace some or all of the transitions.

1. Apply a theme and find a transition you'd like to switch out.

2. Click the transition button for it and hit the Delete key.

3. Drag another transition into its place. A dialog box appears asking what you want to do. Click **Turn off Automatic Transitions** to place your new transition.

   You'll only have to click that button once.

Transitions and themes are just a few of the cool things you can do with your video projects. iMovie is rich with features—too many to detail here. If you're interested in learning more, check out *iLife '09 Portable Genius* by Gary Hart-Davis (Wiley, 2009).

Make a link

Project Properties includes access to the preset Themes.
Transitions in each Theme can be switched around.

Share your movies

iMovie lets you export your movie in a variety of different ways, depending on *where* you want it to be viewed. You've already gotten a glimpse of this. Remember in the Project Properties window, when you chose an aspect ratio? That was in preparation for sharing your movies.

There are several ways to share your movie; the one you choose depends on how you want to share the video. You can:

→ **Export it as a movie file**. Save your movie in Apple's QuickTime (.MOV) format, so that it can be played on both Windows PCs and Macs.

→ **Save it to YouTube**. iMovie can put your movies right onto YouTube, the top video-sharing site.

→ **Post it to your MobileMe gallery**. If you have a MobileMe account, you can post your movie there.

→ **Burn it to a DVD**. The iLife suite includes a companion application called iDVD that makes it easy to craft professional-looking DVDs that can be played on computers or standalone DVD players.

→ **Store it in the Media Browser**. The Media Browser is a feature shared by other iLife programs, such as iWeb and iDVD. When you're ready to use a movie, you can retrieve it from here without having to open iMovie.

Export your movie

When you export a movie, it's saved as a file on your Mac's hard drive that you can attach to an e-mail, save to a disk or flash drive, or copy to another computer on your home network.

1. Have your project loaded in the Project window, then click **Share > Export Movie** in the Menu Bar. The Export window appears.

2. Give your movie a name in the **Export As** field.

3. If you want to store it someplace other than the Movies folder, use the Where drop-down menu.

4. **Select the size** of the movie, depending on where you want to display it. The bigger the size, the longer it will take to export, and the bigger the file will be.

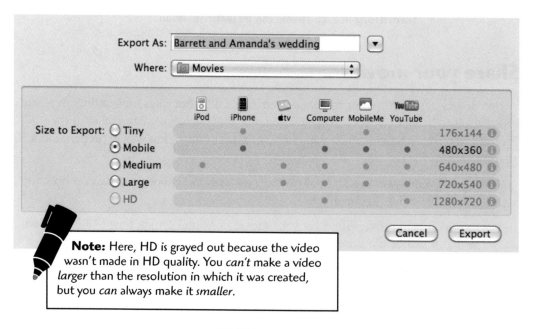

Note: Here, HD is grayed out because the video wasn't made in HD quality. You *can't* make a video *larger* than the resolution in which it was created, but you *can* always make it *smaller*.

5. When you're ready, click the **Export** button.

A window appears to show you the progress of the export process, and tells you how long it will take.

Macs with slower processors and less memory will take longer than those with faster processors and more memory. Preparing video is one of the most processor-intensive tasks a computer can do.

By default, the video is saved in the Movies folder as a file with an .M4V extension. This file can be played in iTunes and in QuickTime on a Mac or Windows.

Tip: If you're sending the video to someone who doesn't have QuickTime or iTunes on their Windows PC, they may not be able to play the file with the .M4V extension. Fortunately, this is easy to fix.

Before you send your friend the file, select the file in the Finder, press Enter and change the extension to **.MP4**, which most modern video-playing programs can play.

Play with it

Would you prefer to save the file in a different format? iMovie can export in many different formats:

1. Click **Share > Export Using QuickTime**.

2. Give the file a name in the **Save As** dialog box.

3. Choose your format:

   a. If you just click **Save**, the file will be exported as a **QuickTime file** with a .MOV extension.

   b. Is there another format you'd like to use instead? If so, click the **Export** drop-down for a slew of choices.

4. Select a file format. For this exercise, choose AVI, which is a format that's friendly for Windows Media Player.

5. Click the Use drop-down to tell iMovie if the file will be posted to the Web. If you don't plan on doing that, just use the Default Settings.

6. Click Save.

Exporting can take quite a while, depending on the quality of the format.

When it's done your .AVI file will be stored in the Movies folder on your Mac.

Movie to 3G
Movie to Apple TV
Movie to AVI
Movie to DV Stream
Movie to FLC
Movie to Image Sequence
Movie to iPhone
Movie to iPhone (Cellular)
Movie to iPod
Movie to MPEG-4
✓ Movie to QuickTime Movie
Sound to AIFF
Sound to AU
Sound to Wave

Upload your movie to YouTube

If you want to share your video with a *lot* of people, export it directly to YouTube. The process is similar to uploading photos to Flickr and MobileMe in iPhoto.

1. Click **Share** > **YouTube**. The YouTube upload window appears.

2. Click the **Add** button next to the account field and enter the name of your YouTube account, then click **Next**. (Don't have one? Sign up at www.youtube.com/create_account.)

3. Back at the YouTube uploader, give your movie a name, add a description and some **tags**—keywords that help people find your movie.

4. **Choose a size** for the movie, just as you did when you initially exported it.

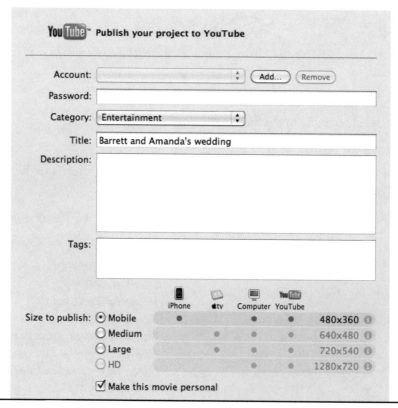

Warning

The *minimum resolution* you can upload to YouTube from iMovie is 480x360, but you can upload high-definition video. Uploading takes longer for bigger files and upload speeds are often slower than download speeds. You may be in for a marathon session. Also remember that if your Internet provider has a bandwidth cap, uploads count against those limits.

5. If you don't want anyone else to see your movie, check the **Keep this movie personal** box. This will hide the movie on your YouTube page, and share it with a limited number of people.

6. Click **Next**.

7. Click **Publish** to agree to YouTube's terms of service, and to begin the uploading process.

The export progress dialog box appears and when the export's done, another box reports the upload. When both are completed, go to your YouTube page to see your video.

Don't see it immediately? YouTube sometimes takes a few minutes to process the video at its end.

Burn your movie with iDVD

Sure, sharing your videos electronically is cool, but nothing beats watching your creation on a living room screen, particularly if you have an HD camera and an HDTV.

iDVD is a companion program to iMovie. You can burn DVDs directly from iMovie by going through iDVD or iDVD can create DVDs from standalone video.

To burn an iMovie project using iDVD:

1. In iMovie, click **Share > iDVD**. The progress-bar dialog box appears. (This time, you don't get a chance to pick the resolution.)

2. When the video process is complete, iDVD launches.

3. iDVD applies a default theme for the menu screen that opens your DVD. In the right-hand column is a selection of other themes, which will change the menu screen's presentation. Scroll through them and click on any of them to preview how they'll look in the larger pane on the left.

Tip: Don't see one you like? Click the 7.0 Themes drop-down at the top of the right-hand column to choose from themes offered with past versions of iDVD.

4. Insert a DVD in your Mac's SuperDrive or external DVD burner, and wait until it spins up.

5. Click the button on the bottom iDVD toolbar that looks like a closed camera iris.

6. A dialog appears and shows you the progress of the burning process. This may take a while if you're burning a long movie to DVD.

When iDVD is finished, you can eject the DVD by pressing the Eject button on your Mac's hard drive, dragging the disk to the Trash, or pressing Command+E. Now, take it to a DVD player connected to your TV... and enjoy!

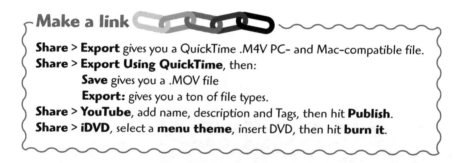

Make a link

Share > Export gives you a QuickTime .M4V PC- and Mac-compatible file.
Share > Export Using QuickTime, then:
   Save gives you a .MOV file
   Export: gives you a ton of file types.
Share > YouTube, add name, description and Tags, then hit **Publish**.
Share > iDVD, select a **menu theme**, insert DVD, then hit **burn it**.

Take a break

It's time to take a break. Seriously. You need to give your brain time to filter and organize all of this new material so you can recall it just when you need it most. So, go watch TV or play a game of solitaire—something that doesn't require you to learn a new skill. You've done enough learning for a little while.

Review

Roll the iMovie titles, import, and organize video

↺ To import video into iMovie from a folder on your Mac you click
.... > .... > ....

↺ Why might you want to reduce the resolution of videos when you import them into iMovie?

....

↺ By default, each video thumbnail in the Event Browser represents
.... seconds. Drag the .... to change the amount of time represented by each thumbnail.

↺ To make a video using your Mac's iSight camera into iMovie, click
.... Movie, then ....

↺ How do you combine multiple events into one?

....

↺ How do you split an event into two?

....

Make a movie

↺ To combine clips into projects, go to the .... and Browse
....

↺ List the two ways you can move clips from the Event Browser into a project.

1. Hit the .... key.

2. .... and ....

↺ What does an orange line under a clip in the Event Browser mean?

....

↺ The [▶] button plays the movie ....

↺ The [▶] button plays the movie ....

↺ To add a theme, right-click a clip in the ....
and choose ....

Continues, flip the page

↺ To add transitions to a project manually, apply a ...., click the .... button for the transition you want to replace, ... another transition from the .... Browser.

Share your movies

↺ List three of the ways you can share your movie:

1. ....

2. ....

3. ....

↺ What format does iMovie's Export option produce?

.... format.

↺ To send an exported movie to someone who doesn't have QuickTime or iTunes on a PC, change the file extension to ....

↺ To export a movie in a different format, hit Share > ....
....

↺ What do the themes in iDVD style?

....

How did you do?

Did you forget anything? It's hard to remember it all. Go ahead and re-read the sections covering what you overlooked. Your brain might need a bit more time to absorb all the information.

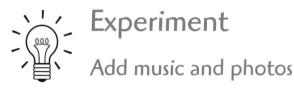

Experiment

Add music and photos

Every great movie needs a great soundtrack. iMovie gives you the tools to add music to your project through a feature that isn't immediately apparent from just glancing at the iMovie window.

iMovie includes a music browser, similar to those found in other Mac apps. Adding songs is as easy as dragging and dropping.

Look at the buttons on the right of the iMovie toolbar that includes the Transition Browser. Which button do you think would give you access to your music? Hold your cursor over the buttons to see the descriptions and see if you were right.

Click the Music Browser button, and the browser opens.

Find some music you want to use and drag it into the Project window. What visual changes do you see there?

Do you want to add some photo stills to break up the pace of your movie? You can do that, too. Use the Photo Browser button. Find photos you like, and drag them into place.

When you're done moving photos and music into place, click the icons that look like gears to get access to more detailed settings. Explore them to see what they do.

Remember, you can always undo with Edit > Undo. Nothing's permanent until you export or upload your movie.

Front Row

- Movies
- **TV Shows**
- Music
- Podcasts
- Photos
- Settings
- Sources

14 A Front Row seat

Now that you've got your video organized and you're maybe even making your own movies, you want to be able to watch them in style. If you've got a widescreen iMac, can you make your video use all that screen real estate? Or maybe you've got a Mac Mini or a MacBook Pro that you'd like to connect to a big monitor, or TV. How can you display your video so it takes advantage of these large-sized screens?

No Problem!

Every Mac comes with Front Row, a program that turns your computer into a movie theater. It's specifically designed to work with large screens but it works just as well on a smaller monitor or a notebook display. Front Row also makes it easy to enjoy other kinds of media, not just movies. With Front Row you can:

⇨ Watch movies and TV shows from iTunes and on DVDs.

⇨ Watch movie trailers.

⇨ Listen to music and podcasts.

⇨ Look at your favorite photos.

Watch movies

Are you coming to the Mac from a Windows PC that included Windows Media Center? It's found in some versions of Windows XP and Vista, and all versions of Windows 7. Media Center is actually a little more feature-rich than Front Row but you'll appreciate the Mac program's simplicity.

Front Row integrates with all the media-oriented Mac programs you've already learned about. It can access the movies, TV shows, podcasts and music you have on iTunes; the movies you've edited in iMovie; and the photos you organized and edited in iPhoto. All these can be displayed using the simple, clean interface of Front Row.

Note: Until early 2008, Apple included a small, simple remote control with its notebooks and iMacs, specifically for use with Front Row. It's now sold for $19 as an option, but the Apple Remote is worth every penny if you plan to use Front Row. It's much easier than hunting for the right keys on your keyboard, and it's essential if you plan to hook your Mac to a TV.

The Apple Remote controls are a lot like iPod controls.

The Menu button brings up Front Row, and also lets you back out of nested menus. There's a stop/start button, and the ring controls fast forward/reverse and the volume.

If you want to use Front Row with a large monitor or TV, you'll need to buy an adapter that connects the DisplayPort on your Mac to the screen you're using. The adapter you need will depend on the type of display you have (and may be a different type if you have an older Mac), but you can buy many different types at Apple's online store at http://store.apple.com. They start at around $29.

Finally, if you're linking your Mac to a TV, you'll also need to think about the audio. You can connect powered speakers directly to your Mac, they'll work in the headphone jack on all Macs. (On iMacs, the headphone jack also has digital audio-out capabilities.) You can also buy adapters for connecting audio to a home theater system or directly to your TV from the Apple site, as well as at most electronics stores.

Unlike the other applications we've looked at so far, Front Row doesn't yet have an icon on the Dock. It's in the **Applications** folder, but you *can* launch that from the Dock and once Front Row's launched, you can anchor its icon to the Dock. Or, just drag the Front Row icon to the Dock to anchor it there before you start.

Click Front Row's icon in the folder to launch it.

You can also use **Command+Esc** on your keyboard or, if you have the **Apple Remote** just press the **Menu** button while aiming the remote at your Mac to start Front Row.

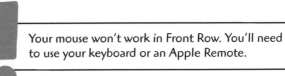

Your mouse won't work in Front Row. You'll need to use your keyboard or an Apple Remote.

It may take a few seconds for Front Row to launch, but when it does, the top menu takes over your entire screen.

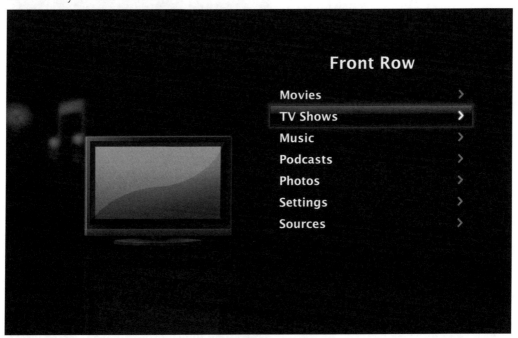

Use the cursor keys on your keyboard to move through the list on the right. (If you have an Apple Remote, click the top and bottom of the controller ring to step through the menu items.) When you do, what happens to the image on the left?

Select **Movies** using the cursor keys and hit **Enter**, **or** use the **Play** button on the remote. The Movies menu appears.

Step through each menu item to get a preview of the item on the left side of the screen. If you have any videos in your Movies folder, you'll also see them on the menu.

The first two items on the list, **iTunes Top Movies** and **Theatrical Trailers**, let you watch **movie trailers** over the Internet. If you're connected to the Internet, you'll see movie posters scroll by as you highlight the items.

Hit **Enter or** press the **Play** button on the remote for **iTunes Top Movies**.

Select a trailer for one of them and hit Enter or Play.

> **Warning: Speed bump ahead**
> Front Row streams movie trailers over the Internet, and the quality of the video you see is directly related to the speed of your connection. If you're on a congested or slow connection, what you see won't be as clear or as smooth as it would be over a quality connection.

Use the play/fast forward/reverse keys on your Mac's keyboard, or the corresponding buttons on the Apple Remote to control the video. It works just like your DVD player or the DVR on your TV.

iTunes Top Movies is a list of the current most popular movies in the iTunes Store.

To **exit**, hit the **Esc key** on your keyboard or the **Menu button** on the remote, and you'll return to the iTunes Top Movies list. Hit Esc again to go back to the Movies menu (are you starting to see a pattern?).

Play with it

Repeat the same steps for both the **Trailers** and **Movies** Folder items. If you've rented or purchased video content in iTunes, you'll find those items there, too. The way you view all video in Front Row is the same.

Do you want to see what movies are currently in theaters, or coming soon? Apple updates the previews in the Trailers category frequently, so check back often to see what's new.

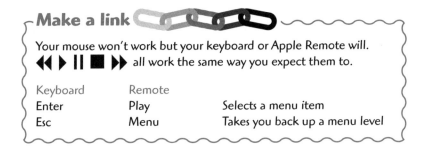

Make a link

Your mouse won't work but your keyboard or Apple Remote will.
◀◀ ▶ ‖ ■ ▶▶ all work the same way you expect them to.

Keyboard	Remote	
Enter	Play	Selects a menu item
Esc	Menu	Takes you back up a menu level

Watch TV shows

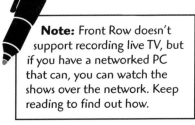

Note: Front Row doesn't support recording live TV, but if you have a networked PC that can, you can watch the shows over the network. Keep reading to find out how.

Apple sells single episodes of shows, and even full seasons of TV shows, as well as movies on iTunes. If you've got your Mac connected to your TV, it's a great way to catch up on your favorite shows, or sample new ones you've been meaning to try.

Individual shows start at around $1–$2. The price of entire seasons—called a Season Pass—varies based on how many episodes are included. TV shows bought via iTunes are yours to keep and many of the shows are available in high-definition (though they're more expensive).

Have you bought some TV shows on iTunes? Go back to Front Row's top menu, select the **TV Shows** category and click Enter or Play to see any TV shows you've purchased.

See the **Date** and **Show** buttons over the list of TV shows? If you've got multiple shows, and multiple episodes in a series, click the **Show** button and watch what happens. You can sort your collection based on the show, or on the date it first aired.

When you're ready to watch a TV show find one you want to watch in your list, then hit Enter or press Play. Sit back and enjoy.

And as with the Movies section, you can see the most popular shows on iTunes in the **Top TV Shows** area. Take a look. This time around, you get a 30-second clip of a recent episode from the series.

Watch DVDs

Insert a movie DVD into your Mac's optical drive and the movie immediately begins playing in fullscreen mode. To see the program's controls hit the **Esc** key and the movie continues to play in a smaller window, with the DVD control panel visible.

That's not Front Row! By default DVDs play in the standalone **DVD Player** program that's part of Mac OS X.

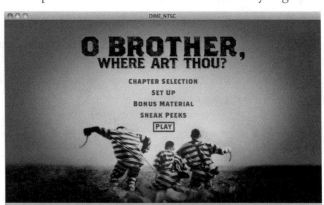

© Touchstone Pictures / Universal Pictures

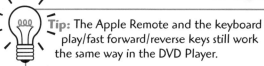

Tip: The Apple Remote and the keyboard play/fast forward/reverse keys still work the same way in the DVD Player.

Play with it

Would you rather your Mac automatically launched Front Row when you inserted a movie DVD? To do that, you need to make Front Row the default player for DVDs:

1. Open **System Preferences**.

2. Click the **CDs & DVDs preferences** icon.

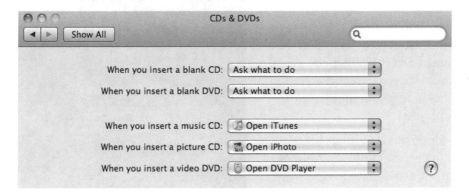

3. Click the drop-down next to **When you insert a video DVD** and choose **Open Front Row**.

4. Close the preferences pane.

5. Eject the DVD, quit Front Row, and then reinsert the DVD. This time, Front Row opens. Select **DVD** and hit **Enter or** press **Play**.

    The movie begins to play, or goes to the DVD's own menu, depending on how the DVD is designed.

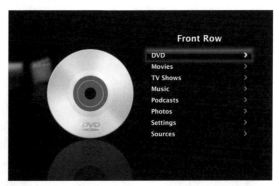

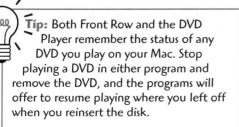

Tip: Both Front Row and the DVD Player remember the status of any DVD you play on your Mac. Stop playing a DVD in either program and remove the DVD, and the programs will offer to resume playing where you left off when you reinsert the disk.

Make a link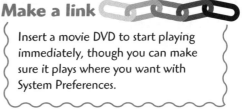

Insert a movie DVD to start playing immediately, though you can make sure it plays where you want with System Preferences.

Listen to music

If you've got your Mac hooked up to a TV and home theater audio system, Front Row is a super way to play your music. While you can't do more advanced things, like buy and organize songs, it does offer most of the playing features found on iTunes.

Launch Front Row and select the Music item in the top menu. The **Music menu** should look familiar.

The music categories are the same as in iTunes. Select **Playlists** to access all the playlists you've set up on iTunes, including your most recent Genius playlist.

The Music section also includes most-popular "Top" lists from iTunes, both for songs and music videos. Go into those areas and watch samples of the videos or hear snippets of the songs.

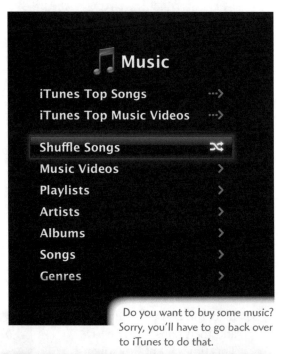

Do you want to buy some music? Sorry, you'll have to go back over to iTunes to do that.

Want to **play** some music? Go ahead and select the **Shuffle Songs** item. The first song appears, along with its album artwork, if available.

Not happy with a song? Hit your **right cursor key**, or the **right side** of the Apple Remote controller ring, to go to the next song.

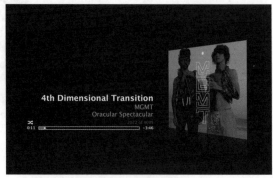

All the playlists and the other categories of music work the same way. Explore the list of composers, artists, songs and albums to see how they're organized.

Tip: Do you have other Macs on your home network? Or, do you have Windows computers or a home media server that supports the DLNA media-sharing protocol? If so, you may be able to access music on those devices through Front Row.

First, make sure sharing is enabled on the computer or server that has music (how you do this depends on the device and the software it's using).

Launch Front Row and select the last item on the main menu, Sources. You'll see a list of devices that will allow you to access the available media.

Select the one whose content you want to access via Front Row's **Movies**, **TV Shows**, and **Music** categories.

Play with it

You can also use Front Row to listen to podcasts. See the Podcasts item on the main menu? It works similarly to the TV shows Front Row feature, grouping podcasts as series.

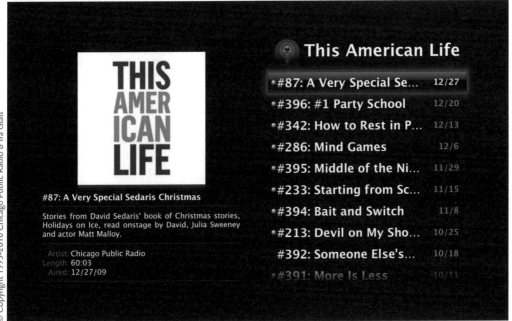

View your photos

Slideshows look great on a big monitor, or TV. If you want to share photos with a group of friends, or turn your TV or big monitor into a giant digital picture frame, Front Row is the way to go.

Front Row lets you play a quick slideshow from any event or selected group of photos, or you can create slideshows and add specific folders to them, and then play them full screen, complete with music just like you can in iPhoto. The only difference is that Front Row grabs the last piece of music you selected for an iPhoto slideshow.

Go to the **Photos** item in Front Row's top menu and **hit Enter** or press **Play**. See a list of folders and slideshows? Do they look familiar?

They're the same ones you see in the left-hand column in iPhoto. Select them to see big thumbnails of the photos in each grouping on the left. The Photos item is your "master" list containing all the photos Front Row knows about.

Go into a folder or one of the iPhoto slideshows. The photos automatically display in a quick slideshow. Hit the Mute key on your keyboard, or hold down the Down button of the Apple Remote controller ring for a few seconds to mute the sound.

You may find as you use Front Row that it becomes the way you usually play your movies, TV shows, music, and photos. It's classic Mac: simple, elegant and fun.

- -

Take a break

It's definitely time to take a break. Your brain needs time to sift through what you just learned. We're nearly at the end of the chapter, anyway. So walk away and give your brain something else to focus on for just a little while. Then, come on back and try your hand at the review and the experiment.

Review

Watch movies on Front Row

↺ Write down the kind of adapter you will need to connect your Mac to a TV to help you remember what you need from your next trip to the Apple Store.

....

Watch movies and TV shows

↺ Your Internet .... affects the quality of the video you see when you watch movie trailers.

↺ Name the two ways you quit watching a video:

1. Press the .... key.

2. Press .... on the .... Remote.

↺ TV shows in Front Row are organized by: .... and ....

Listen to music

↺ Where does Front Row get its list of music categories?

....

↺ Front Row's Top Songs item shows you .... and its Top Music Videos item shows you ....

↺ To skip a song in a playlist, press .... or ....

↺ To access music on other Macs or home media servers that are set up to share, select the .... item on the main Front Row menu.

View your photos

↺ Where does Front Row get its list of image folders and slideshows?

....

↺ To mute the slideshow music in Front Row, press the .... key or press and hold the .... on the Apple ....

↺ The .... item in the Photos menu gives you access to all your pictures.

How did you do?

Take some time to re-read your links, or if you didn't remember them, consider creating a new link that's bigger, sillier, scarier, more extreme, anything to make it more memorable.

Experiment

Add extensions to Front Row

If you're a fan of Windows Media Center for its plug-ins that add new features, you're in luck because Front Row offers a way of accessing new features, too. In Front Row they're called extensions and while there aren't quite as many Front Row extensions as there are Windows Media Center plug-ins, there are some you may want to explore.

Do you have a Netflix account? If so, there's a way to stream movies from Netflix using an extension called Understudy.

1. You can download a copy of Understudy from
   `code.google.com/p/understudy/`

2. Run the installer package.

3. Before you launch Front Row, go to the Netflix website using Safari and log in to your account. Now you can launch Front Row. What's different about the top menu?

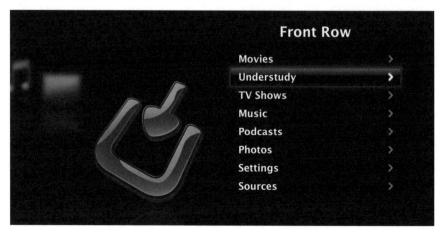

4. Now you need to add some feeds, so select Understudy > Manage Feeds.

5. Select Add Feeds. You'll get a list of sources, including Netflix.

6. Select Netflix. You'll get a list of options for different feeds from that service. To watch movies instantly, select **New choices to watch instantly**.

7. Hit the Escape key (or the Menu button on the Apple Remote) until you're back to the Understudy menu, and you can see the **New choices** item that's appeared.

8. Select it to see a list of movies you can watch from Netflix. When you find one you want, select it to begin watching.

Check out some of the other sources under the Manage Feeds > Add Feeds area of the Understudy menu. The feeds include Hulu (from **www.hulu.com**), which lets you watch many current and past TV shows for free.

Search for more Front Row extensions

Check out the other extensions, or for even more, use your favorite search engine and look for "Front Row extensions." Experiment with different ones to see what else you can add to Front Row.

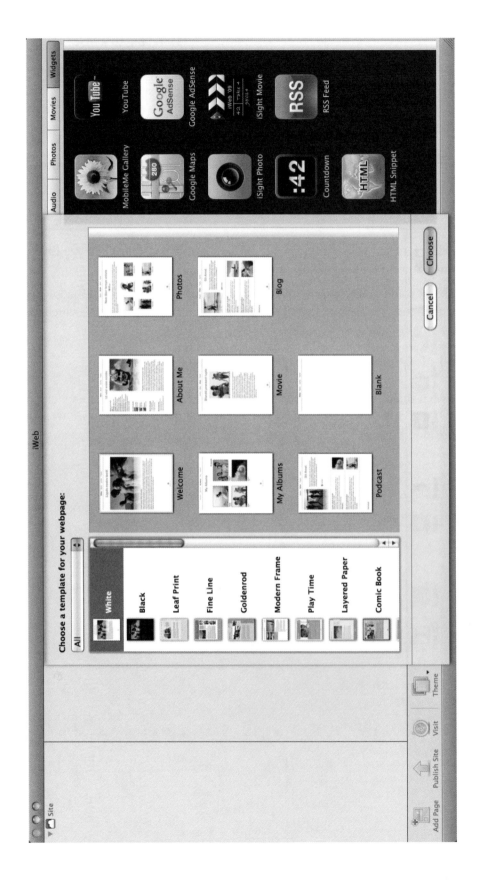

15   **Build an iWeb site**

You've always wanted your very own website, either for creative expression or for a business, but a couple of things have gotten in your way. You may know your way around the Web, but building your own online presence is another matter. You aren't interested in learning HTML, CSS or Javascript. And your PC didn't come with any software for building websites.

No Problem!

You're the proud owner of a Macintosh now, and your Mac comes with an application called iWeb as part of the iLife suite. It makes building a website as easy as creating a presentation or a graphics-rich word processing document. In fact, it may be even easier.

With iWeb you can:

⇨ Easily build your own site.

⇨ Add photo albums to your site.

⇨ Start a blog, complete with comments.

⇨ Publish your site to the Web.

Build a website

iWeb makes what was once very difficult—creating professional quality web pages—a snap. Working in iWeb is ridiculously simple: select a template, drag in photos or other media, write some words in text boxes, and click the Publish button. If you understand those basic concepts, you can build a website. Really.

Dive into the Applications folder and double-click the iWeb icon.

A window inviting you to sign up for MobileMe appears. If you have a MobileMe account, go ahead and click the

iWeb's icon doesn't really look like a web page...

Sign In button. You'll be taken to the MobileMe preference pane where you can enter your login name and password. If you don't have an account and don't want one yet, click **No Thanks**. Want to give the free 60-day trial a run? Click **Learn More** to go to the MobileMe website, where you can research the service and sign up.

Note: You'll need a place on the Internet for your site to live. With iWeb, there are two ways you can do that: the simplest is with a MobileMe account. The second route is to arrange for your own web hosting.

MobileMe is the simplest route, and for $99 a year, you get *lots* of other really useful services. If that sounds good, you may want to sign up before you start this chapter. If you're still unsure, you can try MobileMe free for 60 days. See www.apple.com/mobileme for details.

If you want to play around with iWeb before you pay for any kind of web hosting, you can enable web sharing. This lets you see the website on your own computer. Click **System Preferences > Sharing**, then select **Web sharing** in the list of items on the left. Your web page will appear in a folder called Sites inside your Home folder.

After you've cleared that window, there's the familiar iLife Welcome screen. Close it to go to the initial iWeb window.

To clear this drop-down you'll need to choose a template. iWeb makes it easy to work out what to do.

The iWeb window is similar to other iLife programs, but also different. What parts have you seen before, and what's new?

→ As with other iLife titles the **Left sidebar** is where you manage the pages you've created. As you add new pages and components to your website, they'll be added here.

→ **Templates** is a drop-down, and the starting point for working in iWeb. Choose a design template here, and once it's selected, you'll work on it in the center area now hidden behind it.

→ When you're ready to add pictures from iPhoto, video from iMovie or music from iTunes or GarageBand, you'll find it in the **Media browser** on the right. The browser also holds widgets that let you add social networks and other nifty features to your site.

Choose a template

Let's take a closer look at the template chooser and start building your site.

On the left-hand side of the drop-down are thumbnails for different design themes. Click on a few of them. When you select each template, the various page templates you can use with this design appear in the bigger window on the right.

1. You can use any theme you like but for now, go ahead and **select** the *Leaf Print* **theme** in the left-hand column. The right side of the selector shows your options.

2. Choose a **page template**. Click on the Welcome page.

3. Click the **Choose** button. The drop-down slides up, and the page you've chosen appears in the center iWeb pane.

Once you're in the Welcome page, double-click text boxes to change their contents.

4. Each of the text boxes holds placeholder text that can be changed by double-clicking on it. To start, double-click the words "Welcome to my site."

5. Type a new title for your site.

6. Do the same for all the other text elements, until the placeholder content has been replaced with your own stellar verbiage.

Now that you have the text in place, would you like to swap out the placeholder photo with one of yours?

1. Click on the **Photos** button at the top of the **Media Browser** on the right.

2. Find a photo you like by navigating through the folders at the top and the images down below. Drag the image onto the placeholder photo in the welcome page to replace it.

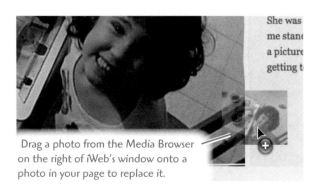

Drag a photo from the Media Browser on the right of iWeb's window onto a photo in your page to replace it.

3. Click on the photo you've added. A zoom slider appears below it, along with a button labeled **Edit Mask**.

4. Move the slider back and forth to zoom the image in and out. Click the **Edit Mask** button to reposition the photo inside the window.

5. When you're done adjusting the picture, click outside the box to lock in your changes.

Congratulations! You just built your first web page. Yes, it's simple and basic, but it's all yours.

Play with it

Even though it's a template, your page can be customized even more. Would you like to rearrange a few things?

Each of the text boxes and images can be moved around on the page. Say, you want to move the caption from the right side of a picture to under it. You'll need to make room for the caption by moving the text boxes below the photo first.

1. Click *once* on the main body of text under the photo. The borders of the box appear, along with square **"nodes"** that let you grab the corners, top, bottom and sides of the box.

2. Click on the top middle node, hold down your mouse button and drag downward. The box reduces in size from the top down.

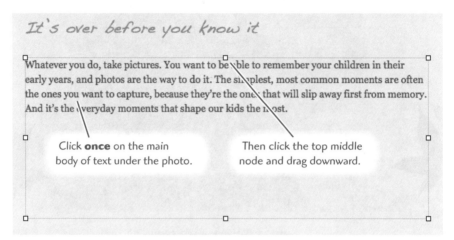

3. Next, click anywhere on the headline above the text body. This time hold down your mouse button and drag the whole box down until you have some space beneath the picture.

4. Click on the caption to the right of the photo and drag it below the photo. Guidelines appear that help you center it.

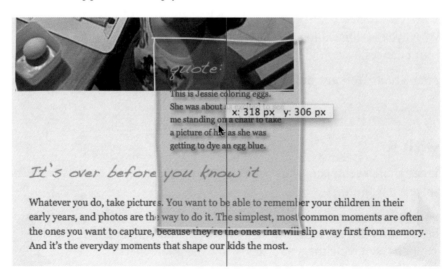

5. Use any of the nodes to resize and reshape the caption box.

6. Adjust the other text boxes below it until you have everything aligned how you like it.

You can move and resize anything on any page this way, including the photo. In fact, taking what you've learned, why don't you resize the photo and center it, then re-center the caption underneath it?

Make a link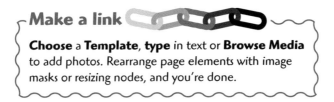

Choose a **Template**, **type** in text or **Browse Media** to add photos. Rearrange page elements with image masks or resizing nodes, and you're done.

Add a photo page

iWeb makes it easy to showcase your pictures online. There's a special photo-page template you can use that automates a lot of the setup work.

Click the **Add Page icon** in the toolbar at the bottom of the iWeb window. Select the **Photos page** in the Leaf Print theme from the template chooser drop-down, and then click the **Choose** button.

What happens when you click on any one of the placeholder pictures?

The photos are laid out on a grid, and the control that pops up lets you handle spacing, how many lines you have for captions under each picture, and more.

Grab some photos from the Media Browser and drag them to the middle pane to replace the placeholder images.

Tip: You can add photos one at a time, but what if you have an entire Event's worth of pictures you'd like to put on the page, that's going to take *forever*.

iWeb feels your pain. Click on **Events** at the top of the Media Browser, select an Event and drag it onto the photo page. *All* the images in that Event are added, and automatically arranged so they all fit on the page.

Double-click on one of the photos. What happens?

iWeb has automatically created a large photo page linked from each smaller image on the main photo page. There's even a slideshow button that will play your photos once the site is published.

Click on the **Back to Photo Album link** in the top left of the large photo page. Back on your main photo page, click on the text underneath each photo and add a short caption.

Will your website have more than one page of photos? Select **My Albums** from the pages in the template chooser, and drag and drop photos or Events onto the photo area.

This page also serves as an index for all your photo pages. Your visitors can get to any of the albums from this page just by clicking on the photo album's main photo.

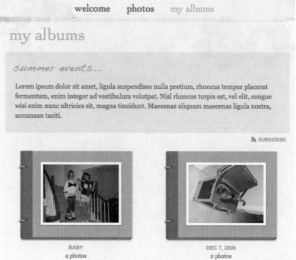

Play with it

Now that you've got a couple of pages under your belt, look at the area at the very top of any page. A series of words that correspond to the names of your pages has appeared. As you add pages, iWeb automatically adds links to them in the navigation menu that appears on every page.

Talking of links, do you want to create any text links on your pages? Click on your Welcome page in the left-hand column. To create a link out of any text in iWeb:

1. **Highlight** the text you want to link.

2. Open the **Inspector** window by clicking on the **i** icon on the bottom toolbar of the iWeb window.

   Inspector

3. Click the **Link Inspector** button ⊙ at the top of the Inspector window that pops up.

4. Check the **Enable as a hyperlink** box at the top of the window.

5. In the URL field, type or paste your destination web address.

   > **Tip:** By default, iWeb sets the link to an *external* link (a page outside of your site), but at step 5 you can also link to another page in your site, a file for users to download, or even create an e-mail link that users click to make their e-mail program send a message to whatever address you specify.

6. Check the **Make hyperlinks active** box at the bottom of the Inspector window.

The Inspector is a powerful set of tools that lets you get creative within iWeb. Spend some time clicking on its tabs at the top, then seeing what tools appear below them. See how it works with text, photos, RSS feeds, links, videos, and more.

Make a link

Use the **Media Browser** to add photos *one at a time*, or add a whole *Event*. An **Album** page is a good place to offer users links to your photo if you have more than one photo page.

Blog in iWeb

iWeb includes a simple blogging platform. No one's going to confuse this with Blogger or WordPress, but it gets the job done.

Adding a blog works just the same way as adding any other page in iWeb. In the **template chooser**, find your **theme**, click the Blog **template page**, and then click **Choose**.

See the new pane at the top? A blog's made up of multiple entries, and this area shows you the various entries or posts in your blog.

Play with it

What do you think will happen when you click the Add Entry button under the top pane? Try it to see if you were right.

You've now got a duplicate of the base page. Click on the names of the entries in the top pane to switch between them.

Go ahead and use what you've learned about adding photos and text to your pages to add the same elements to a few new entries. Make each entry different, and be sure to give each a unique title.

Turn on comments

Let's turn on comments so that users, can, uh, *comment* on your blog.

Note: Comments only work when you use MobileMe to host your site. Comments are not available for iWeb sites located at other hosting services.

1. Open the **Inspector**. (Hint: remember how you added a link earlier?)

2. Click on the **RSS button**.

3. Click the **Blog** tab.

4. Check the box next to **Allow comments**. A drop-down appears telling you that comments are now allowed.

5. Click OK to close the drop-down.

> **Warning**
> When you turn on comments, the **Allow attachments** item becomes active right underneath the option to turn on the comments. It's a good idea *not* to check that box if your blog is going to be public. Why do you think that is?
>
> The attach feature lets visitors who comment on your site include an attachment. This could be something as harmless as a photo, but it may also be a file that includes spyware or a virus. Or, it could be copyrighted material that neither the commenter, nor you, has the right to distribute.
>
> If your blog is going to be private—only MobileMe sites can be made private and you'll learn how in a little while—this may not be a big concern, if you trust your visitors. But if it's public, it's smart to leave this unchecked.

Publish your iWeb site

Once you have your site's pages just the way you want them, getting them onto the Web is simple, it just takes a couple of clicks.

Publish your site with MobileMe

If you have a MobileMe account:

1. Click the **Publish** button on the toolbar at the bottom of the iWeb window.

   A drop-down appears telling you that you need to have rights to distribute any content you post to the Web.

2. Check the box next to **Don't show again** if you don't want to see this drop-down again, and then click **Continue**. A prompt for MobileMe appears.

3. Click **Sign In** if you're already a member. If not, click **Learn More** to be taken to the MobileMe website, where you can sign up.

The MobileMe preference pane appears.

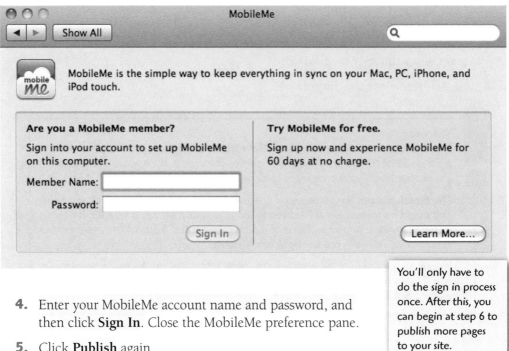

4. Enter your MobileMe account name and password, and then click **Sign In**. Close the MobileMe preference pane.

5. Click **Publish** again.

6. You'll get the Content Rights window again (unless you checked "Don't show again"). Click Continue.

> You'll only have to do the sign in process once. After this, you can begin at step 6 to publish more pages to your site.

7. iWeb begins the upload process, and a dialog box tells you publishing will continue in the background. Click OK.

8. After a few minutes, depending on the size of your site and the speed of your connection, a dialog box announces that your site is ready.

9. Click OK to simply end the process. Click **Announce** to bring up your default e-mail client so you can send out an announcement that your site is published. Or click **Visit Your Site Now** to go direct to your site on the Web.

iWeb is a WYSIWYG editor: What You See Is What You Get, and it's true, the published site looks exactly like it did in iWeb while you were editing it.

Tip: Do you want only certain friends and family to see your site? You can make it private, but only if you're using MobileMe.

1. Click on the **Site** link in the upper left-hand corner of the sidebar in iWeb, and the **Site Publishing Settings** window appears.

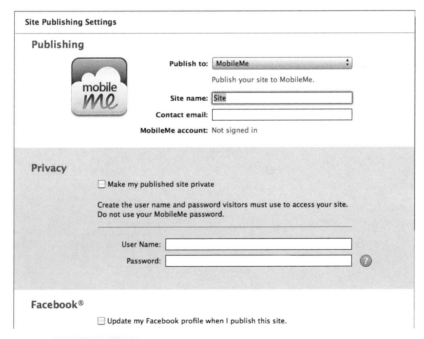

2. Fill in your **MobileMe login** info.

3. Under the **Privacy** heading, check the box next to **Make my published site private**. Fill in a user name and password, *but don't make it the same as your MobileMe login!* Now, when you tell someone about the site, give them that user name and password.

Publish your site to an ISP with FTP

Did you arrange for hosting other than through MobileMe? If so, you'll need to use the File Transfer Protocol (FTP) to publish your site. This method is also easy, though you'll need to have your ISP's FTP details on hand.

1. Click the **Site** link in the sidebar on the left, and the **Site Publishing Settings** window appears.

2. Change the **Publish to** drop-down to **FTP Server**. The settings area below changes.

3. You'll need to get the settings for the Server address, Directory/Path, Protocol and Port from your hosting provider. You'll also need to know your user name and password.

4. Enter all the details into the correct fields and click the **Test Connection** button. You'll be told if the settings are correct in a drop-down. Click OK.

5. Fill in the **main web address** for your site in the **URL** field. If you're unsure about this, contact your hosting provider.

6. Click the **Publish** button. A drop-down appears telling you that you need to have rights to distribute any content you post to the Web. Click Continue.

7. iWeb begins the upload process, and a dialog box tells you publishing will continue in the background. Click OK.

8. After a few minutes, depending on the size of your site and the speed of your connection, a dialog box announces that your site is ready.

9. Click OK to simply end the process. Click **Announce** to bring up your default e-mail client so you can send out an announcement that your site is published. Or click **Visit Your Site Now** to go directly to your site on the Web.

You now have a live site on the Web, a place to call your very own. You'll want to keep it updated frequently of course, but, uh, how do you do that?

Play with it

You can update your site once it's been published. All you need to do is open the page in iWeb, make your changes, and then repeat the steps to publish the updated page to your site.

If you have a blog, you can also update it by going directly to your site and working on it from there, just as you could with any other blogging platform. Let your friends know there will be new stories, photos, and more there often!

- -

Take a break

It's time to take a break. Take some time, walk away and give your brain some much needed time away from learning new things. This is a great time to go for a walk or catch up with that pile of mail sitting on the corner of your desk. When you're ready, come back for the review and experiment to test your newly learned skills.

Review

Build a website

↻ To get extra themes in iWeb, click the .... in the ....
....

↻ To change text in an iWeb template, simply .... it.

↻ List the six steps to add a link:

1. .... 4. ....

2. .... 5. ....

3. .... 6. ....

↻ Use the .... to add photos.

↻ What do you need to do to adjust the size and placement of a photo in iWeb?

....

Add a photo page

↻ Does adding photos to a photo page work the same as adding photos to an album page? Yes / No

Blog in iWeb

↻ Can users comment on a blog that's not hosted on MobileMe? Yes / No

↻ Why would you *not* want to allow attachments to comments?

↻ To add new entries to your blog, click the .... button.

Publish your iWeb site

↻ How do you view your site once it's published both on MobileMe and on an alternate ISP?

....

How did you do?

Did you forget anything? It's hard to remember it all. Go ahead and re-read the sections covering what you overlooked. Your brain might need a bit more time to absorb all the information.

Experiment

Add photos, videos, and music to your blog

iWeb allows you to add all kinds of things to your website. As well as photos, text, and blogs, you can also add video and music, all from the **Media Browser**. The process to add all of these is similar to adding photos: just drag and drop.

Don't worry if you add something you later decide you don't want. You can always delete the component.

Widgets give your blog extra functionality

Another type of addition you can include is a widget—a small feature that does specific things. Click on the Widgets button on the Media Browser to see them.

iWeb includes widgets for adding a MobileMe gallery, a YouTube video, a Google map, a countdown timer, an RSS feed, and more. Want to make a little extra cash? There's even a widget that lets you put Google AdSense ads on your site.

Experiment with dragging and dropping these onto pages on your site and see what happens. If you find some you want to add permanently, set them up the way you want them, then click the Publish button.

267

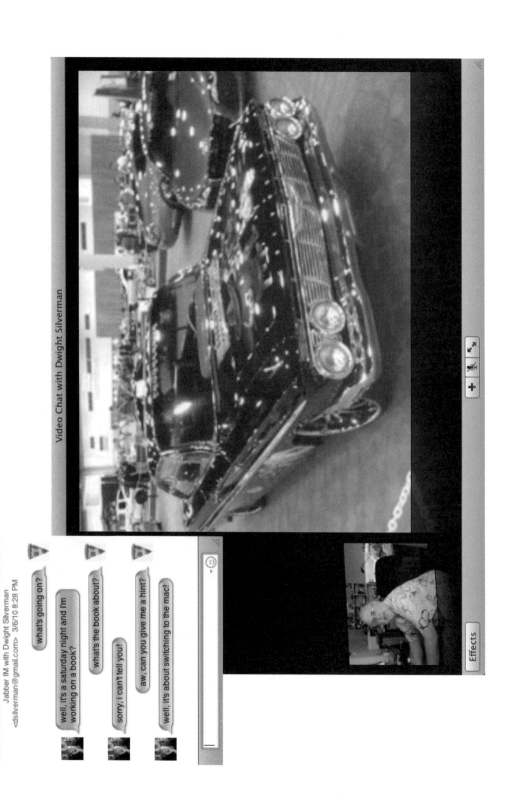

16 Talk via text, audio, and video with iChat

You've got friends scattered all over town, across the country, maybe even around the world. They're online and you're online, but talking to them easily, and cheaply, can be a challenge. You're a social animal, so how can you stay in touch with friends and family, and do so with one elegant program?

No Problem!

Your Mac comes with a handy, versatile program called iChat that lets you communicate in a variety of ways and using more than one chat service. It makes your social circle just a little more unified.

With iChat you can:

⇨ Set up IM accounts on different services.

⇨ Have audio and video chats.

⇨ Access a friend's desktop.

⇨ Show the contents of documents.

⇨ Transfer files to your friends.

Set up iChat

Instant messaging (IM) has been around for a long time, so there's a good chance you already have an account on one or more services. iChat supports three of them, so if you're already signed up on any of these, you're golden.

You don't have an account? Well then, here are your choices in iChat:

→ **AIM (Aol Instant Messenger)** is one of the most popular chat networks. It's also the one used by Apple's MobileMe IM service.

→ **Jabber** is a **protocol** or communication system that is used by a lot of other services. For example, it works with **Gtalk**, the chat feature paired with Google's Gmail.

→ **Bonjour**, which you can use when you've got multiple Macs on a network. However, since Bonjour doesn't work over the Internet, this doesn't get as much use as the other two (though it can be handy in an office when everyone is using a Mac).

Warning
Unfortunately, the Windows and MSN Messenger network isn't one of the chat services supported in iChat. But you *can* download a Mac version of Messenger at www.microsoft.com/mac/products/messenger/default.mspx.

iChat doesn't support Yahoo Messenger either, but you can get a Mac version of Yahoo Messenger at messenger.yahoo.com.

If you used Skype, on your Windows PC, you can also get a Mac version at www.skype.com/download.

If you don't have an account with any of these, how do you choose which service to use? Talk to your friends, and see which ones they use. Both AIM and Jabber can be used by people using almost any kind of computer. Many smartphones will also work with these services, so you can make a strong argument for your pals to sign up.

Sign up for AIM at www.aim.com, or get a Jabber account by signing up for Google's Gmail at www.gmail.com. If you signed up for MobileMe, you can use that e-mail address.

Got an account? Great, let's set up your iChat account for the first time.

1. Click the **iChat icon** in the Dock.

2. The Welcome to iChat window appears. Click **Continue**. The Account Setup window appears.

3. Click the **Account Type** drop-down, and choose the service you want to use. We're using Google Talk.

4. Enter your **screen name** and **password**, and then click Continue. The Conclusion screen appears.

5. Click **Done**.

That's all there is to setting up your first account.

Play with it

Want to set up an additional account? Click **iChat > Preferences > Accounts**. Click the plus (+) icon at the bottom and repeat the process you followed for creating your initial account.

You can only be signed in to one account at a time, so you'll need to choose which account to sign in to in the Preferences window once you're done setting up the alternate account.

Look on your desktop, what's appeared there?

That's your buddy list, showing the people who you communicate with on the service. If you just signed up for an account, you won't have anyone on the list yet, so you'll need to add some buddies. Do you have their screen names or e-mail addresses? Once you have either of those, adding friends as buddies is easy.

Look for the **plus (+) icon** at the bottom of the Buddy List window then choose **Add Buddy**.

Enter your buddy's account name (their screen name), and then the way you want the name to appear in your list. Click **Add** when you're done.

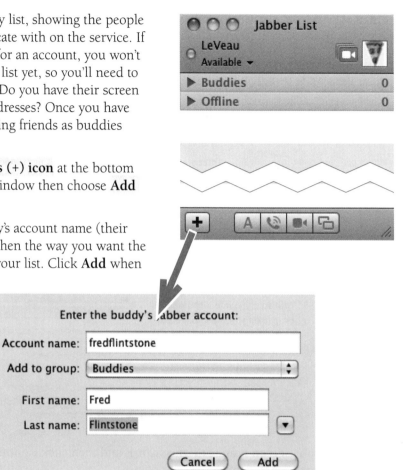

Note: Depending on the service you're using, and the settings your friend has in his or her own chat software, you may not see the name in your list right away. Some services, like Gtalk, require users to authorize your request to add them to a buddy list first. Even then, you may not see someone if they're not online. Click the Offline drop-down in your buddy list to see friends who are not connected to the service.

Make a link

Change the account you use in iChat **Preferences**.
It's simple to add new buddies with the + button.

Text chats

Have you used IM before? If so, you'll know how to use iChat to talk to someone else. It works just like AIM, Skype, Windows Messenger or any other chat software you may have used.

Double-click the person's **name** in your buddy list, and a chat window pops up. **Type** your message into the box at the bottom of the window and hit **Enter**.

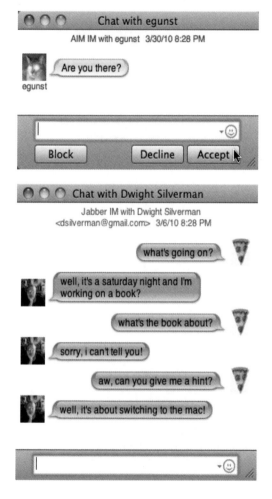

On the other end, your friend will see your initial message, and has the option to **Accept** or **Decline** the chat. (If the recipient clicks Decline, you'll never know. You won't see a notification that you've been turned away, you just won't get an answer to your message.)

Once your friend accepts, as you chat, your comments and your friend's replies appear in a series of alternating cartoon bubbles.

Play with it

Sure, the cartoon bubbles are cute. But if you don't like cute, do you want to see your chats in another style? Right-click in the chat window to get a menu that lets you change the style.

Go ahead and play around with the various styles until you find one you like.

Do you want to change the look of iChat even more? Click **iChat** in the Menu Bar, then **Preferences > Messages**. What do you see there that you want to change?

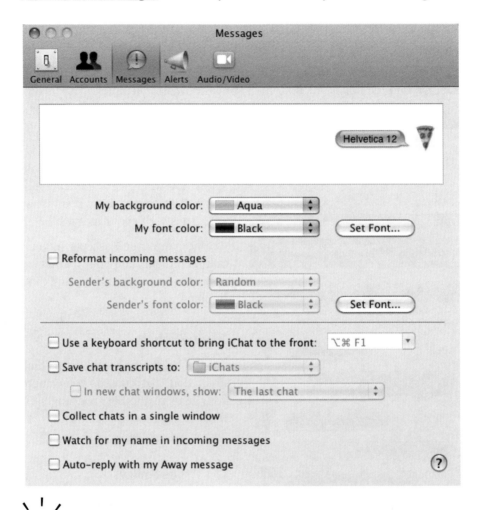

Tip: One of the most popular features of AIM's Windows software is its ability to have one window for multiple chats. If you're chatting with four people, rather than have four little windows cluttering up your screen, you've got just one with four tabs.

Good news AIM fans, iChat will do the same thing. See the checkbox in the Messages settings window marked **Collect chats in a single window**? Check it to have one window for all your chats, but *be careful!* It's easy to type a message to the wrong person...

Video chats

If you own an iMac or a Mac notebook, you've got a built-in webcam. Why not take advantage of it to do video chatting? (And even if you don't have a Mac that includes a camera, webcams are plentiful and inexpensive.)

Find a friend in your buddy list who also has a webcam. How? When one of the people on your buddy list has video capabilities, you'll see a small camera icon next to their Buddy Icon.

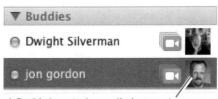

A Buddy Icon is the small photo or image representing your friend. Click the camera next to it to start a video chat.

Click the **camera icon** to **start a chat**. A window pops open to show what your webcam's seeing. And since it's *your* webcam, it's you on screen in the Preview.

On the other end of the connection, your friend sees a video request notification. What it looks like depends on the operating system and chat software they are using, but if it's iChat on a Mac, it looks like this:

When the invitation is accepted, the picture of you shrinks as the image of your friend fills the window instead. You'll be able to see and hear each other.

Sending video over the Internet is always better with a faster connection. The faster your Internet service, the better the picture. And your friend's connection speed is also a factor. If your Internet service is slow or unreliable, the video image may stutter, or even look like it's dissolving in tiny square blocks, an effect known as *pixelation*.

Tip: Want to have more fun with video chats? Add special effects. Click the **Effects** button in your video chat window and browse through options that will distort the image your buddy sees in some way. You can even add custom backgrounds, just as though you were sitting in front of a Hollywood "green screen."

Again, this works better if you have a fast connection and a more powerful Mac.

When you're done chatting, just close the window to end the conversation.

Group video chats

You can invite more than one person to a video chat at the same time. Click each participant's video icon after the first person has joined in. You'll see everyone in one window as well as your small preview box.

Make a link

Add participants to a video chat *after* the first person's joined: just click their camera icon.

For the other participants to see this as a grouped video session, each will need to have iChat. If they're using AIM or some other program, they'll see each person in a separate window.

If you receive an invitation, you don't have to accept it. Did you just get out of the shower? Having a bad hair day? Click the **Decline** button at the bottom of the preview window, or click the Text Reply button to tell your buddy, "Audio chats only today!"

Audio chats

Now that you know how to start a video chat, you can easily do the audio version. Audio chats work almost identically to video chats, except you **click the telephone handset icon** instead of the camera icon in your buddy list.

What if you only see the camera icon? **Right-click** on your friend's name in the buddy list and select **Invite to Audio Chat**. Your friend will still need to accept your invitation to participate.

> **Note:** For an audio chat, you'll need a microphone and speakers. They're built into iMacs and Mac notebooks and most webcams will send audio without sending video. You may still want to use a headset with a built-in microphone, to improve the sound quality and keep the other party's half of the conversation for your ears only.

> **Tip:** iChat lets you save a copy of your video or audio chat, *but your friend will have to give permission.*
>
> Click **Video** in the Menu Bar > **Record Chat**. A permission box appears in your friend's video chat window. When they click **Allow**, recording begins. The resulting .MOV file is saved in the iChats folder in the Documents folder.

Share a screen

How many times have you tried to help a friend or family member figure out how to do something on their computer over the phone? How much easier would it be if you could *see what they're seeing on their screen*? Why it would be almost as good as sitting next to them and explaining . . . iChat has a solution to this problem: **Screen Sharing**.

If both you and your friend have Macs, and are running Mac OS X 10.5 or later, you can access each other's desktops through iChat. This is great for tech support, collaborating on a project, or checking software a friend has that you're considering buying. Be careful, though: *you should only share screens with someone you trust.*

 Look at the bottom of the Buddy List window. See the row of buttons there? This toolbar provides other ways to launch voice, video, and text chats. But right now, we're interested in the one on the far right, which invokes screen sharing.

> **Tip:** Right-click on a buddy's name in the buddy list for an alternate way to access all these types of chat.

Click on the name of a buddy whose screen you want to see, then the **Screen Sharing** button, and choose **Ask to Share [your buddy's] Screen**.

Your friend gets a notification.

When they click Accept, your desktop shrinks to a small preview box in the lower right or left corner of your screen, and your friend's desktop fills your screen. Screen Sharing also launches an audio chat so you can still talk to each other.

Play with it

Move the mouse around. What happens? Try moving windows, opening folders, even launching programs. You can do anything on your friend's computer that they can.

To exit Screen Sharing, click the small X in the upper left-hand corner of your desktop's preview box.

Want to share your screen with someone else? Just choose **Share My Screen…** instead of **Ask to Share…** to reverse the process.

Share more in iChat Theater

iChat also lets you present documents to your friends through a cool feature called **iChat Theater**. What can you share this way? Many different kinds of documents and files can be presented in iChat Theater, including Word and Excel documents, photos, movies, and even music. In fact, if you can see a file or document in Quick Look (which you learned about in chapter 6), you can show it in iChat Theater.

When would you use this feature? Let's say you're chatting with a friend and want to show them a document or photo, without actually sending the file. In iChat Theater, your friend can "look but not touch."

> As with Screen Sharing, iChat Theater only works if both you and your friend are using iChat on a Mac, running Mac OS X 10.5 or later.

1. iChat Theater needs you to do a video chat. So, start video chatting with a friend first, then:

2. Click **File** in the Menu Bar > **Share a file with iChat Theater . . .** A Finder window appears, showing your Documents.

3. **Find the file you want.** If it's not in the Documents folder, navigate to the folder where it lives. Select the file and click Share.

4. The document fills the video chat window, while the image of your friend shrinks to preview size.

Your friend can see the document, but can't alter it or even scroll through; only you can do that (and you have to use the scroll wheel or ball on your mouse; you can't grab the scroll bar on the right in the video chat window). This allows you to control the presentation.

When you're done, click the small X in the upper right-hand corner of the document to close it. The video window showing your friend returns to its regular size.

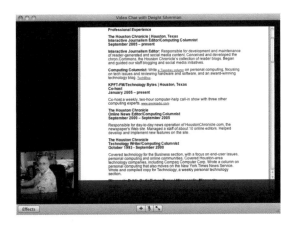

Play with it

One of the best uses for iChat Theater is to share songs or movies. You may be chatting with your friend and mention a great song you just bought from iTunes. Use iChat Theater to play the song for your friend.

The song plays on both your Mac and your friend's. You see controls for pausing, playing, volume, and moving to specific parts of the song. (The video player is similar.) But your friend only sees the album artwork or video screen and the file information.

Send files with iChat

Sure, iChat Theater gives you a chance to *show* documents and files to your friends. But what if you want to send them a copy of a file without ducking out of iChat and over to Mail? Just like you can with most other IM programs, you can send files using iChat.

Find the file in a Finder window and leave that window open. Start a text chat with your friend, and drag the file onto their chat window. Hit Return, or type a few words of explanation first. Your friend sees a chat bubble with a down arrow.

When they click on it, the file is downloaded to your friend's computer. The speed of the download depends on your and your recipient's Internet connections.

Make a link

iChat Theater doesn't allow audience participation, but you can drag and drop a file onto a text chat window to send it to your buddy.

Take a break

It's time to take a break. Seriously. You need to give your brain time to filter and organize all of this new material so you can recall it just when you need it most. So, go watch TV or play a game of solitaire—something that doesn't require you to learn a new skill. You've done enough learning for a little while.

Review

Set up iChat

↺ What chat services does iChat support?

....

↺ To set up additional accounts, click .... > .... and add the account details.

↺ .... +click the .... to change the style of your chat windows.

↺ To group chat windows, you need to check the "Collect chats in a single window" option, but where do you find this option?

....

Video chats

↺ List the four ways you start a video chat:

1. Click the .... icon next to a buddy's name in the buddy list.

2. Right-click a buddy's name in the ...., then choose ....

3. Click .... in the Menu Bar > ....

4. .... an invitation from a buddy.

↺ To add others to an iChat video session, start a video chat with one buddy, and then click the .... of the other people you want to add.

Continues, flip the page

Share a screen

↺ What do the following options do?

→ Ask to Share… ....

→ Share My Screen… ....

↺ What other type of chat session launches when you're sharing screens?

Text / Audio / Video

↺ What can you do on someone else's computer when you share screens?

....

Present files with iChat Theater

↺ What kind of chat session is required with iChat Theater?

Text / Audio / Video

↺ To start an iChat Theater session, click .... > ....

↺ How do you end an iChat Theater session?

....

How did you do?

Did you forget anything? It's hard to remember it all. Go ahead and re-read the sections covering what you overlooked. Your brain might need a bit more time to absorb all the information.

Experiment

Share a slideshow

Launch iPhoto and create a new slideshow you would like to show off.

You learned how to make an iPhoto slideshow complete with music special effects in chapter 11. Well, you can share any iPhoto slideshow via iChat with other Mac users (OS X 10.5 or later). They'll even hear the music that goes along with it!

Set up a video chat with a friend then click File > **Share iPhoto with iChat Theater...** A window showing your list of Events, Photos and Slideshows will appear. Select the show you want to present, and then click Share. iPhoto itself will open.

Once your friend accepts, your selected slideshow will display on their Mac.

You can share whole events and photo galleries this way. Play around by selecting different elements to see what happens.

Parental Controls

Show All

Jack Silverman

System | Content | Mail & iChat | Time Limits | Logs

☐ Use Simple Finder
Provides a simplified view of the computer desktop for young or inexperienced users.

☐ Only allow selected applications
Allows the user to open only the selected applications. An administrator password is required to open other applications.

Select the applications to allow

▲ ☑ iLife
▲ ☑ iWork
▲ ☑ Internet
▲ ⊟ Widgets
▲ ⊟ Other
▲ ☐ Utilities

☐ Can administer printers
☑ Can burn CDs and DVDs
☑ Can change password
☑ Can modify the Dock

🔒 Click the lock to prevent further changes.

17 Stay secure on the Mac

In the Windows world, security is a constant concern. It feels like you're under assault at every turn from viruses, spyware, poisoned web pages, bugs in the operating system, and programs that open doors for hackers. If you're using Windows, you spend an awful lot of time, energy, and even money keeping the bad guys at bay. One of the reasons you switched to a Mac was to get away from this hassle. Are you really safer using a Mac?

No Problem!

Macs have a reputation for being more secure than PCs. The Mac OS comes with powerful, simple programs and a design all meant to keep you safe online and give you peace of mind, such as:

⇨ Built-in antivirus protection.

⇨ A sophisticated software firewall.

⇨ Accounts with limited features.

⇨ Parental controls.

⇨ Password tools.

Your Mac and malware

The Mac's current OS, Snow Leopard, has quite a few features that protect you from malicious code, especially viruses and spyware—collectively known as **malware**. You've run into some of them already.

→ Whenever a software installer begins to run, a pop-up **installation warning** alerts you to that fact. *Nothing* proceeds without your approval, and in some cases, you have to enter your login password (or that of an administrator) before the installation can proceed.

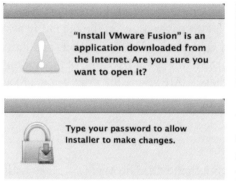
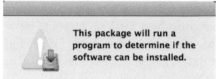

When you start a program that uses a drag-and-drop installation, you'll see a similar warning the first time you launch the program.

→ Snow Leopard's applications use 64-bit code (that determines how much information can be handled at once) and changes important memory locations at random so viruses can't easily target important system features.

→ Snow Leopard has **antivirus software** that automatically checks for a handful of Trojans (malware that masquerades as something else), and only works with some Mac programs (Safari, Mail, iChat, and Microsoft's Entourage, among others). When any targeted malware is encountered, the antivirus software pops up a warning and lets you abort saving it to your hard drive.

→ Apple sends out security updates several times a year. The Mac OS has a Software Update feature that alerts you to the updates. Whenever the updates appear you should install them right away.

> Although the Mac has a reputation for being malware-free, as more Windows users switch to the Mac, the platform will become a more tempting and potentially lucrative target for malware authors.

With all these measures in place, do you really have to worry about malware on your Mac?

It's always better to be safe than sorry, and even if a virus doesn't infect your Mac, that doesn't stop you accidentally sending infected files to your friends with PCs who really won't thank you for it. You can find both free and paid security software for your Mac, for example:

→ **Norton Antivirus for Mac.** One of the most popular titles for Windows is also available for the Mac. It looks for Mac malware as well as bad Windows software to make sure you're not passing it on to your friends who still have PCs. It costs $50, and requires an annual subscription fee. Available at www.symantec.com/norton/macintosh/antivirus

→ **iAntivirus for Mac** is free software that only scans for Mac OS malware. It runs in the background and uses very few system resources. Available at www.iantivirus.com

Of course, staying safe is a lot more than just protecting yourself from malware. And there are other features in the Mac OS that are watching out for you.

Turn on the firewall

When you set up a Windows XP, Vista, or Windows 7 computer the firewall is turned on by default. It can block attempts to access a computer from across a network, or it can alert you when software on your computer is trying to make an outside connection.

The Mac's built-in software firewall is *turned off by default*. If you want its protective features, you've got to turn it on yourself.

Before you do, consider this: you may not need it. If your home network has a router—a device that connects a group of computers to the Internet—then you're already protected by a firewall. All modern routers have them, but if yours is older and you're not sure it has a firewall, the built-in one in your Mac can offer protection.

If you travel with your Mac, and particularly if you connect to public networks, you may want to consider turning on the firewall.

1. Open **System Preferences**, find the **Security** icon, and click it.

   The Security preference pane opens.

2. Click the **Firewall** tab.

3. Click the **lock icon** in the bottom left corner of the pane.

4. **Enter your password** in the pop-up that appears, and click OK or hit Return.

5. Click the **Start** button. The firewall will begin monitoring the incoming and outgoing connections on your Mac. Depending on what you have installed on your computer, you may immediately get a pop-up asking you to approve an application's connection to the Internet.

Do you want the application "Microsoft Entourage.app" to accept incoming network connections?

Clicking Deny may limit the application's behavior. This setting can be changed in the Firewall pane of Security preferences.

(?)   (Deny)   (Allow)

6. If you get one or more of these pop-ups, click **Allow** to let it talk to the Internet. If you don't recognize what it is and you're concerned, click **Deny**.

Your Mac's firewall is now working. You'll probably see a lot of these pop-ups at first as the apps on your computer try to access the Internet. Once you click Allow or Deny, you won't be bothered again for that particular app.

Warning
Do other users access your Mac in separate accounts? If you turn on the firewall in your account, it will be on in theirs as well and it could affect how their applications communicate with the Internet.

Play with it

Do you want more control of the firewall's features? Click the Advanced button on the Firewall preference window and you'll get three different options.

☐ **Block all incoming connections**
The only things that get in are those services required for basic Internet connectivity.

☐ **Automatically allow signed software to receive incoming connections**
Lets software with official security certificates talk to the Internet.

☐ **Enable stealth mode**
Your computer won't respond in any way to attempts to access it.

Make a link
The firewall keeps your Mac safe when you travel. Turn on the firewall via System Preferences as it affects the whole system.

Keep your kids safe (and your Mac safe from kids!)

In Windows, you were able to set up different types of accounts to control access. And in some editions of Windows Vista and in Windows 7 you also had parental controls. Are those available on the Mac?

Why, yes! Yes, they are . . .

→ **Managed accounts** lets you create accounts that have limited capabilities. This feature is also available in Windows, so you may have some experience with it.

→ **Parental controls** lets you decide exactly what programs and websites your kids can access, and even what hours they can use the computer. A similar feature is also found in Windows Vista and Windows 7.

Set up a managed account

If you have multiple people using your Mac, it's a good idea to give each user his or her own account. You can set up accounts with varying degrees of capabilities:

→ **Administrator** can perform any action and launch any program. You can't, however, get into other users' folders unless they've turned on sharing for them. (This is the default account type when you initially set up your Mac.)

→ **Standard** users can install software that only works for them, but can't set up other accounts and can't make critical system changes.

→ **Managed with Parental Controls** is best if you want to control which websites kids can visit, what programs they can run and what changes they can make to the Mac.

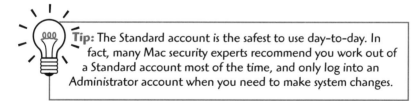

Tip: The Standard account is the safest to use day-to-day. In fact, many Mac security experts recommend you work out of a Standard account most of the time, and only log into an Administrator account when you need to make system changes.

To set up an account with limited capabilities:

1. Go to **System Preferences > Accounts**. The Accounts page appears, showing your current account in focus.

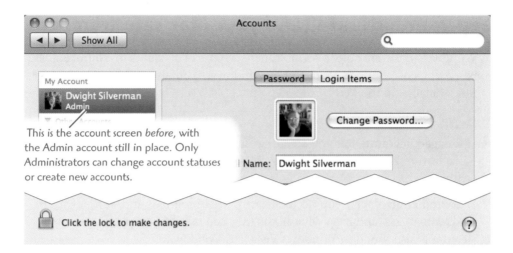

This is the account screen *before*, with the Admin account still in place. Only Administrators can change account statuses or create new accounts.

2. As you did earlier in this chapter, click the lock icon at the bottom of the screen and enter your password so you can make changes to accounts.

3. Click the plus (+) icon to add a new account. The New Account window appears.

4. Click on the **New Account** drop-down. You'll see the various accounts you can create. Select **Managed with Parental Controls**.

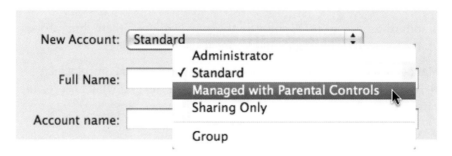

5. Fill out the rest of the form. You may recognize the process from when you first set up your Mac.

6. Click the **Create Account** button when you're done. You're returned to the Accounts preference pane, and your new account is in focus.

7. If the user has a MobileMe account, enter the user name in the MobileMe field.

Although you've created a managed account, if you were to log in now to the account you created *without* applying the parental controls, it would look like your own account. That's because, without any controls applied, it's the same as a Standard account.

Set Parental Controls

Did you have Parental Controls turned on in Windows 7 or Vista? If so, you'll understand the concepts behind Apple's use of the same feature. If you've never worked with Parental Controls features before, you'll find they're simple to set up and effective.

To set the Parental Controls on the new managed account, go back into the **Accounts preference** pane. Unlock it so you can make changes, and then click the name of the new account. Check the **Enable parental controls** box and click the **Open Parental Controls** button.

The first of several Parental Controls panes appears.

The first four tabs across the top tell you what you can control.

→ **System. Use Simple Finder** is good for a very young child. If you click just this, and no other options on this pane, you'll see just about the most limited desktop you can imagine.

Select **Only allow selected applications** to decide which programs can be used in this account.

Tip: It's a good idea to uncheck the **Can change password** box.

→ **Content.** Here you can control what children see in the Mac's Dictionary application. It also lets you designate what websites your child can visit, and which are always off limits.

This pane gives you a list of child-friendly websites when you select **Allow access to only these websites**. But if you select **Try to limit access to adult websites automatically**, you can enter your own set of allowed and off-limits sites.

> **Warning: Safari only!**
> The website limits *only* work with Apple's Safari browser. Your child could use any other browser, like Firefox or Google's Chrome, that you may have installed to visit any site on the Internet. You may want to use the **Only allow selected applications** feature in the System controls pane to allow only Safari to appear in your child's managed account.

→ **Mail & iChat.** Use this to control whom your child can chat with and e-mail using Apple's Mail and iChat applications.

Check the **Send permission requests to** box and fill in your e-mail address. When your child tries to chat with or e-mail someone not on the list, you'll get a notification.

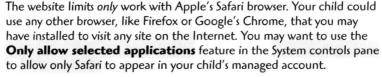

→ **Time Limits.** The **Time Limits** feature can block access to your child's account during hours you specify.

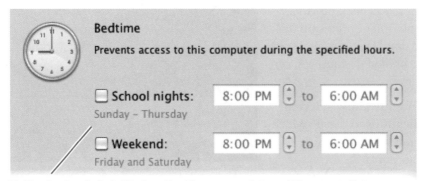

Unlike the time limits in Windows 7 or Vista, you can't have different cutoff times on different days of the week. The Mac's limits are set by weekdays or weekends only.

Once you've turned on Parental Controls, the fifth tab, Logs, lets you see what your child has done in the account. It tracks websites visited—as well as attempts to access blocked sites—programs launched and chats.

Seeing what sites your child is trying to visit, and whom he or she is talking to, gives you a better handle on your child's life online. You can use this information to allow more sites… or take a few more away.

Make a link

Create a Managed with Parental Controls account and control which parts of the system and what content your kids can access, who your kids can chat to, and at what times.

Create and keep strong passwords

How easy to guess are *your* passwords? Your new Mac has two cool features that make it easy to create strong passwords and store them. The **Password Assistant** will generate passwords of varying strengths for you, and the Mac's **Keychain** can store them for you.

Use the Password Assistant to create strong passwords

For this exercise, we'll work on the password for your own account, but you can use this approach to change any account password. In fact, you can use the **Password Assistant** to generate a password to be used with something other than an account. The Password Assistant is a great way to always ensure you've got a strong password.

1. Go back to the **Accounts preference pane** and click the **Change Password** button. The Change Password window slides down.

2. See the **key icon** next to the **New Password** field? That's your key to the Password Assistant. Click it. The Password Assistant appears.

Old password:	
New password:	🔑
Verify:	
Password hint: (Recommended)	

(Cancel) (Change Password)

3. Click the **Suggestion** drop-down for more suggestions. When you find one you like, select it.

The **Quality** bar changes color to indicate how strong that password is. **Red** is weak, **orange** and **yellow** a little better, **green** is best.

4. Want an even stronger password? Move the Length slider to the right and you'll get suggestions with more characters.

5. Click the **Type** drop-down at the top to change how the suggestions are generated. The default is Memorable, but you can also create passwords with letters and numbers, just numbers, and purely random characters. You can even have passwords that meet federal standards (FIPS-181) for strong passwords.

How strong is your own password? Select **Manual**, and then enter it in the **Suggestions** field. The color bar will show you how strong it is.

6. Once you've decided on a password, *write it down*, or copy and paste it into a spreadsheet or word processing document. Once you close the Password Assistant, the password won't be visible again.

7. Click the red button in the upper left corner of the Password Assistant. The password you selected will be inserted into the New Password field.

If you do want to continue and change your password, fill out the rest of the New Password window and click Change Password. If not, click Cancel.

The Keychain stores passwords securely

Now you've got a strong password, let's look at a safe place to store it. Some versions of Windows have the Credential Manager, which lets you store login and password information that can be used with other computers and websites. The Mac's Keychain is better integrated with the operating system, and also allows other programs to work with it.

As you use your Mac over time, you'll be asked to enter logins and passwords often. You may already have seen evidence of the Keychain. When you enter a new login or password for a website, Safari asks you if you want to store it. When you say yes, it's kept in the Keychain where you can access and even edit the login info.

Don't worry. The Keychain is secure. Before you can make any changes, you'll need to enter your login password. You can't access any information in the Keychain without it.

The Keychain Access application is found in the Utilities folder, which is inside the Applications folder. Once in the Utilities folder, double-click the Keychain icon to launch Keychain Access.

This window follows the same conventions as many other Mac programs: general items on the left, specifics in the main pane.

Suppose you've *forgotten a password for an application or website*. For this exercise, we'll focus on the item called **Passwords** in the left sidebar. Select it and find an item you'd like to examine in the main pane, then double-click on the item. The **Attributes** window appears.

Check the **Show password** box to see what the password is. (You'll be prompted for your login password.) You can change the listed password if you like. In fact, you can change any of those fields. When you're done, click the Save Changes button.

If an application doesn't automatically work with Keychain, you can still store your password for that app securely. You'll have to manually fish it out, but you'll know where to find it.

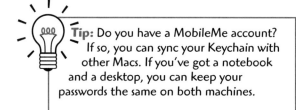

Tip: Do you have a MobileMe account? If so, you can sync your Keychain with other Macs. If you've got a notebook and a desktop, you can keep your passwords the same on both machines.

Click the **plus (+) icon** at the bottom of the main Keychain Access window, and the **Keychain Item** window will slide down.

Fill out the information—the Password Assistant is even provided—and you can later come back to the Keychain and check on the password if you've forgotten it.

Keychain Item Name:

Enter a name for this keychain item. If you are adding an Internet password item, enter its URL (for example: http://www.apple.com)

Account Name:

Enter the account name associated with this keychain item.

Password:

Enter the password to be stored in the keychain.

Password Strength: Weak

☐ Show Typing

(Cancel)   (Add)

Make a link ⬤⬤⬤⬤

Use the Password Assistant to create a strong password, then save it in the Keychain.

- -

Take a break

Your brain needs time to sift through what you just learned about keeping your Mac secure. Time to take a break. You're nearly at the end of the chapter. All that's left is the review and the experiment. So, walk away. Seriously, get up and move around. Your brain will thank you for it.

Review

Your Mac and malware

↺ .... and .... are collectively known as malware.

↺ Name two ways the Mac OS protects you from malware.

   1. ....

   2. ....

Turn on the firewall

↺ The Mac's firewall is on / off by default.

↺ To turn on the Mac's firewall, go to .... > .... >
.... , enter your password and hit Start.

↺ Why do you start seeing pop-ups when you turn on the Mac's firewall?

....

Keep your kids safe (and your Mac safe from your kids!)

↺ Name two of the four types of accounts you can set up on a Mac.

   1. ....

   2. ....

↺ The safest useful, account you can set up is the .... account.

↺ Name the four areas you can control with Parental Controls.

   1. ....

   2. ....

   3. ....

   4. ....

↺ What do the Parental Controls logs show you?

....

....

....

Continues, flip the page

Create and keep strong passwords

↺ What constitutes a strong password?

....

↺ To get to the Password Assistant, go to .... and click the .... button so that the Change Password window slides down. Click the .... icon next to the .... field to open the Password Assistant.

↺ In the Quality bar, a red color tells you a password is .... , while green means the password is ....

↺ The Keychain Assistant is in the .... folder.

↺ Click .... > .... to see login and password details.

How did you do?

How did you do? If you'd like to improve your recall on any of these you should spend a little more time on that part of the chapter. You'll get more familiar with the new information faster if you take a little time to make some strong links to the new information you're learning.

Experiment

Lock down your Home folder

In chapter 5, you learned about the Home folder, where your applications, documents, movies and videos are stored. That makes it one of the most precious folders on your Mac, and it's worth protecting.

The Mac OS X has a feature called **FileVault** that can encrypt everything in the Home folder so it cannot be accessed without a password. If you use a portable Mac, it's a good idea to use this, as it keeps someone from removing the drive and trying to read your data from it.

To start FileVault, launch the **Security** preference pane and click the **FileVault** tab.

> **Warning**
> Once you have FileVault turned on, some utilities may not work properly. For example, backup programs other than Time Machine will see FileVault as one big file. Any time you make a change to a file within it, it will try to update the entire FileVault folder, which will take a long time.

Click the **Turn On FileVault** button. It may take a while for FileVault to start up, and once you launch the app, it may take some time for it to encrypt your Home folder if there's a lot of data in it.

You'll also need a decent amount of free space on your drive. It takes quite a bit of space during the process to generate the encrypted version of the Home folder. Once it's finished, the extra space is no longer needed.

> **Note: Master Password**
> The Master Password lets an administrator reset your password if you forget it. If you're the only user of your Mac, a Master Password isn't needed.

Parallels Desktop
File
View
Virtual Machine
Devices
Window
Help
Sun 4:33 PM
Windows 7 – Parallels Desktop
Recycle Bin
Parallels Share...
My Boot Camp
Windows 7
3:33 PM
3/21/2010
Macintosh HD
BOOTCAMP
Parallels
Windows 7

18 Your Windows strategy

You've worked your way through Mac OS X. You've learned how to do everything from surfing the Web to managing and creating media to communicating with your friends and family. But you may still need your old friend Windows from time to time. Maybe there are games you want to play that don't come in Mac versions, or your work uses some specialized software for which there's no Mac equivalent.

No Problem!

Now that you have a Mac, you've also got a choice of operating systems. You can run Windows just fine on your Mac and you can choose *how* you run Windows. And even if you don't want to run Windows there are plenty of applications that will open Windows files.

With your Mac, you can:

⇨ Boot directly into a copy of Windows.

⇨ Run Windows at the same time you're running the Mac OS.

⇨ Find compatible Mac software.

> **Warning: Intel only!**
>
> Throughout this book, we've figured you're using a new Mac running Snow Leopard, or Mac OS X 10.6, or later. Since 2005, Macs have used Intel processors—the same as you'd find in a PC—and that's why Macs can now run Windows. If you're working with an older Mac that's pre-2005 and uses a PowerPC processor instead of an Intel chip, the techniques described here won't work with your non-Intel computer.

Run Windows on your Mac

Now that you're working on a Mac, are there any programs you miss from your Windows PC? Do you want to play Windows games? Do you have a favorite productivity application that you don't want to give up? Or maybe you have a specialized program for work that's written for Windows with no Mac equivalent? Maybe you have some hardware for which there aren't any Mac drivers.

You're in luck. There are two ways to run your Windows program right on your Mac. How you want to use Windows may decide which option you pick for running it on your Mac:

Note: If you want to run Windows on your Mac, you'll need to purchase a licensed copy of Windows, regardless of the approach you take.

→ **Boot Camp** lets you boot your Mac directly into Windows. You can choose which operating system to use at startup, or you can tell your Mac to always launch with Windows.

→ **Virtualization** creates a "virtual" PC on your Mac. You may then run Windows at the same time as the Mac OS. You can run Windows within a window on the desktop; run it full screen, so it appears that Windows is all you're using; or make the Windows desktop go away, allowing Windows programs to run independently and side-by-side with your Mac apps.

Each approach has pros and cons:

	Boot Camp	Virtualization
Performance	Faster because Windows runs "natively," directly on the Mac hardware. Best approach for running games or other programs with high graphics requirements.	Slower because Windows runs within another operating system. Usable for most tasks, even some 3D games. On an older Mac with a slower processor and not much memory, virtualization may be frustrating.
Convenience	Boots into Windows or Mac, either by choice at startup or as designated primary operating system. May be difficult to access data and files stored in the other operating system. To access the other operating system, your Mac must be rebooted.	Must launch Windows from within the virtualization program. Files may be dragged and dropped between Windows and Mac desktops in most cases. You may also be able to use the same data folders with both operating systems (i.e., one Documents folder for both).

	Boot Camp	**Virtualization**
Cost	Requires a copy of Windows XP, Vista, or Windows 7. The Boot Camp application comes ready-installed as part of OS X.	Requires a copy of Windows XP, Vista, or Windows 7. Also requires a virtualization program (though free, open-source titles are available).
System resources	Can take advantage of all your Mac's memory. You must designate enough hard drive space to allow for Windows and its programs and data (if you plan to store your data on the same drive). On a notebook, running Windows via Boot Camp tends to drain the battery faster than Mac OS X.	Can only use some of your Mac's memory—you'll need to leave enough RAM for the Mac OS to run. Can conserve hard drive space, as the virtual drive expands as needed. On a notebook, virtualized Windows drains the battery faster than just the Mac OS.
Compatibility	Will run all Windows software, and will work with almost all hardware add-ons. Boot Camp only works with Windows XP SP2 or later, Vista, or Windows 7.	Will run almost all Windows software, except for those with the highest graphics requirements. Will work with most hardware add-ons. Works with any version of Windows, as well as other operating systems, including Linux.
Security	Requires antivirus and antispyware software	Requires antivirus and antispyware software. However, if your virtual machine becomes infected, you can easily replace it with a backup copy.

Do you have a better feel for how you might like to run Windows? Let's take a look at each option.

Run Windows in Boot Camp

Have you decided Boot Camp is for you? Except for a copy of Windows, everything you need to get started with Boot Camp is already on your Mac.

To install Windows using Boot Camp, you'll first create a **partition** (dedicated space on your Mac's drive) where your Windows setup will live.

Look in the **Applications > Utilities** folder for the **Boot Camp Assistant**.

1. Double-click to launch the Boot Camp Assistant. The Introduction screen appears.

2. Click the **Print Installation & Setup Guide** button, then follow the prompts to print the 14-page document. Take some time to read the guide before you proceed.

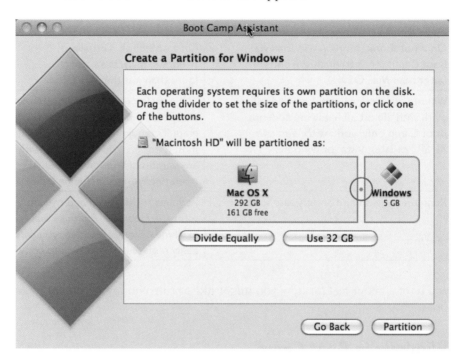

3. When you've read the guide, click Continue on the Introduction screen. The Create a Partition for Windows screen appears.

This screen represents your hard drive. The wide area on the left is the section or partition that will be used for the Mac OS, and the smaller area on the right is the default amount set for Windows. 5 GB is adequate only for Windows XP, and may not be enough if you plan to install additional software in the partition. Click and drag the dot between the two partitions to the left to increase the amount of space for your Windows setup.

Click the **Use 32 GB** button to automatically size the Windows partition to that amount. Or, click **Divide Equally** to split your drive in half.

Tip: When setting up a Windows partition, how much space should you allow? Since *you can't change the size of a Boot Camp partition after you've set it up*, you want to get it right first time.

You'll need to include space for your programs, for data (if you plan to store it in the Windows partition) and for temporary and virtual memory files. Do you plan to use Windows for games? High-end games can take up several gigabytes on your hard drive so you'll need to allow for that, too.

To figure out how much you need, look at the amount the operating system requires; the disk space requirements for the programs you'll install; and the types of data you'll save on the Windows partition, if any. Then, add some padding. Having a 40–60 GB Windows partition wouldn't be unusual.

4. When you've selected the size of your partition, click the **Partition** button. A progress bar appears. The process may take a while to complete. When it's done, you'll get the Start Windows Installation screen.

5. As the instructions indicate, insert your Windows XP, Vista, or Windows 7 disk and click the **Start Installation** button.

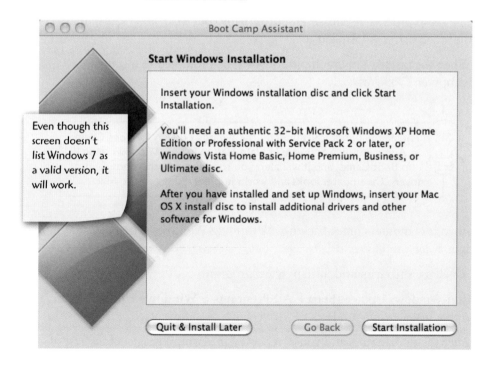

From here, the Windows installation process takes over. Your Mac reboots and begins installing Windows. Follow the Windows setup prompts, and when you arrive at your Windows desktop, insert the Mac OS system disk that came with your Mac. A prompt to start the Windows side of the Boot Camp installation appears.

1. Click the **Run setup.exe** button, and OK on the confirmation pop-up that follows it.

2. The Boot Camp Installer screen appears. Click Next.

3. Check the box next to **I accept the terms in the license agreement**, and click Next. The **Choose additional features** window appears.

4. Click **Install** to allow installation of **Apple Software Update for Windows**. This lets Apple keep the Boot Camp Software up-to-date.

   The setup process installs several drivers for your Mac. Your screen may flash as the video driver is installed.

5. When the installation is completed, you'll be prompted to restart your computer. Click Yes.

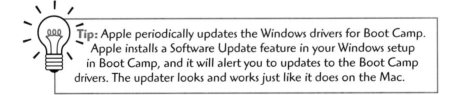

Tip: Apple periodically updates the Windows drivers for Boot Camp. Apple installs a Software Update feature in your Windows setup in Boot Camp, and it will alert you to updates to the Boot Camp drivers. The updater looks and works just like it does on the Mac.

When your computer comes back up, it's running Windows. There are several things to do right away:

1. Install an **antivirus and antispyware program**.

2. Run Windows Update (**Start > All Programs > Windows Update**). The Apple installer only updates the drivers, not Windows itself.

3. After the update runs and you've rebooted the computer, install the rest of the software you plan to use.

Play with it

Wait a second! When your Mac rebooted after using Apple Software Update it booted into Windows. You didn't get a chance to choose whether to use Windows or Mac OS X.

When you want to boot back into Mac OS X, go to the **Boot Camp module** in the **Windows Control Panel** and click the **Startup Disk tab**.

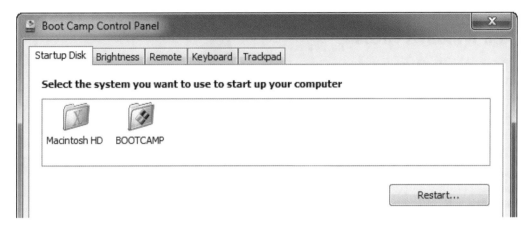

Click the **Macintosh HD** and click **Restart**, and then OK to confirm. Your Mac will now start up in Mac OS X.

But that just makes your Mac boot into Mac OS X when you start it. Does switching between the two operating systems really mean logging in to one, picking the other as the Startup Disk, then rebooting?

There's an easier way to choose the operating system. When you boot up, hold down the **Alt** key when you hear the Mac OS **chime** after you turn on your Mac. Hard drive icons labeled Windows and Macintosh HD appear. Double-click the icon representing the operating system you want to use (or use your cursor keys to navigate and hit Return).

Make a link

To switch between Mac OS X and Windows in Boot Camp, listen for the Mac chime on startup, and then hold down the Alt key.

Boot back into the Mac OS, and you'll see a disk labeled BOOTCAMP on your desktop. That's your Windows partition. Double-click it. What do you see?

You can explore the files in that window, and even copy them to the Mac side by dragging them to your desktop or a Finder folder. But what happens when you try going the other way—copying files from the Mac into the Windows partition? Unfortunately, you can't do it.

If you really need to move files back and forth between Windows and Mac setups, you need to use virtualization.

Run Windows virtually

Are your Windows needs fairly basic? Do you really need the power and speed that running Windows in Boot Camp will give you? Do you want to have the option to switch between operating systems? If so, virtualization may be your best Windows strategy. It's certainly the most versatile, because it allows you to work in both operating systems at the same time.

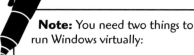

Note: You need two things to run Windows virtually:

1. A licensed copy of Windows (any version will do).

2. A program to set up and run the virtual computer on your Mac, which is called a **virtual machine**, or VM.

The three most popular VM applications are:

→ **Parallels Desktop for Mac.** This VM app can run Windows in a variety of ways. It sells for about $80, though you can find it discounted to around $70. Available at www.parallels.com/products/desktop

→ **VMware Fusion.** Also runs Windows in many different modes, and will work with VMs created by the PC version of VMware Workstation. It's also $80, discounted to around $70.
Available at www.vmware.com/products/fusion

→ **VirtualBox.** This *free* program lacks some key features found in Parallels Desktop and VMware Fusion (you can't drag and drop files between desktops, for example), but it's simple, easy to set up and, of course, you can't beat the price. Available at www.virtualbox.org

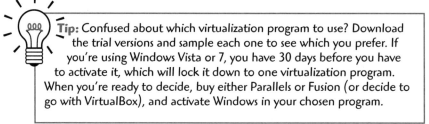

Tip: Confused about which virtualization program to use? Download the trial versions and sample each one to see which you prefer. If you're using Windows Vista or 7, you have 30 days before you have to activate it, which will lock it down to one virtualization program. When you're ready to decide, buy either Parallels or Fusion (or decide to go with VirtualBox), and activate Windows in your chosen program.

Because these apps aren't included with the Mac OS, we won't go through them step-by-step, though the installation process for any of these products is essentially the same. Here's the general procedure (screenshots are from Parallels Desktop for Mac 5):

1. **Install** the virtualization software on your Mac. All three use the installer method. You may need to reboot your Mac.

2. **Launch** the virtualization program after it's installed. You may be prompted to create a new virtual machine, or you can click **File** > **New** to begin the process.

3. Insert your **Windows disk**. You may be asked to tell the program what operating system and version you're using, or you may need to specify it yourself. You may also be asked to enter your Windows activation key. Go ahead, but if you just want to trial the software, decline to activate it immediately in Windows.

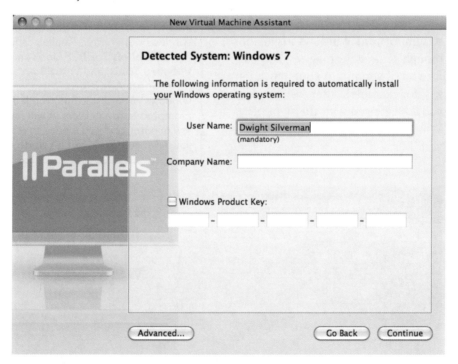

4. You'll be given the chance to **change key settings**, such as the amount of memory and hard drive space you want your VM to use and whether to share document folders with your Mac. You may also get an "express" option that sets these automatically. You can always go back into the VM's setup later and change them.

Tip: The hard drive space guidelines on page 305 will serve you well here, but virtualization gives you an added bonus. All three programs only use as much hard drive space as you need, up to the limit you set. So, if you've designated a 30-GB virtual drive and the files in your Windows VM only require 10 GB, your drive will only take up 10 GB on your "real" hard drive, and will expand as needed.

What about memory? It's generally a good idea to give your VM as much memory as you can without hurting the performance of your Mac. Start by allocating half of your RAM. For example, if your Mac has 4 GB of memory, give 2 GB to your Windows installation.

Let your virtualization program use *all* the available cores in your processor. Most Macs at this writing come with dual-core processors, some with four-core. If your Mac runs slowly, you can always go into the settings and disable some of the cores for your VM.

5. When your settings are tweaked, you'll be able to create your Windows VM. From here, the process is a straightforward Windows installation, though some steps may be skipped for you (if you put in your activation key, for example). After installation, you'll be greeted with the sight of Windows running in a window on your Mac.

Note: Each of the virtualization programs listed here requires you to install a special set of drivers that make Windows work better. Parallels calls them **Parallels Tools**; Fusion's are **VMware Tools**; and VirtualBox calls them **Guest Additions**. When your Windows VM first starts up, you'll be prompted to install them. It will take a few minutes, and you'll need to reboot your VM afterwards, but it's worth it!

Play with it

Once your VM machine is set up and running, you can install your antivirus and antispyware programs, along with the other Windows programs you need.

Your VM is actually just one big file, usually stored in the Documents folder. (VirtualBox stores its files in the UserName > Library > VirtualBox folder.) In chapter 6, you learned how to tell Time Machine *not* to back up specific folders and files. You should include your VM file in those exceptions, because it's a very large file. Just launching the Windows VM will change the file, and cause Time Machine to back it up. This will take a long time, and eat up lots of space on your Time Machine drive.

Instead, consider periodically making a separate backup copy of your VM to another external drive or, if it will fit, onto a DVD. If your Windows installation becomes corrupted or gets infected by a virus, you can just delete the VM file and replace it with your copy.

Mac-compatible software

While being able to run Windows on your Mac is both useful and cool, it may be overkill. What if all you need to do is read and write documents sent to you by Windows users? If that's the case, you may not need to have a copy of Windows on your Mac at all.

If you're working with common document types, such as Microsoft Office files, or image files, like JPG or TIF, there's plenty of Macintosh software to handle those. In fact, some of it's on your Mac already.

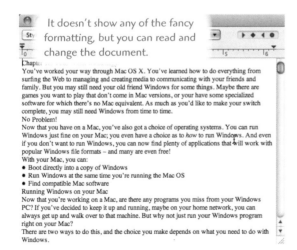

It doesn't show any of the fancy formatting, but you can read and change the document.

For example, if you have a Word document from your Windows PC and you haven't yet installed a Word-compatible word processor, double-click the Word document. It's likely to open in an application called **TextEdit**, found in your Applications folder. Like Notepad or WordPad on the PC, it's a program designed to open simple text documents. But unlike its Windows counterparts, it also can open Word documents, including those saved with the newer .DOCX format from Word 2007 and 2010.

Need a program that works with media files? **Preview** doubles as a basic photo editor and a media player. It will even read PDF files. You can also find it in the Applications folder.

If you need professional programs that will work with Windows-compatible documents there are quite a few to choose from, including some that are free.

Microsoft Office for Mac	
Full-featured office productivity suite that's completely compatible with the Windows version of Office. There are several editions at different prices, but they all come with Word, Excel, and PowerPoint.	
Price	Prices range from $150 to $400, and a free trial is available
Available at	www.microsoft.com/products/office2008

iWork	
Apple's own productivity suite that comes with Pages, a word processor; Numbers, a spreadsheet program; and Keynote, a presentation manager. Though each program has its own native file format, they all work with Microsoft Office documents.	
Price	iWork is a bargain at $79, and a trial version is available
Available at	www.apple.com/iwork/download-trial/

OpenOffice.org	
This free, open-source productivity suite is available for all three major computing platforms: Mac, Linux, and Windows. It's also got a slew of applications: word processing, spreadsheet, presentations, drawing, and a database. It saves documents in its own format but also will save them in Microsoft Office-compatible formats, including the Office 2007 and 2010 versions.	
Price	Completely free
Available at	www.openoffice.org

NeoOffice	
When OpenOffice.org was first released, there was no native version of it for the Mac. Because it was an open-source program, a developer took the code and created this separate Macintosh program called NeoOffice. It has since become a popular and polished suite that includes all the features of OpenOffice.org with a Mac-friendly interface. It also supports all the Microsoft Office formats, including those from the 2007 and 2010 versions.	
Price	Completely free
Available at	www.neooffice.org

Two of these packages are free, and the other two offer trial versions. Why not sample each one until you find one that suits you best? Now that you've got a Mac, you've doubled the choices you have for software!

Take a break

That's it—which means it's time to take a break. You need to give your brain some down time away from the new material. Just make sure to come back to do the review and experiment. They provide a great means to solidify the content in your brain.

Review

Run Windows on your Mac

⟳ Name the two ways you can run Windows on your Mac:

1. ....

2. ....

⟳ You will you need a copy of ...... regardless of the method you choose to run Windows on your Mac.

⟳ List some pros and cons of using Boot Camp or virtualization.

....

Run Windows in Boot Camp

⟳ Find the Boot Camp Assistant in the ....

⟳ To resize the Boot Camp partition, you ....

⟳ What are the first things you should do once you have your Windows installation in place?

....

⟳ To switch between Windows and Mac OS X when rebooting, press the .... key when you hear the Apple chime.

Continues, flip the page

Running Windows virtually

↻ What are "tools" and "additions" in virtualization software? Why do you need them?

....

↻ What's the best way to back up your VM?

....

Compatible Mac software

↻ When would you use compatible Mac software instead of running Windows on your Mac?

....

↻ Microsoft Office for Mac and Apple's iWork both include apps to work with:

1. ....

2. ....

3. ....

↻ What comes with OpenOffice, the free, open-source suite, that doesn't come with Office for Mac or iWork?

....

How did you do?

Did you forget anything? It's hard to remember it all. Go ahead and re-read the sections covering what you overlooked. Your brain might need a bit more time to absorb all the information.

Experiment

Use Boot Camp with virtualization

In this chapter, you learned about the two main ways to run Windows on your Mac: Boot Camp and virtualization. Now, here's a surprise: you can combine the two, and use a Boot Camp installation of Windows with virtualization software.

→ If you installed Windows in Boot Camp, you can install either Parallels Desktop for Windows or VMware Fusion and tell it to use the Boot Camp setup as the source for its virtual machine.

For example, here's the screen from Parallels Desktop 5 that lets you select the Boot Camp installation of Windows.

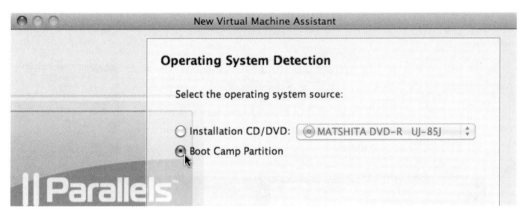

→ You'll still need to install the Parallels or VMware tools components, even though you're working with the Boot Camp installation of Windows.

→ You may also need to run Windows activation twice, once when running in a VM, and again while running directly in Boot Camp.

→ If you've not yet installed Windows, use what you learned in this chapter to first install it in Boot Camp, and then in one of the virtualization programs.

Give Windows some space

Would you like to be able to run both your Mac and Windows desktops full screen, and switch between them quickly? Combine the fullscreen feature available in all virtualization programs with **Spaces**, a **multiple-desktop** feature of Mac OS X, and you can.

First, turn on Spaces. Launch System Preferences, select Exposé & Spaces, then click the Spaces tab. Check **Enable Spaces**, as well as **Show Spaces in the Menu Bar**.

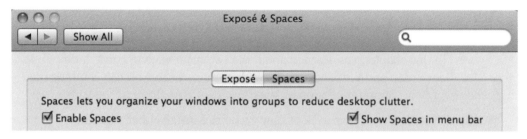

Close System Preferences when you're done. Next, open your Windows VM, click and hold on its title bar and drag it all the way to the right edge of your desktop, and hold it there. It's almost as though you break through a wall into an…. *alternate ~~universe~~ desktop*.

Now, use your VM's view settings to go to fullscreen mode. Once full screen is set up, press Control+1 to go back to your Mac desktop, Press Control+2 to go back to Windows.

By default, you have *four* **Spaces desktops**. To see them, go to **Applications > Utilities** and click the **Spaces** icon.

You'll see a kind of map of your Spaces, and you can see what windows are open in each space. Try dragging one of the windows between spaces. What happens?

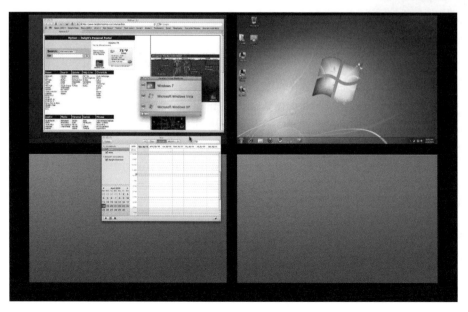

Index

Microsoft Office for Mac, 312
Mighty Mouse, 29
minimizing windows, 6
Mixer button, 201
MobileMe, 3, 252
    iWeb site published with, 261–263
    photos posted to, 182–183
mounts simulated drive, 35
.MOV extension, 207, 227, 229, 232
Movie Maker (Windows), 222. *See also iMovie*
movies, 222–232
    burning (iDVD), 231–232
    export, 228–229
    Front Row and, 238–241
    making, 222–224
    music for, 235
    photos for, 235
    sharing, 227–232
    themes/transitions in, 224–227
    upload (to YouTube), 230–231
Movies folder, 63
Mozilla Thunderbird, 92–93
MP3 format, 131, 135, 207
.MP4, 229
MSN Messenger, 270
multiple-desktop feature (Spaces), 315–316
music. *See also GarageBand*
    for blog, 267
    CD conversion to, 131
    Front Row and, 244–245
    import, 129–131
    iTunes Store, 133–135
    for movie projects, 235
    online stores, 135
    taking music with you, 140–142
Musical Typing keyboard, 204
Music folder, 63
music lessons, 198–201, 208
My Documents folder, 46, 47, 48, 51, 63, 156
My Instrument, 196

N

National Public Radio, 107
NeoOffice, 312
Netflix, 248, 249
New Project window, 195
News.com (CNET), 165

New York Times, 107
Nine Inch Nails, 210–211
non-destructive editing, 180
Norton Antivirus for Mac, 287
Notification Area, 5

O

O2M, 92, 93, 110, 111
One-on-One service (Apple), 47, 92
OpenOffice.org, 312
outgoing server, 90
Outlook Express, 92, 93, 110, 111, 112
Output button, 22

P

Parallels Desktop for Mac, 308
Parallels Tools, 310
Parental Controls, 291–293
partition (Windows partition), 304–305
Password Assistant, 293–294
passwords, 2, 53, 271, 293–296, 299
Path Bar, 34
PC-Mac network, 51–57
PCs. *See Windows PCs*
permissions (folder permissions), 59
personal Genius, 137–140
personalization. *See customization*
Photo Browser, 97, 235
photo page, 257–259
Photos folder, 64
Photoshop, 169
photos/pictures
    background image, 16–17
    for blog, 267
    editing, 180–181
    Events and, 172–174
    Faces and, 175–178
    Front Row and, 246
    import, 168–172
    iPhoto and, 167–191
    keywords and, 190–191
    for movie projects, 235
    Places and, 178–179
    printing, 189–190
    sharing, 182–187
    slideshows, 183–187
Piano icon, 202

Sites folder, 63
Skype, 270, 273
Sleep option, 11
sliders, 21
slideshows, 183–187, 283
Smart Albums, 174
Smart Mailboxes, 100–101, 107
Smart Mailbox Folders, 101
Smart Playlists, 135–137
SMTP server, 98
Snow Leopard (Mac OS X 10.6), 1, 286, 301
software (Mac software), 35–40
software instruments, 196–201, 203–205.
    See also GarageBand
Sound preference pane, 19–21
sound sources, 22–23
Spaces, 40, 315–316
spam, 101–104
Split Event Before Selected Clip, 221
Spotlight, 70
spring-loaded folders, 64
spyware, 286
Stacks, 67–68
Standard account, 289
Start menu/Taskbar hybrid, 4, 5, 6, 11, 27, 66
Status Bar, 151
status indicators, 5
Straighten button, 181
strong passwords, 2, 293–296
subfolders (Home folder), 62–63
synchronization, 140–142, 145
System Preferences, 14, 28
System tab (Parental Controls), 291
System Tray, 5

T

Tab bar, 151
tags, 230
takes, 205
tape camcorder, 219
Tap to Click, 32
Taskbar/Start menu hybrid, 4, 5, 6, 11, 27, 66
templates (iWeb), 253–257
Test Connection button, 264
text chats, 273–274
TextEdit, 89, 311
Theatrical Trailers, 240

themes/transitions, 224–227
Threading, 99
Thunderbird, 92–93
Time Limits feature, 292
timeline, 202
Time Machine, 47–50, 75–85, 311
Top Hit section, 70
Top Movies (iTunes), 240, 241
Top Sites, 149, 153–154
track headers, 202
trackpad, 31–33
transferring files. *See* file transfers
Transition Browser, 226
transition marker, 226
transitions/themes, 224–227
TV shows (Front Row), 241–242

U

Understudy, 248
upload movies (to YouTube), 230–231
User Agent feature, 164
User folder, 46, 47, 48, 49, 51, 52

V

video chats, 275–276
videos
    for blog, 267
    importing, 216–220
    organizing, 221
Viewer (iMovie), 215, 226
views, 67, 132–133
VirtualBox, 308
virtualization, 302–303, 308–311, 315
virtual machine (VM), 308–311
viruses, 286
VMware Fusion, 308
VMware Tools, 310
VoiceOver, 142

W

WAV format, 135
weather widget, 161
webcams, videos imported from, 220
Web Clips, 159–162
web hosting, 252
web sharing, 252
websites. *See* iWeb site